Glassbead Books

JOHN HOLBO, EDITOR

Framing Theory's Empire

Edited by John Holbo

a VALVE book event

Parlor Press
West Lafayette, Indiana
www.parlorpress.com

Parlor Press LLC, West Lafayette, Indiana 47906
Printed in the United States of America

SAN: 254-8879

Library of Congress Cataloging-in-Publication Data

Framing Theory's empire / edited by John Holbo.
p. cm.
"A Valve book event."
Includes bibliographical references.
ISBN 978-1-60235-014-4 (pbk. : alk. paper) -- ISBN 978-1-60235-015-1 (adobe ebook)
1. Criticism. 2. Literature--History and criticism--Theory, etc. I. Holbo, John, 1967-
PN81.F678 2007
801'.95--dc22

2007043878

The book you are holding—*if* you are holding a book—is available as a free PDF download. Visit http://www.parlorpress.com

This book was designed and edited by John Holbo. Text is set in 11 point Adobe Garamond Pro. and printed on acid-free paper.

Parlor Press, LLC is an independent publisher of scholarly and trade titles in print and multimedia formats. This book is available in paper and Adobe eBook formats from Parlor Press on the World Wide Web at http://www.parlorpress.com or through online and brick-and mortar bookstores. For submission information or to find out about Parlor Press publications, write to Parlor Press, 816 Robinson St., West Lafayette, Indiana, 47906, or email editor@parlorpress.com.

Theory's Empire, edited by Daphne Patai and Will H. Corral is published by Columbia University Press (2005).

The pieces in this book were originally blog posts, part of a 'book event' focusing on *Theory's Empire*, hosted mostly on the Valve (thevalve.org), mostly in July, 2005, mostly organized by me, John Holbo. (See the introduction for more information.)

Paper has been a bit of a puzzle. We have opted to make it typographically clear where links appear in the electronic version. Readers of the paper version who wish to follow links can download the PDF version of the book from Parlor Press, or check the original posts.

The material in this book is licensed under Creative Commons (see facing copyright page). What this means (to pick on the likeliest practical application) is that educators who wish to include a piece from this volume in a course reader, or make copies for classroom use, can do so freely, and without filling in annoying forms. This is, of course, a very legally imprecise statement. But it conveys the pragmatic point. We would like academics to become more aware of the fact that there is a legal device that permits such happy things.

Contents

Preface: Framing Framing Theory's Empire

Scott McLemee

The book now in your hands is the product (and/or simulacrum) of an online seminar. It consists of a few rounds of debate, tangential amplification, and afterthought—making this a peculiarly open-ended sort of document, one characterized by the noise of crosstalk, and by opened parentheses that, in some cases, never quite close. As a published work, then, it has a quality of improvisation and experiment. That is perhaps especially true at the level of format, for its very existence reflects a certain amount of shuttling and boundary-blurring between discursive venues.

We might call this a book about a book about books about methods of reading books. That would be putting things in a straightforward way. But in fact to frame *Framing Theory's Empire* more precisely, we'd need to note that it is a volume of texts originally prepared for digital publication in response to a hefty anthology, *Theory's Empire,* which consisted of reprinted texts from (paper-and-ink) journals and essay collections. That anthology in turn being a response to one more hefty still, *The Norton Anthology of Theory and Criticism,* the very title of which marks it as embedded in a kind of "branded" intertextuality we could spend no little time unpacking.

Furthermore, it may bear mentioning that *Framing Theory's Empire*—unlike the other volumes it devolves from, or sublates, or interstitially situates—is being made available as an ebook that can be downloaded for free. This is not a small point. Its significance goes beyond novelty, or even the way it stages a (partial) withdrawal from publication as market process. The shuttling between print and digitality—between formal scholarly publication and some, at times, rather studiously informal modes of comment and elaboration—would be distinct enough if this volume were to exist only as a bound volume. Its further dissemination, *gratis* and all-digital, plants it in some more recursive niche.

In fact, nobody involved in writing the texts below or preparing the collection for publication has any idea when you will encounter this volume, or how. You might be reading it ten years from now, or fifty. You might be doing so in some format not known—or even quite imaginable—in 2007.

All of this bears mentioning if only because it was not always so. The opening salutation above ("The book now in your hands....") would have been at one time would a pretty straightforward thing—a direct, literal way of pointing to a familiar, immediately present experience. It referred to a normative experience that could be taken for granted. Now it is haunted by meta. It points to a normative experience that is lost.

Well, maybe not lost—but one that has grown more complicated, anyway. And I suspect that complexity, and its discontents, may be part of the informing subtext of the material you will encounter in this book.

Debates over the genres, practices, and institutions we have come to call Theory took shape, over the final decades of the twentieth century, against a background of transformations in the circumstances that condition the experience of reading. (And also, just to be explicit about this, of writing.)

At one level, this should seem obvious. Nearly all discussions in the matter of Theory—whether in the form of expositions, polemics, defenses, or what have you—had their moment of narrative reconstruction. There were various stories, and ways of telling stories, about Theory as the response to shifts, large and small, in intellectual history ("Then the limitations of a merely formalist approach became impossible to ignore...") or cultural sociology ("No longer would the authority of dominant group X go unchallenged...") or even a rough-and-ready sort of labor economics ("Mastery of literary theory became a means of attaining a dominant position within the dominated enterprise of academic knowledge production...")

Those alternative modes of emplotment jostled one another, crowding around the topic in ways that were sometimes compatible, sometimes mutually exclusive. But all the while, other kinds of storytelling were pressing upon the attention of everyone—and not just on the relatively few people interested in whether, say, Theory should or should not be spelled with a capital letter.

The status of the book as a definitive sort of cultural artifact was constantly getting a little more difficult to take for granted. And that could be hard to take, especially for those who had undergone the experience of feeling as if the book in their hands was, in some sense, alive. A certain amount of the hostility generated by the genre we are calling Theory came from people who were terribly zealous about preserving a rather literal understanding of the quickening of sensibility that they experienced during encounters with particular books. They might have taken their slogan from Goethe: "All theory is gray, my friend, but green is the tree of life."

Well, perhaps. But efforts to romanticize the experience of reading will only go so far. A large portion of one's reading, however "untheorized," was always bound to be gray. And besides, the genre we are calling Theory had its vitalizing moments, too. A text by Deleuze or Gramsci could be green, in its season. Some of those engaging in the debates on Theory's behalf were just as zealous in defending the integrity of that lived experience.

They might be embarrassed to say so in quite so many words (at least without placing "integrity" or "lived experience" into question first.) Even so, a certain implicit fetishizing of the text was involved, which one might gainsay without thereby quite escaping it.

Meanwhile, "the book now in your hands" (actually or rhetorically) shifts its shape, amidst a changing sensorium conditioned by mass media for which text, literary or otherwise, need not be the primary mode of authorship, let alone embodiment of authority.

What will that mean in five years? In fifty? How will it mark the experience of reading? Of writing? Of interpretation or disputation?

Prophecy is a dangerous line of work. I'm glad to see that the contributors to *Framing Theory's Empire* avoid it—even while remaining quite aware, it often seems, that the longstanding arguments in the neighborhood of literary analysis are now a bit tired, if also hard to transcend.

Before leaving you to their musings, let me close with a quotation from a rather old-school humanist critic one known for his studies of Blake and Shakespeare and the Bible. We find ourselves—as he puts it in a forward-looking passage—conscious of:

> the confused swirl of new intellectual activities today associated with such words as communication, symbolism, semantics, linguistics, metalinguistics, pragmatics, cybernetics, and the ideas generated...in field as remote (as they seemed until recently) as prehistory and mathematics, logic and engineering, sociology and physics. Many of these movements were instigated by the desire to free the modern mind from the tyranny of emotional rhetoric, from the advertising and propaganda that try to pervert thought by a misuse of irony into a conditioned reflex. Many of them also moved in the direction of conceptual rhetoric, reducing the content of many arguments to their ambiguous or diagrammatic structures. My knowledge of most of the books dealing with this new material is largely confined, like Moses' knowledge of God on the mount, to gazing at their spines, but it is clear to me that literary criticism has a central place in all this activity....

The shape of things to come? So it appeared to Northrop Frye in *The Anatomy of Criticism* (1957). Fifty years is a long time. But not always. The next five might be longer.

May, 2007

Introduction

John Holbo

First, my thanks to Jennifer Crewe, of Columbia UP, for saying *yes* when I requested a preposterous two dozen review copies for the sake of an 'event' that must have sounded a bit … unlikely.

I've written ELSEWHERE about why 'book events' are a good thing.[1] I think *Theory's Empire* turned out to be a particularly suitable subject, because *theory* turned out to be. My reasons for thinking so would probably turn out, on examination, to be the same reasons I have for holding the views about theory I do. My contributions to the volume give you enough of that. But I'm confident those with different views will for the most part agree, for their own reasons, that this *style* of conversation complements what we are used to getting in other contexts.

Let me say a few words about organization, contents, and formal issues that arise due to cross-media shifts.

In making book, I haven't aimed at comprehensive inclusiveness. The event seethed and sprawled. I have culled posts and omitted comments on the assumption that book readers are most likely to be interested in a compact artifact, not fanatic completists about the event.

There *is* a 'champagne without the bubbles' quality to posts without comments. But a bit of experimentation has convinced me suspending a few bubbles in amber doesn't convey the flavor either. The real concern, such as it is, is archival, and concerns the whole conversation, not a few comment box *bon mots*. In his contribution to our volume Tim Burke remarks, concerning *Theory's Empire*: "the volume could really use an ethnographic retelling of a conference or conversation from the late 1980s or early 1990s." Trouble is: accurate field notes can be thin on the archival ground. Conversations and even conferences are alms for oblivion; not transcribed (not fully). This book is, to some extent, an attempt to address the ephemerality issue. If they had had 'book events' in the 1980's, we would now have a wealth of that sort of data Burke misses. But if this book contains only a tidied-up select sampling of posts, and no comments, in what sense can it fill the bill?

By the time I got around to collecting material for this book—about nine months after our event—perhaps 10% of the material I recalled seeing at the time had disappeared. Since then, another 10% of the links have broken. Deleted and migrated blogs, crashed comment boxes. No doubt much of this material clings to the bowels of Google—but for how long? At best, it's now a lock to which the key has been lost. My response to the archival issue is as follows: at the back of the book there is a page providing all the URL's for the posts we have included. Last but not least, I have created and included a WebCite Consortium link for each of these. Read about this organization at:

http://www.webcitation.org/

Should the original sites go away (reducing post URLs to sad cenotaphs), WebCite Consortium links should be good. And—the reader should be aware—the Internet Archive 'wayback machine' should still be around as well.

http://www.archive.org/index.php

These are organizations committed to archival preservation … but one still needs to know what to *ask* for. Call this the 'finders-keepers' problems. Search engines are for *finding*, not *keeping*. These archive sites are for *keeping*, but are not search engines. I think for a good long while this book can stand as a marker for a particular set of qualitative search results that might be otherwise unrecoverable. If someone wants to read the comments in 30 years, I hope they will be able to.

Authors have been encouraged to edit and rewrite. Some of the pieces that follow have been substantially made-over. So in many ways this book has become distinct from the event it records. (Yet another reason not to include comments, which properly address original versions. *L'esprit de l'escalier* is a fond dream. Editors should not do anything to make it appear to have been a happy reality.)

I opted for a straightforward chronological ordering, with only a few pieces shifted, as seemed appropriate (original post dates can be found at the end of each.) Mark Bauerlein jumped in early with his review, to which Michael Bérubé promptly responded: they make a nice, contrastive pair—Mark holding out for the great good of *Theory's Empire*, as clarion wake-up call blown in the ear of the drowsy likes of *The Norton Anthology of Theory and Criticism*; Michael doing his best to update Voltaire: 'theory's empire is neither theory's nor an empire.' John McGowan made an early post as well, taking a similar line. Anyone wanting a sense of how disputes over theory tend to play out will find many basic attitudes and arguments tried on for size in these pieces.

Then the event proper: two dozen posts in two weeks (a few more if you consult the full archive.) I led off with "Making Sense of the Theme"—so any reader in need of basic sense-making might start there. (Of course, *some* people thought that post was nonsense.) We have so many contributions, and mostly short ones, that any attempt by me to provide a summary, piece-by-piece guide would be dull (unless I made it very tendentious) compared to the lively, conversational prose you are likely to encounter by sampling directly. But let me say: Tim Burke's modestly titled "Book Notes: Theory's Empire"—quoted above—offers a lovely mix of sharp analysis and personal retrospection on 'the moment of theory'. I know I am not alone in thinking it was the finest piece of writing our little event inspired. Also, I cannot refrain from feigning sincere shock that Michael Bérubé's "Theory Tuesday III", about the advent of structuralism and its place in the history of theory, was not entitled "T3: Rise of the Machines". Last but not least, it is worth mentioning that several participants more or less independently arrived at the conclusion that Stephen Adam Schwartz' "Everyman an Übermensch: the Culture of Cultural Studies" was a particularly valuable contribution to *Theory's Empire.*

The event was over at a certain point but the conversation rolled along. The dividing line, past which the tone became in many ways more acrimonious—but also more humorous, or at least sarcastic—is probably my "Bill the Butcher as Educator" post. It might be argued that I should have omitted more of what followed (I *did* omit the angriest.) But, as Nietzsche says: it may only be by letting oneself go, in a manner one learns to regret, that one learns what one really thinks and feels. Only the wide orbit of excessive formulation eventually returns you to yourself. We bloggers better hope so. (A wholehearted embrace of Nietzsche's philosophy of eternal recurrence is very helpful in coming to terms with the nature of discussions of theory.)

Finally, I have included two posts by John McGowan, discussing the well-known case of Martha Nussbaum's *New Republic* attack on Judith Butler. I thought his posts were good, and it is only by some accident that Nussbaum's piece doesn't actually appear in *Theory's Empire*. (Daphne Patai tells me they tried, but it didn't work out.) I responded to John, in a post tangled up with more general issues: I've teased that specific thread of response out and included it as a final entry.

And I would like to thank the *Theory's Empire* editors, Daphne Patai and Will H. Corral, for contributing an "Afterword".

June, 2007

NOTES

1 I delivered a paper on the subject, "Form Follows the Function of the Little Magazine, v. 2.0," at the 2006 Annual MLA Conference. The text of my talk is available HERE.

Framing Theory's Empire

1. Review of Theory's Empire

Mark Bauerlein

This spring [2005], Columbia University Press published an anthology of literary and cultural theory, a 700-page tome entitled *Theory's Empire* and edited by Daphne Patai and Will Corral. The collection includes essays dating back 30 years, but most of them are of recent vintage (I'm one of the contributors.)

Why another door-stopper volume on a subject already well-covered by anthologies and reference books from Norton, Johns Hopkins, Penguin, University of Florida Press, etc.? Because in the last 30 years, theory has undergone a paradoxical decline, and the existing anthologies have failed to register the change. Glance at the roster of names and texts in the table of contents and you'll find a predictable roll call of deconstruction, feminism, new historicism, neopragmatism, postcolonial studies, and gender theory. Examine the approach to those subjects and you'll find it an expository one, as if the job of the volumes were to lay out ideas and methods without criticism (except when one school of thought in the grouping reproves another). The effect is declarative, not "Here are some ideas and interpretations to consider" but "Here is what theorists say and do."

If the theories represented were fresh and new, not yet assimilated into scholarship and teaching, then an introductory volume that merely expounded them would make sense. The same could be said if the theories amounted to a methodological competence that students must attain in order to participate in the discipline, or if the theories had reached a point of historical importance such that one studied them as one would, say, the utopian social theories surrounding communist reform, no matter how wrongheaded they were. But Theory lost its novelty some two decades ago, and many years have passed since anybody except the theorists themselves took the latest versions seriously. And as for disciplinary competence, the humanities are so splintered and compartmentalized that one can pursue a happy career without ever reading a word of Bhabha or Butler. Finally, while the historical import of Theory remains to be seen, indications of oblivion are gathering. Not only are the theorists largely unread outside of graduate classrooms, but even among younger scholars within the humanities fields the reading of them usually doesn't extend beyond the anthologies and a few landmarks such as *Discipline and Punish.*

One wouldn't realize the diminishing value of Theory by perusing the anthologies, though. In fact, one gets the opposite impression—and rightly so. For, while Theory has become a humdrum intellectual matter within the humanities and a nonexistent or frivolous one without, it has indeed acquired a professional prestige that is as strong as ever. This is the paradox of its success, and failure. Intellectually speaking, twenty-five years ago Theory was an adventure of thought with real stakes. Reading "Differance" and working backward into Heidegger's and Hegel's ontology, or "The Rhetoric of Temporality" and sensing the tragic truth at the heart of Romantic irony, one apprehended something fundamental enough to affect not just one's literary method but one's entire belief system. No doubt the same was true for an earlier generation and its interpretation of Wordsworth or T. S. Eliot. But this time it was Derrida and Baudrillard, and the institution was starting to catch up to it, with "Theory specialist" entries in the MLA Job List, Introduction to Theory and Interpretation courses for first-year graduate students, and press editors searching for theory books to fill out their next year's catalogue. In an inverse way, the public seemed to agree when William Bennett initiated the academic Culture Wars with *To Reclaim a Legacy*, an NEH report that decried Theory for destroying the traditional study of literature with politicized agendas and anti-humanist dogma. He was right, and a public outcry followed, but that only confirmed to junior theorists the power and insight of their practice.

Ten years later, however, the experience had changed. As theorists became endowed chairs, department heads, series editors, and MLA presidents, as they were profiled in the *New York Times Magazine* and invited to lecture around the world, the institutional effects of Theory displaced its intellectual nature. It didn't have to happen, but that's the way the new crop of graduate students experienced it. Not only were too many Theory articles and books published and too many Theory papers delivered, but too many high-profile incursions of the humanities into public discourse had a Theory provenance. The academic gossip in *Lingua Franca* highlighted Theory much more than traditional scholarship, David Lodge's popular novels portrayed the spread of theory as a human comedy, and *People Magazine* hired a prominent academic feminist as its TV critic. One theorist became known for finding her "inner life," another for a skirt made of men's neckties, another for unionizing TAs. It was fun and heady, especially when conservatives struck back with profiles of Theorists in action such as Roger Kimball's *Tenured Radicals*, sallies which enraged many academics and soundly defeated them in public settings, but pleased the more canny ones who understood that being denounced was better than not being talked about at all (especially if you had tenure.)

The cumulative result was that the social scene of Theory overwhelmed the intellectual thrust. Years earlier, the social dynamic could be seen in the cult that formed around deconstruction, and a comparison of "Differance" with the section in *The Post Card* in which Derrida ruminates over a late-night call from "Martini Heidegger" shows the toll celebrity can take on a brilliant mind. By the mid-nineties, the social tendencies had spread all across the humanities, and its intellectual consequences surfaced in the desperation and boredom with which Theorists pondered the arrival of The Next Big Thing. When a colleague of mine returned from an MLA convention in Toronto around that time, he told a story that nicely illustrated the trend. One afternoon he hopped on a shuttle bus and sat down next to a young scholar who told him she'd just returned from a panel. He replied that he'd just returned from France, where he'd been studying for a semester.

"What are they talking about?" she asked.

"Hmm?"

"Is there any new theory?"

"Yeah, in a way," he answered. "It's called 'erudition.'"

"What's that?" she wondered.

> "Well, you read and read, and you get your languages, and you go into politics, religion, law, contemporary events, and just about everything else." (He's a 16th-century French literature scholar who comes alive in archives.)
>
> She was puzzled. "But what's the theory?"
>
> "To be honest, there isn't any theory," he said.
>
> "That's impossible." He shrugged. "Okay, then, give me the names, the people heading it."
>
> "There aren't any names. Nobody's heading it."

A trivial exchange, yes, but it signals the professional meaning and moral barrenness Theory accrued in the nineties. The more popular Theory became, the less it inspired deep commitments among searching minds. The more Theory became enshrined in anthologies ordered semester after semester, the more it became a token of professional wisdom. The only energy Theory sustained during those years issued from a non-philosophical source: the race/gender/sexuality/anti-imperialism/anti-bourgeois resentments tapped by various critics giving different objects of oppression theoretical standing.

This raises another discrepancy between Theory's intellectual content and its institutional standing. Theory in its political versions claimed to be subversive, egalitarian, anti-hegemonic, and ruthlessly self-critical, but in their actual working conditions theorists presided over one of the most hierarchical, prestige-ridden, and complacent professional spaces in our society. Theory promised to bring a fruitful pluralism to the field, yet the proliferation of outlooks created the opposite, a subdivision into sects that didn't talk to one another. Theory purported to supply intellectual tools to dismantle the contents of humanities education and undo the power structures of institutions, but while the syllabus and curriculum changed, the networking, factionalism, and cronyism only intensified. No doubt the infusion of corporate approaches into the university, along with the growing isolation of humanities professors from American society, played a role in the process, but while Theorists critiqued moneyed interests and bourgeois conventions, they enjoyed the perks of tenured celebrity as much as anyone. One can't blame them for that, but one can blame them for enlisting Theory in the service of social justice while insulating themselves from genuine social problems.

The personality rituals, the routine discoveries of radical approaches, the abhorrence of dissent, the discordance of word and deed—they enervated Theory and the intellectual stakes evaporated. The outcome shouldn't surprise anybody. It isn't the first time a philosophy rose to prominence in an institution at the same rate that it lost its power to inspire. But only recently, and far too late, have theorists begun to admit it, for example, at the April 2003 *Critical Inquiry* symposium in Chicago. Even their hesitant admissions, though, differ from previous reactions to criticism, for while others have made these points for years, Theorists and their votaries managed to make their charges look random and eccentric, outside the principal scholarly dialogue. Theory may appear at first to be a diverse collection of psychoanalysis, Marxism, feminism, and the like, but while the different schools were allowed to spar with one another (feminists criticizing psychoanalysis, political critics chastising deconstruction, and such), whenever a non-theorist tackled a Theory (Fred Crews on psychoanalysis, John Searle on deconstruction), his or her arguments were denounced as anti-intellectual bile. Theory quickly seized the vanguard terrain and cast its detractors as merely anti-Theory—retrograde, bitter, superseded.

What the latter group lacked, among other things, was a potent and lively volume such as Josué Harari's best-selling early collection of programmatic and illustrative essays, *Textual Strategies*, or a bulky anthology suitable for a survey of all the reigning approaches such as *The Norton Anthology of Theory and Criticism.* Individual critiques such as Eugene Goodheart's *Skeptic Disposition* might punch holes in one theoretical premise and another, but the institutional might of Theory remained firm. Only when an anti-or counter-Theory expression found a medium with sufficient institutional heft would the lock of Theory upon the humanities begin to loosen.

This is, of course, a heavy burden to place upon *Theory's Empire.* The purpose of the anthology, however, is not to replace existing collections but to complement and contrast with them. Despite its apparent pluralism, Theory has become a set of Establishment factions, and while in ordinary circumstances factions maintain their vitality by rivaling one another for influence, the protections of the academy permitted academic sects to coexist and turn inward. The loss of real intellectual challenge followed the time-tested laws of human nature; as John Stuart Mill put it: "Both teachers and learners go to sleep at their post, as soon as there is no enemy in the field."

In the past, yes, Theory thrived on enemies, the "anti-Theorists," but they were conveniently interpreted as outsiders. Theory needs new antagonists whose intelligence is unquestioned—not the conservative and (classic) liberals in the public sphere who unite in despising academic Theorists for their posturing and abstractedness, and not the isolated traditionalist professors who lament the hijacking of their profession with cartoon jibes on their office doors. Essays by a broad array of critics, philosophers, social scientists, and public intellectuals who question Theory's logical and empirical contents and diagnose its institutional status, gathered into a single, course-friendly volume, will restore some respect and vigor to the field. The second thoughts of preeminent theorists of the past are inadequate, and we require more to make metacriticism interesting once again.

Theory's Empire is a start. It is weighty enough to preempt the anti-intellectual tag and count as more than idiosyncratic musings on the subject. The contributors are diverse enough in their interests, training, and politics to escape the standard labels applied to critics. The contributions are informed and broad enough to bring a wider perspective to fundamental problems. Some of Theory's premises will be expelled, some names discredited, but others will be strengthened. That is the natural and healthy evolution of a discipline, and Theory has been able to resist it for too long. In a few weeks, the anthology will be the subject of a weblog discussion at The Valve, where several distinguished voices and lots of commentators shall initiate a process long overdue.

Originally posted July 2005

2. Theory of Everything

Michael Bérubé

Today, it's time to get back to Mark Bauerlein's *Butterflies and Wheels* essay on *Theory's Empire*. But first, the bad news: as hideously long as this post is (over 3500 words, nearly Holbovian in heft), this is only a warm-up. I've agreed to participate in The Valve's distributed-intelligence review of *Theory's Empire* sometime between July 12 and July 14, and I told John Holbo that I would confine myself to commenting on Bauerlein's essay, "Social Constructionism: Philosophy for the Academic Workplace". Mark your calendars, or don't. I'm also slated to review the entire volume for *The Common Review* later this year, so I'll attend to the other 700 pages of the book then, in 2000 words or less. And last but not least, Bauerlein's *B&W* essay raises a number of interesting points about the institutional status of literary theory these days, and I'm going to save those questions for another post. I'll explain why as I go.

To the text, then. Bauerlein opens by explaining why we need *Theory's Empire*:

> Why another door-stopper volume on a subject already well-covered by anthologies and reference books from Norton, Johns Hopkins, Penguin, University of Florida Press, etc.? Because in the last 30 years, theory has undergone a paradoxical decline, and the existing anthologies have failed to register the change. Glance at the roster of names and texts in the table of contents and you'll find a predictable roll call of deconstruction, feminism, new historicism, neopragmatism, postcolonial studies, and gender theory. Examine the approach to those subjects and you'll find it an expository one, as if the job of the volumes were to lay out ideas and methods without criticism (except when one school of thought in the grouping reproves

> another). The effect is declarative, not "Here are some ideas and interpretations to consider" but "Here is what theorists say and do."

I'll start with the trivial point first. Thirty years? Literary theory has been in decline for thirty years? That would take us back to ... let me think ... 1975. How strange! In 1975, deconstruction was still just a-rumbling in a few seminar rooms at Yale; feminism was still larval; New Historicism had not been invented; nobody except Fredric Jameson was doing Marxist anything on these shores; postcolonial criticism was still on the horizon; the work of Raymond Williams and Stuart Hall was still largely unread in the U.S.; and queer theory would have to wait another decade to be invented. In 1975, the hottest items in the theory store were reader-response criticism (Wolfgang Iser, *The Implied Reader*, 1974) and structuralism (Jonathan Culler, *Structuralist Poetics*, 1975). Oh yes, and Susan Sontag was reading Roland Barthes. But that's about it. Now, of course it's possible to lament the appearance of deconstruction, feminism, New Historicism, postcolonialism, queer theory, and cultural studies, and possible to say that theory ruined everything (whatever you imagine "everything" to be). But it's quite odd to characterize the explosion of theory as always already the decline of theory. It's a little like saying that the Beatles were all downhill after 1962. (I choose my analogy carefully: after all, it's entirely plausible to say that the Beatles peaked in 1966, though of course the point is worth arguing.)

Now for the more important point. Bauerlein's complaint about theory anthologies is that they are not sufficiently critical of theory, except when—and this is a remarkable escape clause—"one school of thought in the grouping reproves another." For some reason, this kind of "criticism" is not enough: it simply doesn't count when a feminist criticizes a deconstructionist or a queer theorist criticizes a feminist. But why not? And why doesn't it count when a feminist criticizes a feminist or a postcolonialist criticizes a postcolonialist, as happens roughly ten or twenty times a day?

The reason it doesn't count is that Theory is monolithic—indeed, a monolith made up of monoliths. Theory, as Bauerlein argues toward the end of his essay and as Patai and Corral argue in the introduction to *Theory's Empire*, does not admit of criticism; and likewise, the different schools of Theory do not permit dissent from their premises.

Thus, the only way a student can get a reliable assessment of what's what in Theory is to read the work of people who are hostile to every branch of it. This is a strange view of the theoretical enterprises of the past thirty years, and as I'll explain in a moment, it seems to me to be driven more by the curious phenomenon of theory-celebrity than by the actual theoretical-critical work on the ground.

Bauerlein continues:

> If the theories represented were fresh and new, not yet assimilated into scholarship and teaching, then an introductory volume that merely expounded them would make sense. The same could be said if the theories amounted to a methodological competence that students must attain in order to participate in the discipline, or if the theories had reached a point of historical importance such that one studied them as one would, say, the utopian social theories surrounding communist reform, no matter how wrongheaded they were. But Theory lost its novelty some two decades ago, and many years have passed since anybody except the theorists themselves took the latest versions seriously.

Actually, most of the introductory volumes began to appear in the early 1990s. Before then, all we had was Terry Eagleton's *Literary Theory: An Introduction*, a book so glib and unreliable that I would not inflict it on any serious student. But as I've learned from *Theory's Empire*, the event that inspired the volume was actually the publication of *The Norton Anthology of Theory and Criticism*, which was published in 2001 and which is, if anything, the least expository volume in the business. That's the reason I've assigned selections from the *Norton* in my "Intro to Graduate Study" course over the past two years: as opposed to dreary introduction-to-theory volumes that offer chapter after expository chapter on how Queer Theory Says X and New Historicism Does Y, the *Norton* simply gives students excerpts from the primary texts themselves, accompanied by detailed headnotes.

But, it turns out, that's precisely what Bauerlein et al. are objecting to—not the expository nature of the *Norton Anthology*, but the *Norton*

Anthology nature of the *Norton Anthology*. That'll become clearer in a moment. In the meantime:

> And as for disciplinary competence, the humanities are so splintered and compartmentalized that one can pursue a happy career without ever reading a word of Bhabha or Butler.

This is quite true, and I'll say more about it in my follow-up post. One of my first-year students said much the same thing to me as we were reading the *Norton* last year—or, rather, she informed me that one of her other professors had said much the same thing. Why bother with Derrida, she asked, when three-quarters of the faculty in the English department know next to nothing about Derrida?

A fine question, and it could be asked of the work of Bhabha and Butler as well. But then that would mean that Theory doesn't quite have the kind of stranglehold on the study of literature that the term "empire" is clearly meant to suggest.

> Finally, while the historical import of Theory remains to be seen, indications of oblivion are gathering. Not only are the theorists largely unread outside of graduate classrooms, but even among younger scholars within the humanities fields the reading of them usually doesn't extend beyond the anthologies and a few landmarks such as *Discipline and Punish*.

This, by contrast, is palpably untrue. The people in my wing of the enterprise have witnessed a very different phenomenon, one related to the splintering and compartmentalizing Bauerlein noted above: almost every young assistant professor at Illinois or Penn State, over the past ten years, has been thoroughly conversant in one or two areas of theory. They didn't pray to a specific Theory God every morning and evening, but they were generally familiar with debates in one or another area of the field, and often contributed to those debates themselves.

This is a phenomenon worth remarking on in more detail, so again, I'll save it for the follow-up post. But I'll say this much for now: beginning in the late 1970s, the University of Illinois had a "Unit for Criticism and Interpretive Theory" (it was responsible for the 1983 Marxism conference and the 1990 cultural studies conference) and when I arrived in 1989, the Unit simply invited assistant professors to "affiliate" with the Unit if they had any interest in matters theoretical. By the late 1990s, however, a good number of new hires in Communications, History, Anthropology, Sociology, and even Kinesiology—as well as the stalwarts from English and the modern languages—were affiliating with the Unit as a matter of course. This is not a triumphalist narrative; on the contrary, it underscores Bauerlein's next point. Theory had in fact "declined" at Illinois between the late 1970s and late 1990s, but only because one or another of its aspects had become another name for business as usual.

> One wouldn't realize the diminishing value of Theory by perusing the anthologies, though. In fact, one gets the opposite impression—and rightly so. For, while Theory has become a humdrum intellectual matter within the humanities and a nonexistent or frivolous one without, it has indeed acquired a professional prestige that is as strong as ever. This is the paradox of its success, and failure.

Reread this passage slowly if you want to figure out what's going on. The first sentence tells us that theory's value is heading south, and the anthologies mask this fact; the second tells us that the masking itself gives us the right impression, and the third that theory's prestige is as strong as ever. Theory's value, then, remains high in the humanities—but only because the humanities as a whole have been so devalued. How have the humanities been devalued? By Theory.

And then things get confusing.

> Intellectually speaking, twenty-five years ago Theory was an adventure of thought with real stakes. Reading "Différance" and working backward into Heidegger's and Hegel's ontology, or "The Rhetoric of Temporality" and sensing the tragic truth at the heart of Romantic irony, one apprehended something fundamental enough to affect not just one's literary method but one's entire belief system. No doubt the same was true for an earlier generation and its inter-

> pretation of Wordsworth or T. S. Eliot. But this time it was Derrida and Baudrillard, and the institution was starting to catch up to it, with "Theory specialist" entries in the MLA Job List, Introduction to Theory and Interpretation courses for first-year graduate students, and press editors searching for theory books to fill out their next year's catalogue.

Five years into its decline, in other words, theory was an adventure of thought with real stakes—and Bauerlein's examples are Derrida and de Man. One apprehended something fundamental enough to affect not just one's literary method but one's entire belief system: jeez, you know, it sounds as if this stuff might just be worth teaching to people today, even if only to say, "here's what Theory was like when Theory was worth doing." But then the very next passage casts its lot with Bill Bennett:

> In an inverse way, the public seemed to agree when William Bennett initiated the academic Culture Wars with *To Reclaim a Legacy*, an NEH report that decried Theory for destroying the traditional study of literature with politicized agendas and anti-humanist dogma. He was right, and a public outcry followed, but that only confirmed to junior theorists the power and insight of their practice.

Now, I know enough of Bauerlein's work to know that he hates it when people simply declare things that they need to argue, so I have to think that the pat announcement that Bennett was right is simply a mistake. And as for that public outcry: well, actually, there was no "public" outcry. There was an outpouring of right-wing screeds that eventually gave us the P.C. controversy of the early 1990s and the full flowering of the career of Dinesh D'Souza, yes, but most of the general public did not actually rise up and say, "see here, we liked reading 'The Rhetoric of Temporality' and sensing the tragic truth at the heart of Romantic irony, but this anti-humanist dogma has to go."

And then I come around to agreeing with Bauerlein's account of things again:

> Ten years later, however, the experience had changed. As theorists became endowed chairs, department heads, series editors, and MLA presidents, as they were profiled in the *New York Times Magazine* and invited to lecture around the world, the institutional effects of Theory displaced its intellectual nature. It didn't have to happen, but that's the way the new crop of graduate students experienced it. Not only were too many Theory articles and books published and too many Theory papers delivered, but too many high-profile incursions of the humanities into public discourse had a Theory provenance. The academic gossip in *Lingua Franca* highlighted Theory much more than traditional scholarship, David Lodge's popular novels portrayed the spread of theory as a human comedy, and *People Magazine* hired a prominent academic feminist as its TV critic.

I think this is really the heart of Bauerlein's complaint. In the early 1990s, the profession witnessed for the first time the phenomenon of theory-celebrity, and it was weird and often odious. Some theorists hated it, and some reveled in it. It was actually weirder than Bauerlein lets on, too: for one thing, the machinery of theory-celebrity was put together, in part, by the workings of the P.C. scaremongering itself, as more and more academics came forward to explain just what it was that they were doing. That machinery put Henry Louis Gates on the cover of the *New York Times Magazine*, and it produced Hurricane Camille Paglia at the same time. It was kind of indiscriminate that way.

And then, oddly, just when Bauerlein gets to the celebrity phenomenon (where he can score any number of points, having written perceptively in the past on *epigonism* and territorialism in the field), there are a couple of false notes.

> One theorist became known for finding her "inner life," another for a skirt made of men's neckties, another for unionizing TAs. It was fun and heady, especially when conservatives struck back with profiles of Theorists in action such as Roger Kimball's *Tenured Radicals*, sallies which enraged many academics and

> soundly defeated them in public settings, but pleased the more canny ones who understood that being denounced was better than not being talked about at all (especially if you had tenure).

Suddenly it's time for Spot the Theorist! The one with the inner life is Jane Tompkins. The one with the necktie-skirt is Jane Gallop. And the one having heady fun by unionizing TAs is, I think, Cary Nelson. Now, I've seen people sneer at the idea of graduate student unionization before this—I recall the fatuous Alan Wolfe describing it, in the pages of the *New Republic*, as "advocating class struggle within the university," and I was grateful at the time that Professor Wolfe did not call out the Pinkertons to begin busting heads. But I have never seen it likened to Gallop's or Tompkins' forms of "self-actualization" (or whatever that's called.) I leave it to you, O readers, to make of this what you will.

As for Roger Kimball, the idea that he soundly defeated anyone in a public setting is absurd—unless you mean "public setting" more or less as a synonym for "public outcry" above, in which you're probably invoking an obscure sense of the term in which "public" means "the forums of the American Enterprise Institute." But Louis Menand's *New Republic* review of *Tenured Radicals* was sufficiently devastating to persuade most intelligent readers that Kimball was a less than reliable guide to the contemporary scene.

On a side note, keep Bauerlein's complaints about academic celebrity in mind when, a bit later on, he speaks of the "growing isolation of humanities professors from American society." You would think that the phenomenon of humanities professors working with unions, writing for the popular press, and being the subject of magazine gossip would suggest, both for good and for ill, that humanities professors were less isolated from American society than were their predecessors in 1975. As it happens, these days Bauerlein himself is doing (by all accounts) terrific work as a researcher with the National Endowment for the Arts when he's not teaching at Emory. So perhaps he meant that humanities professors are increasingly isolated from American society with one notable exception. But I think he meant that he doesn't like the way humanities professors are isolated from American society and he doesn't like the way they aren't.

And now it's time for the Telling Anecdote.

When a colleague of mine returned from an MLA convention in Toronto around that time, he told a story that nicely illustrated the trend. One afternoon he hopped on a shuttle bus and sat down next to a young scholar who told him she'd just returned from a panel. He replied that he'd just returned from France, where he'd been studying for a semester.

"What are they talking about?" she asked.

"Hmm?"

"Is there any new theory?"

"Yeah, in a way," he answered. "It's called 'erudition.'"

"What's that?" she wondered.

"Well, you read and read, and you get your languages, and you go into politics, religion, law, contemporary events, and just about everything else." (He's a 16th-century French literature scholar who comes alive in archives.)

She was puzzled. "But what's the theory?"

"To be honest, there isn't any theory," he said.

"That's impossible." He shrugged. "Okay, then, give me the names, the people heading it."

"There aren't any names. Nobody's heading it."

A trivial exchange, yes, but it signals the professional meaning and moral barrenness Theory accrued in the Nineties.

Hmm. Either this is a trivial exchange, or it signals the professional meaning and moral (!) barrenness Theory accrued in the Nineties. I think Bauerlein wants to go with (b), myself. But I'm not going to fault him for predicating this part of the argument on a story that a colleague told him, for, as it happens, I was on that very shuttle bus, and I can tell you that the conversation unfolded almost exactly this way.[1] If anything, Bauerlein is being too kind to this *jejune* young woman, for as I recall, she couldn't even spell "erudition." She didn't simply ask, "what's that?" she asked Bauerlein's colleague to write the word on a pad of paper for her.

Now, seriously. Why would Bauerlein relay this trivial exchange as a sign of moral barrenness and so forth? What is gained by portraying young would-be Theorists as blithering idiots, and non-Theorists as distinguished, erudite folk who come alive in archives?

Many things, surely, but this above all—the one thing about the history of the profession that Bauerlein neglects to mention. In the 1980s, most of the literature professors who were most horrified by theory were not, despite a Christopher Ricks here and a Frederick Crews there, a very impressive bunch. On the contrary, in those days, we upper-level undergraduates and graduate students had a whole mess of people who'd gotten tenure in the 1960s back when there was a severe shortage of college professors (I know it sounds strange) and the standards for tenure were, shall we say, quite low. Some of those professors didn't produce any scholarship of note between 1970 and 1985 (some didn't produce any scholarship at all), and guess what? Assistant professors came up for tenure who were working in feminism or deconstruction, and some of their elders had the task of reviewing their work even though they didn't even know how to distinguish a good feminist or deconstructive argument from a bad one, or a derivative one, or a brilliant one. Meanwhile, graduate students like me were not inspired by faculty members who complained that New Historicist readings of Wordsworth were destroying the integrity of "Tintern Abbey" (a real example) or that feminists were interested in nineteenth-century British novels only because they were hostile to marriage (another real example). We decided, on the basis of a preponderance of the available evidence, that the "anti-Theorists" of the 1980s consisted largely of dodderers and deadwood. (And we knew what "erudition" was, too!) So when Bauerlein writes that "Theory quickly seized the vanguard terrain and cast its detractors as merely anti-Theory—retrograde, bitter, superseded," he surely does so in the knowledge that twenty years ago, a good number (though not all!) of literature professors who denounced every kind of theory as "froggy nonsense" (yet another real example) were simply not the most intellectually active or curious people in the department. They certainly weren't reading "Différance" and working backward into Heidegger's and Hegel's ontology.

Bauerlein registers this only indirectly, by insisting that "Theory needs new antagonists whose intelligence is unquestioned," and that *Theory's Empire* is just what the doctor ordered. For the record, the volume's lineup is quite strong (though I wouldn't call all of these folks "new antagonists"), and it was sometimes true, as Bauerlein charges, that "whenever a non-theorist tackled a Theory (Fred Crews on psychoanalysis, John Searle on deconstruction), his or her arguments were denounced as anti-intellectual bile." The charge of anti-intellectualism was thrown around especially carelessly, as I recall, just as the charge of "elitism" is thrown around with abandon today. (Imagine being charged with anti-intellectualism one decade, and elitism the next. It must be vexing.) And so now, it appears, the charges will be reversed: "The more popular Theory became," Bauerlein writes, "the less it inspired deep commitments among searching minds." So now it's the anti-Theorists who are the smart kids, the searching minds. People still reading and writing about Theory are just camp followers.

Which reminds me that there's one other thing missing from Bauerlein's account, and it's central to his argument that Theory brooks no dissent: namely, the work of many of the scholars of his and my generation (he earned his doctorate a year before I did). Let me put it in the form of a challenge. Anyone who thinks that theory has lost its power to inspire searching minds simply hasn't read, or hasn't heard of, books like Amanda Anderson's *The Powers of Distance: Cosmopolitanism and the Cultivation of Detachment*, John Frow's *Cultural Studies and Cultural Value*, Rita Felski's *The Gender of Modernity*, or Grant Farred's *What's My Name? Black Vernacular Intellectuals*. (And if it's stinging dissent from Theorists you want, check out Anderson's "Debatable Performances: Restaging Contentious Feminisms" or Tim Dean's "On the Eve of a Queer Future".) Sometimes I wonder if I'm simply leading a charmed life: how is it that I happen to hang out with people like Amanda and Grant, and how is it that I'm surrounded by books like Bill Maxwell's *New Negro, Old Left* or Rachel Adams's *Sideshow U.S.A.* or my esteemed co-blogger's *Democracy's Children* or essays by James

Berger and Joseph Valente and Janet Lyon? Am I just lucky in my choice of friends and associates, or do the anti-Theorists have their radar tuned exclusively to the Celebrities and their Epigones?

Probably both. Hey, I am leading a charmed life!

Originally posted on July 06, 2005

NOTES

1 Unfortunately, my anecdote is not "true." I was not on that bus. But my anti-anecdote (or antidote) might serve a useful purpose nonetheless, not merely because it calls attention to how very convenient it was that Mark Bauerlein had an erudite friend who happened to ride an MLA shuttle bus next to an ephebe so ignorant of scholarly erudition as to be unfamiliar with the word "erudition," but also insofar as it suggests that it may not be a good idea, after all, to try to narrate the intellectual history of the 1990s by means of anecdotes.

3. Theory's Empire

John McGowan

Initial disclosure: I am one of the editors of *The Norton Anthology of Theory and Criticism*. Even more germane, perhaps, is the fact that Blackwell asked me to tell them whether I thought *Theory's Empire* was worth publishing. I was given the introduction and a table of contents. I expressed a few reservations (about which there is more below), but recommended publication. Blackwell thanked me for my opinion (and sent me a few books as payment) and that was that. I did not hear from them again—and, so, did not know that they had ignored my advice until I saw the book advertised by Columbia University Press.

Let me start with the good news. *Theory's Empire* collects some excellent work that addresses some thorny theoretical issues like truth, realism, and reference; that offers plausible narratives of the history of literary criticism as a discipline; and that presents useful descriptions of the kinds of work that literary critics do. Contributions from Morris Dickstein, John R, Searle, Vincent Descombes, Susan Haack, Paisley Livingston, and Marjorie Perloff are particularly praiseworthy. The Coda, Wayne C. Booth's "A Hippocratic Oath for the Pluralist," presents a very appealing ethics for literary work. Anyone engaged in literary studies can learn a lot from this book.

But the book is marred by its special pleading for its significance. It is, of course, in the nature of introductions to oversell the importance of the enterprise. Nothing, really, for the reviewer to get hot and bothered about. Better to keep in mind that anthologies are textbooks and, as Thomas Kuhn pointed out years ago, textbooks embody the received wisdom of the field, not its cutting edge research. Anyone even moderately versed in Theory (I will follow the editors' usage and speak of Theory with a capital T, although uneasy with that phrasing) will be familiar with most everything said in *Theory's Empire*. The same, I hasten, to add is true of *The Norton Anthology of Theory and Criticism*. Such volumes are useful compendiums—and are created, obviously, with the classroom in mind. To repeat, *Theory's Empire* has much to recommend it for classroom use.

But the editors feel compelled to make another claim, one that is reflected in their book's title. The material they collect has been suppressed; theory's hegemony is such that dissenting voices have not been heard. Theory has dismissed out of hand various compelling arguments against its assumptions, its sacred cows. As a result, literary studies has become captive to a lot of bad thinking and bad faith, a whole generation (or is it two or three generations by now?) of would-be philosophers and radical politicos who have lost any ability to be good literary critics and who never had any chance to be good philosophers or effective political agents.

I feel very tired at this point. The misunderstandings pile up so fast that it would take a book to unravel them—and I want to keep this under 3000 words. Suffice it to say two things: 1) Theory with a capital T does not exist—at least not as a coherent body of methods, beliefs, assumptions, or predilections. Here's a brief, but telling, argument for that claim. Recall that Fredric Jameson's *The Prison-House of Language* (1971) was, for many American literary critics, their first introduction to structuralism and post-structuralism. And recall, crucially, that Jameson had reservations about structuralism and was strongly against post-structuralism. Similarly, Edward Said's *Beginnings* (1975) and *The World, the Text, and the Critic* (1984) were strongly directed against Derrida and DeMan while also registering uneasiness with Foucault's understanding of power. Are Jameson and Said with Theory or against it? We are only led to ask such a nonsensical question if we reify the notion of Theory. There are ongoing disciplinary and interdisciplinary debates about various issues. Jameson and Said were engaged in those debates and, as strong debaters tend to do, worked hard to frame the issues in distinctive ways that made their arguments seem compelling. They were neither buying nor trying to sell some soap called Theory.

2) But Theory is not utterly a chimera. It is the (unfortunate) name given to a particular phenomenon: the end of the short-lived (1945 to 1965) and never uncontested rule of New Criticism. Theory is a misleading name because it suggests that one thing replaced New Criticism. But there are a plurality of practices and methodologies evidenced by the literary criticism of the past forty years. Theory is an even more unfortunate name if it leads one to think that there is some foundational or transcendent (in Kant's sense of that term) conditions the theorist claims to have identified as the necessary a priori to critical practice. This is not to deny that some literary theorists of the past forty years have had Kantian ambitions. But none has succeeded in producing a set of categories (and/or forms) that has won anything

like wide-spread acceptance in the field. Theory much more plausibly names the proliferation of multiple reasons for doing literary criticism at all and the equally profuse proliferation of accounts of what it means to do literary criticism. That's why Theory is so confusing and so terrifying. It marks a field (literary studies) where the center has not held.

Theory, then, is not—and has never been—an empire. Yes, certain theorists have been particularly influential and much scholarly work has been done under their spell. But that's only to say that *Discipline and Punish* was as inspiring in its day as *The Well Wrought Urn* was in its. And, of course, second-rate, imitative work was—and will continue to be until the last trump sounds—done. Is predictable Foucauldian work (all that productive power!) more pernicious than predictable new critical readings (all those ambiguities and paradoxes!)?

I was taught by Yale Ph.Ds who had studied with Brooks, Warren, and Wellek. You can't convince me that literary studies has been in serious decline since their heyday. They were bad teachers because they disdained our unsophisticated interest in what literature had to say to us in their determination (or so it seemed to my twenty-year old self) to drain all the life from poetry. Luckily, I had some maverick professors, memorably one who taught Blake as a true believer, and another who went right from Wayne Booth's *The Rhetoric of Fiction* to Roland Barthes' *Writing Degree Zero* (this in 1972) as he gave us William Burroughs, John Barth, Doris Lessing, and Thomas Pynchon to read. Those professors were the ones who indicated to me a field, a discipline, that was opening up—and thus seemed exciting and vital to pursue. And I experienced the advent of theory as fulfilling that promise.

This has already gotten too long. So I will close with three final points—and come back on Wednesday with one last bone to pick with the overarching self-understanding of the book (as represented by the editors.)

The first point is that *Theory's Empire* is marred by the inclusion of a number of contributions that are best described as peevish. True, we can get into the pot calling the kettle black on this score. Searle's attack on Derrida is very smart, but he certainly showed little rhetorical savvy when he displayed an arrogance and impatience that was bound to drive off readers he might otherwise have convinced. Derrida, of course, has nothing on Searle on this score, as Reed Way Dasenbrock detailed in his wonderful essay, "Taking It Personally: Derrida's Responses".[1]

(Foucault and Habermas, by way of contrast, were always thoughtful and respectful in their replies to critics.)

The larger question is why is peevishness so prevalent? Far too many academics assume an aggrieved air of being unheard, unappreciated, and conspired against. One can only conclude that we are professionals in a brutal business—brutal because the judgment of our work is so constant and the ladder of prestige is so visible and so hierarchical. But let's not reduce everything to professional pique (which is not to dismiss it either.) Let's give credit to a more noble cause. The contributors to this volume really believe that something valuable—literary criticism as they wish to see it practiced—is in the process of being trashed. And yet their colleagues and students don't see it that way. Nothing seems capable of awakening the discipline to the work of destruction in which it is not just blindly, but gleefully, engaged. The best analogy here is to liberals on today's American scene. They keep jumping up and down to try to catch the populace's attention; our country is imperiled by the antics of the Bush Administration. But the populace either hasn't noticed or doesn't care—or, worse still, actually wants what the Administration has to offer. As one of those frantic liberals, I can (through this thought experiment) feel the pain of those who truly do believe that Theory (as they insist on understanding it) is doing irreparable harm to something they love. But I do want to extend to these suffering and increasingly desperate souls the same advice I tender to my fellow liberals and to myself: no whining. It doesn't become either you or I, all of whom have a very privileged life in a world where billions do not, and each of whom has his classroom as his castle and various outlets for the publication of his views. If those views do not prevail, there is little reason to produce conspiracy fantasies and even less reason (because it is counter-productive to the rhetorical work of persuasion) to whine.

Point number two begins with a concession to the editors of *Theory's Empire*. There is evidence of group-think out there. Let me give an example that bugged me for years. For a long time (happily that time now seems over), lots of people in literary studies knew that if Habermas said it, it must be wrong. The man couldn't get a fair hearing in certain circles. The reasons for this failure in open-mindedness are many and complex. But we certainly should not discount the bad effects of a lousy job market and of the increasing pressure to publish. Conformity will result when it is very hard to get—and to keep—a place at the table. Furthermore—and more interestingly it seems to me—the effect of theory generally was to place everything into question. So, when you went to get a piece published, there was this horrible sense that you had to have an elaborate argument for every single assertion you made. Under such conditions, younger scholars especially latched on gratefully to any port in the storm, any assertion or argument that seemed solid in a world of shifting sands. The results were often not edifying, although very understandable.

The larger point is that most of the work in any discipline is derivative. It elaborates on the pioneering work of the few—or it works to revise (more or less aggressively) that work. Academic work is necessarily double-voiced (at least): it plays its institutional role in credentialing the writer as well as attempts to contribute to knowledge. All of us who review work submitted to presses and journals for publication know the difficulties of honoring these two not very compatible purposes. A lot of work gets published because the writer is worthy of a job and of tenure; the work is, in fact, justified, because it keeps the writer's hand in and thus keeps him or her an active, contributing member to the pedagogical tasks undertaken by the discipline. But the work is not first-rate.

All of this is relevant because *Theory's Empire* deals far too often in generalizations about "theory" and not often enough in engagement with specific theorists. But it makes all the difference whether you are engaging with first-rate work or with the general run-of-the-mill work of the vast majority of practitioners in the field. And once you think about mounting arguments against—but also carefully engaged with—the work of Derrida, Foucault, or Said, the notion that such arguments have not been undertaken or have been suppressed is just absurd. The bookshelves are lined with works that do just that. I'm the author of one of them myself. (*Postmodernism and its Critics* (1991).)

Which brings me to point number three—a point I did bring up in my report to Blackwell. One major source of critique of French theory was Habermas; another was the hermeneutic tradition, notably Gadamer and Ricoeur. *Theory's Empire* is relentlessly Anglo-American (although E. P. Thompson and Raymond Williams, who had their arguments with the French, are notably absent, perhaps because their work inspires cultural studies). One problem, I guess, is figuring out whether Habermas and Gadamer and Ricoeur are Theory or not. It would be funny to call them co-conspirators in Theory since they so resolutely set themselves against other figures who are always associated with Theory: Derrida and Foucault most notably. But it would also be funny to say that they are not involved in Theory. What name would you give to their work? Habermas, in particular, is both more overtly political and more indifferent to literature than Derrida ever was. So, because Habermas doesn't fit the Manichean frame of the volume, he must be passed over in silence. Who cares that he wrote the most detailed critique (in *The Philosophical Discourse of Modernity*) of the theorists that this book wants to argue with?

But I bring up Habermas and the other Continental thinkers only partly to score that last point. More importantly, Habermas suggests and Ricoeur develops in great detail very interesting understandings of how texts produce and disseminate meanings. The biggest problem of *Theory's Empire* is that it is so relentlessly negative—all about the deficiencies of what is currently being done in literary studies. First of all, such constant carping makes you wonder if these people have read any of the work done by literary scholars in the past fifteen to twenty years. Sure, there is lots of crap. But there is lots of wonderful and exciting work as well. Are we really to believe that it is an unrelieved wasteland? And, second, there is very little in the way of any constructive statements about what we should be doing—beyond appeals to sustain the love of literature against the assaults of Theory. There are some lesser-known alternatives to Derrida and Foucault out there. *Theory's Empire* would be a much stronger—and much more appealing—book if it showcased some of those alternatives. Somehow I think that the aspiring literary critic who read this volume in its current form straight through, even if she found her love of literature reaffirmed, would certainly flee the academic pursuit of literary criticism.

Originally posted on July 11, 2005

NOTES

1. Reed Way Dasenbrock, "Taking It Personally: Derrida's Responses," *College English* 56:3 (1994): 261-79.

4. Theory's Empire, Making Sense of the Theme

John Holbo

Our *Theory's Empire* event started early, with Mark Bauerlein's B&W review and Michael Bérubé's vigorous riposte. Let me join the discussion by way of introducing my general thoughts on the value and coherence of the volume's theme.

Bérubé:

> Bauerlein's complaint about theory anthologies is that they are not sufficiently critical of theory, except when—and this is a remarkable escape clause—"one school of thought in the grouping reproves another." For some reason, this kind of "criticism" is not enough: it simply doesn't count when a feminist criticizes a deconstructionist or a queer theorist criticizes a feminist. But why not? And why doesn't it count when a feminist criticizes a feminist or a postcolonialist criticizes a postcolonialist, as happens roughly ten or twenty times a day?
>
> The reason it doesn't count is that Theory is monolithic—indeed, a monolith made up of monoliths. Theory, as Bauerlein argues toward the end of his essay and as Patai and Corral argue in the introduction to Theory's Empire, does not admit of criticism; and likewise, the different schools of Theory do not permit dissent from their premises. Thus, the only way a student can get a reliable assessment of what's what in Theory is to read the work of people who are hostile to every branch of it. This is a strange view of the theoretical enterprises of the past thirty years, and as I'll explain in a moment, it seems to me to be driven

> more by the curious phenomenon of theory-celebrity than by the actual theoretical-critical work on the ground.

Theory-celebrity is indeed curious and discussion-worthy. Geoffrey Galt Harpham's "The End of Theory, the Rise of the Profession: A Rant in Search of Responses", is a good place to start: "the bad effects of 'the star system', by which a few conspicuously useless queen bees absorb vast resources that might go to building the institution" (381).

Bérubé's thesis is that global indictments of 'Theory' tend to be mistargeted complaints about institutional deformations, not proper critiques of intellectual formations. I will argue this is mistaken. The anti-Theory line Bauerlein is pushing on the volume's behalf is sound. But Bérubé makes reasonable points. He faults Bauerlein for succumbing to the temptations of the telling anecdote. The woman on the bus. In comments, Bauerlein cops a plea to 'hasty historicizing' and mixing serious and side issues. So no need to argue more about that. Bauerlein is still right that the problem with Theory anthologies is that they are insufficiently critical of Theory.

Here's another route to the same conclusion. Some of you have read that mock-Platonic dialogue I've circulated in draft form for some time. At the tail end I poke myself with Nietzsche, letting a little air out of the balloon: "At times one remains faithful to a cause only because its opponents do not cease to be insipid." In my case, anti-Theory. As Bérubé puts it: "So now it's the anti-Theorists who are the smart kids." He doesn't think so, obviously, but he's provoking the reasonable thought that—were it so—what would it prove? You can't really settle anything by letting the debate devolve into a duel between competing senses of who is comparatively less insipid. Yet: even granting Bérubé his point, Bauerlein is still right that Theory suffers from a pernicious incapacity for self-criticism. Yes, even though Theorists are a perennially squabblesome lot, as Bérubé points out. That's not good enough because they don't squabble in the right way.

What I am going to do now is, in effect, restate elements of my dialogue's argument to this conclusion. (If you want the mock-Platonic full dress version, please consult the original.) This will amount to a defense of the editorial wisdom of an anthology entitled *Theory's Empire, an Anthology of Dissent.* This is a book that is sure to be judged by its cover. And, up to a point, rightly. The title lodges, by implication, a sweeping charge. If that turns out to be invalid, misguided, just plain over the top—a too-cute transvaluation of values (they think theory is a site of dissent! *we're dissenting from them!*)— the sum will be less than the parts; although perhaps reasonably priced at $29.95.

This seems to be Michael's view. "The volume's lineup is quite strong." And, in comments:

> No doubt a future edition of the *Norton* will include some *Theory's Empire* contributors; at the same time, I have to remark that TE—and Bauerlein's essay about it—practically invites that response. What's more, some of the contributors, like Anthony Appiah, are already considered to be people who helped to build the theoretical edifice.

Michael's sense is that, at the end of the day, it is absurd to posture as if you are 'outside theory'—let alone part of a small band of scrappy rebels, darting nimbly past the rigid defenses of some sinister monolith. Whatever is intellectually valuable in a book like *Theory's Empire* will eventually be acknowledged and taken up, and not in some nightmarish 'you-will-be-assimilated' way either.

This is wrong for a reason so simple it is hard to take seriously. But it should be taken seriously.

Let capital-T 'Theory'—as in *Theory's Empire*—denote a moderately culturally coherent cluster of philosophically-inflected academic writings. Certain figures, arguments and ideas; theme and variation on an intellectual style and sensibility, interlocking with shifting but not totally unsettled sets of questions, issues and subjects. Theory was born around 1965 and anything written before then is 'Theory' only in a somewhat strained, anachronistic sense. (To adapt Nietzsche, 'some Theory is born prenatally,' if you simply must shoehorn in Adorno, Heidegger, Nietzsche, Raymond Williams, Novalis, or whomever you insist 'did Theory' before anyone really did. For that matter, Heraclitus was the first Romantic.) Despite its philosophic and academic character, Theory has never exerted significant influence on Anglophone academic philosophy. But Theory achieved considerable dominance of English departments, especially in America, by about 1985; after which its influence declined to some degree.

Nothing new here, and feel free to quibble. I don't want to insist on more than the following: 'Theory' is a name for an academic movement, or school or style of thought, or cluster of them. As such, it is *prima facie* reasonable to consider that a different school or style might be superior, or at least might be worthy of consideration as a competitor. The problem is that defenders of Theory have gotten into the bad habit of foiling the formulation of this thought.

The easy, one-step procedure: misinterpret anti-Theory arguments as if the target were theory in a lower case sense; what we might call 'Coleridgean theory': 'The meanest of men has his theory; and to think at all is to theorise.' Terry Eagleton's *Literary Theory, An Introduction* gives us the classic formulation of the T-to-t fallacy.

> The economist J. M. Keynes once remarked that those economists who disliked theory, or claimed to get along better without it, were simply in the grip of an older theory. This is also true of literary students and critics. There are some who complain that literary theory is impossibly esoteric – who suspect it is an arcane, elitist enclave somewhat akin to nuclear physics ... Some students and critics also protest that literary theory 'gets in between the reader and the work.' The simple response to this is that without some kind of theory, however unreflective and implicit, we would not know what a 'literary work' was in the first place, or how we were to read it. Hostility to theory usually means an opposition to other people's theories and an oblivion to one's own. One purpose of this book is to lift that repression and allow us to remember.[1]

But when we plug in the relevant, distinct senses of the word we get: those opposed to one particular style of thought must think there is some other way of thinking that is preferable (or at least worthy of consideration.) As a defense of Theory, let alone a proof of false consciousness, this is a non-starter. Yet it is advanced as a decisive objection to 'resistance to Theory'.

Am I saying Keynes is making a bad argument as well? No. Keynes is not employing 'theory' as a proper name for one school of thought.

This point is a bit more complicated, admittedly. We'll return to it below.

When Bérubé describes Eagleton's *Literary Theory, an Introduction*, as "a book so glib and unreliable that I would not inflict it on any serious student," I despair of time I've wasted teasing out implications of Eagletonian claims. But then I read in comments to Michael's post: "The best thing in [Eagleton], iirc, is his Keynes quote or paraphrase, to the effect that those who claim to be theory-free are just in the grips of some theory they're unconscious of. And that's at the very beginning, so you can skip the rest of the book." So there is at least *one* soul in need of saving from this bad argument. And whoever wrote the introduction to *The Norton Anthology of Theory and Criticism* makes two. (Vincent Leitch, I presume.) I just discovered this passage the other day.

> In recent decades, theory and criticism have grown ever more prominent in literary and cultural studies, treated less as aids to the study of literature and culture than as ends in themselves. As Jonathan Culler notes in *Framing the Sign: Criticism and Its Institutions* (1988), "Formerly the history of criticism was part of the history of literature (the story of changing conceptions of literature advanced by great writers), but ... now the history of literature is part of the history of criticism." This dramatic reversal, which occurred gradually over the course of the twentieth century, means that the history of criticism and theory increasingly provides the general framework for studying literature and culture in colleges and universities. Some literary scholars and writers deplore the shift toward theory, regarding it as a turn away from literature and its central concerns. These "antitheorists," as they are called, advocate a return to studying literature for itself—yet however refreshing this position may at first appear, it has problems: it itself presupposes a definition of literature, and it promotes a certain way of scrutinizing literature ("for itself"). In other words, the antitheory position turns out to rely on unexamined—and debatable—theories of litera-

> ture and criticism. What theory demonstrates, in this case and in others, is that there is no position free of theory, not even the one called "common sense".[2]

The problem here is the same as for Eagleton. The first sentence notes the growth of Theory. The last notes that the incidence of 'thinking at all' is probably pretty constant. The impression is generated that to oppose Theory would be to stand athwart the train of thought yelling 'halt'! Obviously this is confused.

In an earlier POST, I suggested *Theory's Empire* fulfills its function of being a beam in the eye of the *Norton*. The above paragraph underscores this. If you honestly believe what this paragraph says, you will think that the 'antitheorists' are an intensely simple, naive, unreflective, philosophically untutored, anti-intellectual tribe. To open *Theory's Empire*, then, could be nothing less than a staggering revelation. Not one page of this 700 page volume is remotely like what the *Norton* leads you to believe every page of it must be like! Oh, Brave New World!

On the other hand, if you did not believe what this paragraph says; if you already knew perfectly well this is a not a dispute between those who think and those who don't—and if you wrote that paragraph anyway? Well, that would be a tad ... imperialistic.

It may be helpful, for comparison purposes, to consider how absurd the following would be: a volume entitled *The Norton Anthology of Analysis and Philosophy*, containing classic works of philosophy from the pre-socratics down to the 20th Century; then, starting in the 20th, nothing outside the core 'analytic' tradition that starts with Moore, Russell and Frege. If anyone wants to argue that analytic philosophy has general shortcomings the introduction has a canned response: to think is to analyze. So to be opposed to the Anglo-American philosophical tradition—the analytic tradition—is to be convicted of absurd delusion. No criticism of analytic philosophy allowed, you say? But here is David Lewis arguing with W.V.O. Quine. And some people think Kripke is terribly important, while others think he is less so. Why doesn't that count as 'criticizing analytic philosophy'?

The point that Theory anthologies are insufficiently critical of Theory is sound because it is analogous to the sound points that would be made against this hypothetical anthology.

Let's now attempt an experimental blunting of the anti-Theory point. Sticking with my silly hypothetical: if analytic philosophers were to ignore, say, Heidegger on the basis of bad puns on 'analytic', this would add insult to, but perhaps be no more injurious than, the situation we've got: analytic philosophers ignoring Heidegger. So: how much extra damage does it *really* do if Theorists are in the habit of defending themselves with bad puns, rather than just plain ignoring their critics like any normal person?

From Mill's *On Liberty*, chapter 1:

> Unfortunately for the good sense of mankind, the fact of their fallibility is far from carrying the weight in their practical judgment, which is always allowed to it in theory; for while every one well knows himself to be fallible, few think it necessary to take any precautions against their own fallibility, or admit the supposition that any opinion, of which they feel very certain, may be one of the examples of the error to which they acknowledge themselves to be liable. Absolute princes, or others who are accustomed to unlimited deference, usually feel this complete confidence in their own opinions on nearly all subjects. People more happily situated, who sometimes hear their opinions disputed, and are not wholly unused to be set right when they are wrong, place the same unbounded reliance only on such of their opinions as are shared by all who surround them, or to whom they habitually defer.

In *theory*, Theory is self-critical; keenest of the keen when it comes to emphasizing epistemological limits. In practice, Theory is appallingly imperial. Well, it's not so bad as that. Apart from a few celebrity Theorists who really do seem to think they are entitled to unlimited deference, ordinary practitioners are willing to be set right now and again, by others within the circle of those who 'do Theory'. But they still assume those outside their little circle—'antitheory' types— must be wrong. Bog-standard dogmatism of our species, in other words.

This may seem like a pretty good argument that Theory is not especially un-self-critical—merely human, all-too human. But let me sharpen the anti-Theory point back up again.

Making bad puns on 'theory' in fact causes significant injury, over and above the insult. By habitually misrepresenting their critics, defenders of Theory end up obliged to misrepresent themselves. *If your first move is to elide the distinction between membership in a particular academic tribe and 'thinking at all', there are no good second moves when it comes to discussing that academic tribe.* Any sharp or insightful observation you make will expose the absurdity of the first move. So you *don't.* J. L. Austin quips that 'in philosophy, it is usually all over by the bottom of page 1'. Eagleton never really gets clear about what he's talking about, having gotten off on the wrong foot with Keynes. The *Norton* is substantially sunk by the first paragraph of its introduction. To be fair, introductions to big anthologies are doomed to stiffness. But they needn't be so muffled and uninformative as this one manages to be, swaddling its subject in *ersatz* necessity.

Let me take this opportunity to let Bérubé off the hook. His post is lively and interesting, isn't it? I am very grateful to him for accepting my invitation to be part of this conversation, and I think he has already done a lot to ensure that an intellectually productive tone is set. Aren't the comments good? Even Kevin Drum says it's interesting! For starters, no bad puns. But that's just a warm-up. Michael is refreshingly frank when it comes to recalling and reconstructing for his audience some main aspects of the history of Theory—some strange twists and turns and odd dynamics that have gotten us where we are. Theory anthologies and introductory discussions are consistently bad at that. The obligatory, habitual pretense that somehow Theory is automatically superior to the only alternative—gross, antitheory naivete—is herbicide to serious, critical consideration of Theory, should such a thing attempt to spring up in the cracks.

Which gets us back to *Theory's Empire*. The volume is useful not just because it refutes the notion that everyone in it must be a naive idiot, but because it turns out to be on the whole pretty good at this thing theory introductions and anthologies are pretty bad at: being intelligently frank about Theory; being canny and clear-eyed about a peculiar product of academic culture. The volume contents are not uniformly successful. Sometimes it tips over into over-aggression. We'll talk about it.

Anticipating a couple objections will get me to stage two of my argument.

First, there are many more than two senses of 'theory'. Talking as if there are just two—Capital-T and Coleridgean—is confused. Yes, but multiplying senses of 'theory' will only make *worse* Eagleton's bad assumption that there is only one, which is the *Norton*'s assumption. It is important to see this argument is bad, and see the bad effects it really does have.

Second, by this late date Theory—i.e. that cluster of more or less distinctive academico-philosophical literary formations—is too tangled and heterogeneous to be usefully subjected to global critique. Saying 'this is what's wrong with Theory' is inevitably going to be intellectual injustice. But that's exactly why what you want is something like—well, like *Theory's Empire*. Something hefty enough that you can hope it begins to achieve coverage of this sprawling subject. Because even if global criticism risks overreach, piecemeal criticism will surely fall short. Because it isn't *just* the pieces. It's how they fit together, and what brought them together. The issue is not a figure or idea or argument or book or article but a distinctive style and intellectual sensibility—yes, hard to pin down, but the attempt must be made.

A nice passage from Valentine Cunningham's *Reading After Theory*, which appears in *Theory's Empire*:

> Theorists have indeed managed to pull off what is, by any standards, an astounding coup, or trick; have managed to wedge together a great many various subjects, concerns, directions, impulses, persuasions and activities that are going on in and around literature, and squeeze them all under the one large sheltering canopy of 'Theory'. They have managed to compel so many divergent wings of what they call Theory under the one roof, persuaded so many sectional variants of interpretative work to sink their possible differences around a common conference table, in the one seminar with the sign Theory on its door. So while setting their faces, usually, against Grand Narratives and Keys to All Mythologies, as delusive and imperialist, and all that, Theorists have managed to erect that Grandest Narrative of all – Theory – the greatest intellectual colonizer of all time. How this wheeze was pulled off, how you can have the political and

> the personal subjects of literature – representations of selfhood and class and genre and race: the outside-concerns, the outward look of writing, the descriptive and documentary, the reformist intentions and the ideological instrumentality of writing – envisioned and envisionable as absolutely part and parcel of the often quite opposite and contradictory functions of writing – the merely formal, or the technically linguistic, or (as often) a deeply inward, world-denying, aporetic writing activity – rather defies ordinary logic. Foundationalism and anti-foundationalism, shall we say roughly the Marxist reading on the one hand, and the deconstructionist on the other, make awkward bed-partners, you might think. But Theory deftly marries them off, or at least has them more or less cheerfully all registered as guests in the same hotel room. (27-8)

When it comes to analyzing this trick, the *last* thing we should do is *fall* for the trick. If any sense of inevitability and necessity attaches to Theory, in the above sense, we fell for the trick, picked the wrong card. Theory anthologies always fall for the trick by picking the 'theory is necessary' card. Oddly enough, Cunningham falls for the trick. Or very nearly. He more or less reconciles himself to living in Theory's Empire, per the above passage, on the grounds that the alternative is naive idiocy. Here is a passage from *Reading After Theory* that didn't make it into *Theory's Empire*.

> There is, of course, a common fantasy of the independent, the natural reader, of men and women quite alone with the text, making sense of it by their own unaided efforts, uncontaminated by givens and presuppositions, by prejudices and doctrines, especially not anything that might be called theory, or (especially) Theory. This dream fires many a whinge against current literary education. But no one ever did read de novo, raw, naturally; understanding never came that easily.[3]

Here is a sentence that makes it in: "No simple return to prelapsarian theoretical innocence is ever possible, for that never existed. There never was such a theory arcadia as Theory's opponent's allege." (p. 38).

This is a variant on the Eagleton fallacy, a.k.a. the *Norton* fallacy. The error is twofold. First, it is absurd on the face to suggest that this allegedly 'common fantasy' has a significant subscription rate. Those who criticize Theory do not do so because they suffer some epistemological delusion. (Poke Helen Vendler with a stick; she may emit something about wanting to recover 'the taste on the tongue'—direct contact with literature. But this is a figure of speech, not bad epistemology. It's shorthand for a set of pedagogical preferences that is not delusional, though it is debatable.)

Second, if anyone simply *insists* on fantasizing that this fantasy is common, it ought to be clear that one could—potentially—object to Theory on other grounds. If proof is needed, *Theory's Empire* contains, for the record, exactly zero fantasies about cavorting with texts in the epistemological nude. 'Theory's Empire or delusions of textual arcadia' is emphatically not an exhaustive catalogue of options.

Cunningham will retort that he wants to underscore how Theory's concerns are not discontinuous with those of previous critics. "The offensive concerns of Theory have always been present in some form or another, muted often, differently loaded frequently, but still there. Theory has always been fallen, as it were. What worries some and excites others, about our recent Theory is by no means its innovativeness, but only what are in effect its strong renovations" (p. 38).

But no. This is a plainly inaccurate account of what excites some and worries and offends others about the Higher Eclecticism, as we might call what Cunningham describes. What worries and offends is a strong sense that there is nothing *higher* about it. (Pardon me, what follows is obvious. But since it is denied, it apparently needs to be said.) Intellectually, Theory looks like unseemly irrationalism, an excuse for simple absence of discipline. Stylistically, it looks like metaphysical mannerism—kitsch. I'm not saying this is obviously right. But this is obviously the *complaint*.

Furthermore, Theory looks dogmatic. A passage from the introduction to the standard anthology, *Cultural Studies* (Grossberg, Nelson, Treichler, eds.):

> It is problematic for cultural studies simply to adopt, uncritically, any of the formalized disciplinary practices of the academy, for those practices, as much as the distinctions they inscribe, carry with them a heritage of disciplinary investments and exclusions and a history of social effects that cultural studies would often be inclined to repudiate." Ergo, "no methodology can be privileged or even temporarily employed with total security and confidence, yet none can be eliminated out of hand. Textual analysis, semiotics, deconstruction, ethnography, interviews, phonemic analysis, psychoanalysis, rhizomatics, content analysis, survey research – all can provide important insights and knowledge.[4]

That's Theory to a T. The rhetoric hints at elevated critical awareness—many theories sounds like many layers of critical defense. But peel these back and what one finds—by the editors' own admission—is a group of critics who "would often be inclined" one way, rather than another. The theories constitute no check on these inclinations but instead provide flexible assurance they will *not* be checked.

Getting back to Cunningham—yes, the prospect of critics trusting their noses without theoretic checks is nothing new. But if Theory turns out to be, as it were, a 'strong renovation' of anti-theoretical genteel amateurism—amateurism on stilts, speaking with a mouthful of metaphysical marbles—then this circus-act quality of what goes on under the Big Tent of Theory is no defense, merely another way of stating the case for the prosecution.

In his contribution to *Theory's Empire*, "Changing Epochs", Frank Kermode discusses a book that would appear to represent the frozen limit of the empire's borders, as it were:

> One of the books recently published by Routledge is Thomas Docherty's *After Theory* (1990). Docherty, as his blurb expresses it, contends that the Enlightenment project of emancipation through knowledge has ended in failure by allowing the academy to "become a prison-house for the institutionalization of critique." The agent of this imprisonment is Theory, so he con-

> tends that Theory needs to be liberated in its turn. After theory there needs to be a post-modernism that "questions every manner of binding or framing," which valorizes transgression and "error," "error" being 'criminal' in the eyes of the white fathers, the acknowledged legislators behind the law of the imperialist enlightenment of the dark tropics of discourse; but the criminality remains fully justified if we wish to reject the parameters of an imperialist mode of politics and an imperialist mode of conversation or social understanding." Finally Docherty wants thought to be liberated from all theory. "It is only in the refusal to be answerable to a governing theory that thought, and above all theoretical thought, becomes possible once more." The dismissal of theoretical thought by means of posttheoretical thought in order to make theoretical thought possible, with the consequence adumbrated in the argument (theory liberated by posttheory, in order to be liberated again, and so on for ever) is a characteristically "oppositional" proposal. The association of older modes of thinking with imperialism simply goes without saying, and what used to be thought of as a "primary" text is at no stage involved in the argument. Why should it be, when there simply is no such thing? It is a sign of the times that Docherty is described as a professor of English. (613-4)

It's not hard to connect the dots with Cunningham. The semantic elastic of 'theory' is overstretched and not snapping back into any sort of shape. The obvious reason for suspecting the Higher Eclecticism is not a good idea is that it looks doomed to go somewhere shapeless and dull, not that it seems to be leading away from textual arcadia.

Having now made the case against Theory as bluntly as I can, let me emphasize that it is not open-and-shut. The one thing Docherty is clear about is that his approach aims at a thorough-going rejection of Enlightenment intellectual values and methods. I always quote Friedrich Schlegel at this point in the discussion. He's a little more delicate about it than Docherty: "It is equally deadly to the spirit to have a system and not to have one. One must resolve to combine the two." Now *there* is your positive recipe for Theory—the Higher Eclecticism—in one line or less. Theory is a late-Romantic formation, a true child of the counter-Enlightenment. I say this not to dismiss but to clarify and give Theory credit for its deep intellectual, literary and cultural roots.

Explaining why Theory might be good—that is, why Higher Eclecticism might be a positive value, rather than just some ongoing academic accident—would mean saying why Schlegel is right. It is not much of an exaggeration to say that the question of the value of Theory is the question of the value of the counter-Enlightenment. Calculate the extent of that value and you have surveyed the outermost possible boundaries of Theory's rightful Empire. Period. No more bad puns.

Which brings us back to Keynes, who I imagine has been an itch in the back of some heads. Keynes says those who resist theory are simply in the grips of an older theory. As J.S. Mill says: "whoever despises theory, let him give himself what airs of wisdom he may, is self-convicted as a quack." This is an expression of Enlightenment intellectual ideals. I won't try to spell out what these are, because it would be difficult. A commitment to reason and reason-giving, but not necessarily an aggressive scientism. In the context of the relatively recent history of literary criticism, a number of paired names suggest themselves: Ogden and Richards; Wellek and Warren; Wimsatt and Beardsley. In *Theory's Empire* we get some more. (Why they travel in pairs I couldn't say.) Freadman and Miller; Lamarque and Olsen. And a few individuals: Paisley Livingston, John M. Ellis. They theorize literature but don't 'do Theory'.

The antonym of 'theorist', in the lower-case sense, is probably 'genteel amateur'; the critic who refuses to admit the eclectic and probably contradictory cluster of notions he calls his 'sound instincts' might be inadequate, or amenable to systematic improvement. Like the editors of *Cultural Studies*, the amateur knows better than to let any 'theory' get in the way of what he has decided, in advance, are the proper conclusions.

I am making fun of Theory, yes. But it is important to see that I don't think my implied alignment of Theory with genteel amateurism is utterly decisive. What I do take to be decisive is this: it is deadly to the spirit of the discussion of theory to let Enlightenment and counter-Enlightenment wires get crossed (yes, even though F. Schlegel says it is deadly *not* to cross your wires. He didn't mean to excuse bad puns. The day Romanticism needs puns to keep itself alive is the day it ought to be decently buried. Which is probably every day, which is part of the undying charm of Romanticism.)

Let 'Theory' stand for the counter-Enlightenment side; let 'theory' stand for the Enlightenment side; Theory is anti-theoretical; theory is anti-Theoretical. Neither side is opposed to human mentality, *per se*, so we need another term for the fact that people think. Maybe: *thinking*. Last but not least, there are a great many critics who are not terribly preoccupied with either theory or Theory. This is not any sort of demonstrable epistemological error, merely a preference. Valentine Cunningham's epigraph comes from Virginia Woolf: "To read on a system ... is very apt to kill what it suits us to consider the more humane passion for pure and disinterested reading." I am a little puzzled at this choice of tags because I can only think that Cunningham sees it as confirming his thesis that a rejection of 'theory' can only mean retreat into delusions of purity. But it seems to work better as a *reductio* on his conclusion, because surely we give Woolf credit for being cannier than that.

Originally posted on July 12, 2005

NOTES

1 Terry Eagleton, *Literary Theory, an Introduction*, 2nd ed. (London: Blackwell, 1996), vii-viii.

2 Vincent Leitch, ed., *Norton Anthology of Theory and Criticism* (New York: W.W. Norton, 2001), 1.

3 Valentine Cunningham, *Reading after Theory* (Oxford: Blackwell, 2002), 5.

4 Lawrence Grossberg, Cary Nelson, and Paula Treichler, eds., *Cultural Studies* (New York: Routledge, 1992), 2.

5. Theory's Empire: Ersatz Theoretical Ecumenism & Criticism qua Criticism

Scott Eric Kaufman

If asked to defend the publication of *Theory's Empire* in twenty-six words or less, I'd write:

> "The Politics of Theories of Interpretation," pp. 235-247
> E.D. Hirsch, Jr.
>
> "Is There a Politics of Interpretation?" pp. 248-258
> Walter Benn Michaels
>
> "The Politics of Interpretation," pp. 259-278
> Gayatri Chakravorty Spivak

Pilfered from the September, 1982 *Critical Inquiry*'s table of contents, these twenty-six words represent the value of *Theory's Empire* far more eloquently than I will.

For most of its history, each number of *Critical Inquiry* contained a section entitled "Critical Response."[1] If the small sample above fails to indicate the stature of the those who participated in this forum, the names of the two I omitted—Stanley Fish and Michael Fried—should seal the deal. At this early point in theory's institutional history, representatives of particular theoretical approaches debated the merits of their respective approaches in one of the discipline's flag-ship journals. These debates were, for the most part, civil. Frank Kermode's response to Denis Donoghue is typical: "Like all sensible men I feel that to be read carefully by Denis Donoghue is a privilege rather than an ordeal; but although I am clearly to blame insofar as I allowed him to misunderstand me, I can't at all admit that he has damaged the argument I was trying to develop."[2] When uncivil, they were at least playfully so, as when Walter Davis anticipates a "Fishing": "He'll pounce on some out of the way statement in your essay and cleverly use it to obscure the issues, incorporate every good point you've made, and then leave you in the embarrassing position of either already unwittingly agreeing with him or committed to an impossible position you never took."[3] This decorum provided the proponents of the major theoretical schools a forum in which to test the strengths and weaknesses of their own approach.

I've long thought the pages of early *Critical Inquiry*—peppered with the productive conflict of clashing theoretical models—a far better introduction to literary theory than any of the available anthologies: Hazard Adams' *Critical Theory Since Plato*, David Richter's *The Critical Tradition*, not to mention the latest entry, *The Norton Anthology of Theory and Criticism.* All three of these anthologies attempt to encompass the history of "theory" with a roll-call of primary sources that speak past more often than they speak to each other. (And, as I will explain shortly, they produce scholars who follow suit.) Each anthology glosses the importance of the works it includes in introductions to individuals thinkers, discreet movements or both. But even though they're typically written in the present tense, the rhetoric of these glosses is static and a-historical. Consider Hans Robert Jauss, whose "views of the historical nature of literary evaluation have influenced," according to the *Norton*, "debates over the literary canon in ways important to feminist, African American, and postcolonial critics."[4] Instead of framing the debates in such a manner as to allow an undergraduate to evaluate the terms of these debates, The *Norton* mentions that they are "in ways important" to other methodologies. All of these anthologies devalue argument-*qua*-argument in favor of a rhetoric of settled issues and future collaboration. If all these anthologies posit is that each essay or excerpt between its covers is "in ways important," should anyone be surprised that scholars first introduced to Theory through these anthologies think of all these distinct theories as exclusive but compatible discourses?

What follows is a brief attempt to demonstrate why an anthology like *Theory's Empire* is a desperately needed corrective to the limitations of the aforementioned anthologies. I will trace one formula for reductive reading first through Fredric Jameson and Hillis Miller, then through Homi Bhabha, in order to demonstrate how the philosophical sophistication of the former—acquired in an academic culture amenable to the endless bickering of the "Critical Response"—and the philosophical incoherence of the latter—acquired in the current anthology-happy academic culture—depend as much as the way in which they approach Theory as on the individual merits of each in his capacity as a Theorist.

Writing at the birth of "what has today for better or for worse come to be known as literary theory," i.e. 1978, Fredric Jameson conceded that, "this displacement of traditional criticism and traditional philosophy by what has come to be known as theory turns out to allow the critic himself a wider latitude for the exercise of personal themes and the free play of private idiosyncrasies."[5] Jameson considered this a positive development, as it would allow for the emergence of "virtuoso readers" who would produce "bodies of criticism in which the practice of peculiar and sometimes eccentric textual interpretations is at one with the projection of a powerful, nonsystematized theoretical resonance, and this even where the critic himself ... misguidedly but compulsively submits his materials to a rage for patterns and symmetries and the mirage of a meta-system."[6] These "virtuoso readers"—*e.g.* Kenneth Burke, William Empson, Northrop Frye, Roland Barthes, Walter Benjamin and Viktor Shklovvsky—reject "the older philosophical criticism," the one which "was content simply to 'apply' various philosophical systems to literature in an occasional way."[7] The older philosophical critics, Jameson suggests, lacked Hegelian seriousness: in place of an aggressive commitment to the consequences of their premises, they were "content" to "simply" muse about literature "in an occasional way." They resembled Henry Fielding's "Virtuoso," endlessly engaged by "nicknacks and Curiosities," more than Jameson's *virtuosi.*[8] His sinecured *dilettanti* mass-produced "curiosities of an existential or phenomenological criticism, or a Hegelian or a gestalt or indeed a Freudian criticism."[9] Burke, Empson et al. avoided indenture in the Curiosity Trade, Jameson argues, by processing literature in accordance with a personal interpretive ethos, one resonant with a nonsystemized theory nonetheless compulsively applied in a rage for symmetry.

Jameson's conception of a good virtuoso critic can be summed up thus: a thinker of original temperament, but suitable Hegelian seriousness, whose passion for patterns generates interesting reading of literary works.[10] His notion of a bad virtouso critic: a calicified mind, learned but unoriginal, philosophically fickle, whose passions for other people's patterns generates predictable readings of literary works. But if the current state of theory (ca. 1978) affords more readers access to the tools that *sui generis* critics created or collected through sheer force of intellect, why would Jameson begin the essay so ominously? Why open with portents of scare-quoted scholarship, a future in which the operant terms would be personal and the work the production of "the free play of private idiosyncracies"? The simple answer: he doesn't and they're not there. Contra the general tenor of his thought, Jameson is optimistic here, genuinely believing that the "linguistic turn" will construct for critics in 1978 what his roll of "virtuoso readers" struggled, successfully, to create *ex nihilo*. It didn't. The profession, however, did not linger long in the Curiosity Trade.

In his 1993 survey of the state of Shakespeare criticism, "Masters and Demons," Brian Vickers contends that "the inbreeding of Derridians, Lacanians, Foucauldians, Althusserians, unable and unwilling to understand anyone else's language or concerns" (265) will eventually and irrevocably Balkanize the discipline. Had Vickers' vision materialized, contemporary literary studies would look more like a Jamesonian curio, only the Hegelians would be Foucauldians, the Freudians, Lacanians, &c. But, as Valentine Cunningham argues, Theory has become,

> more or less all things to all women and men, offering something or other to more or less everyone of every gender and racial and class disposition and from every critical background, as some analytical touch or other for all textual occasions and seasons, the claim on the necessity of this or the other critical corner of Theory does indeed tend to dissolve into mere contingency, into questions of what's useful, or just handy, on any particular reading. (33)

This "toolbox" approach entails a number of problems, foremost among them the good possibility of creating dueling determinisms. For example, a critic accounts for the behavior of one character with an appeal to Foucauldian discourse and another with an appeal to Althusserian ideology. Such a reading demands the critic balance two incompatible theories of human subjectivity. Foucault's anti-subjectism would permeate his first line of thought: "discourse is not the majestically unfolding manifestation of a thinking, knowing. speaking subject, but, on the contrary, a totality, in which the dispersion of the subject, and his discontinuity with himself may be determined."[11] Athusser's conception of ideology, however, would entail the existence of subjects:

"Ideology interpellates individuals as subjects."[12] Logic demands that subjects either "exist" as extremely localized discursive events or that they exist as interpellated individuals.

The conventional response to my complaint is that the work justifies the critic's philosophical incoherence; in the first case, the character seems most interesting when read as a production of discursive power; in the second, the character seems more interesting when read as a production of an ideological state apparatus. Such readings devalue not only the work they describe, but the theories through which they describe it.[13] Foucault and Althusser imagined they spoke of the world as it is. Their respective theories of subjectivity are incompatible. But the critic need no more care about stepping on a Theorist's toes than he or she would about stomping on an author's. However, a further problem, one of signal import to the critic, arises: the toolbox approach undermines the critic's argument by appealing to a given Theorists' theoretical authority while simultaneously refuting it. If the explanatory power of Foucault's discursive thought authorizes its application in this one instance, then the explanatory power of Althusser's ideological and interpellative thought cannot cameo; if it does, it invalidates the earlier appeal to Foucault's authority and, co-damningly, vice versa. The consequences of these premises, the "serious Hegelian" would argue, preclude the possibility of a dual billing unless a critic spreads their appearances over his or her entire corpus. That would constitute an actual, as opposed to an ersatz, theoretical ecumenism or, in Cunningham's words, "Theoretical pragmatism" (33).

The appeal to theoretical ecumenism is common enough: *this* theory best explains *this* text, *that* one best explains *that*. The majority of critics who work in this mode now do so from a position entailing some permutation of the philosophical incoherence I described above. However, the vigorous (and rigorous) debates about the value of post-structuralism—initiated by Jameson's *The Prison-House of Language* (1971) and continued through the '70s as described above—forced post-structuralist thinkers like J. Hillis Miller to construct and refine a coherent philosophical position and practice. That it authorized the philosophical incoherence of the toolbox approach is beside the point. The intellectual and interpretive responsibility engendered by these debates distinguishes the work of early post-structuralists from contemporary theorists whose work is indebted to post-structuralist thought. A quick account of the conversion of J. Hillis Miller—an erstwhile structuralist who would become a post-structuralist poster-boy—will suffice to demonstrate the value of the refining fires an anthology like *Theory's Empire* stokes.

Miller began his career as a New Critic with a fondness for Georges Poulet. In a review of his first book, *Charles Dickens: The World of His Novels* (1958), Bradford A. Booth cites the New Critic's influence as the reason "it is not surprising to find in this book an interpretation of Dickens that is highly useful and rather limited.[14] Sylvere Monod's review agrees: "The claims to originality of J. Hillis Miller's [study] will not be called in doubt. But it is originality of a kind the value of which is less than obvious."[15] Both reviewers call attention to the weaknesses attending his approach: Booth blames Miller's method for "his failure to touch on the many-sidedness of Dickens," and for encouraging Miller "to pursue rigorously his own inquiry;"[16] Monod complains that the "justification for any marked departure from the more or less traditional paths of criticism must lie in its enabling the critic to tell something useful (and little that is not fully intelligible can be termed useful) and new [and] wonder[s] whether this is always the case with Miller's approach, especially when he adheres most rigorously to his method."[17] From the beginning of his career, the criticism of Miller is of a methodology too rigorously applied. This commitment to his methodological approach results in what would, less than a decade later, become the highly ironic conclusion Miller draws from his study of Dickens: "Within this whole a single problem, the search for a viable identity, is stated and restated with increasing approximation to the hidden center" of Dickens' world.[18] He produced, qua Jameson, methodological curiosities; however, his commitment to rigor would later enable him to remain philosophically coherent about his philosophical incoherence.

A little more than a decade after seeking "the hidden center" of Dickens' world, Miller would point to the futility of such searches in his review of Irving Howe's Hardy:

> Novels, as much recent criticism both American and Continental has argued, are ... self-referential works, like any other kind of literature. [...] In light of this current interest in the complexities of novelistic form there is something a bit old-fashioned (perhaps to

> some attractively so), in Howe's tendency to assume, for example, that the narrator of Hardy's novels need not ever be distinguished from Hardy himself.[19]

In less then a decade, Miller sheds the attractively old-fashioned belief that the narrator of a literary work possesses an inviolable relation to its author, such that each novel represents a statement and restatement of that increasingly visible "hidden" center of an author's vision. In its place is what he later calls the inherent "deconstruction of metaphysics" in which "there is no center of meaning or informing power preceding a given structure of signs."[20] Miller exchanges a philosophical position which assumes centers of meaning informed by authorial power for one which precludes centers of meaning and informing powers. The terms of that exchange are argumentative, and Miller could be said to have spent the decade after the Hardy review justifying the equity of those terms. Rigorously argued in the idiosyncratic style of the early post-structuralists, these justifications would form the foundation for the uncritical assumptions of future generations of scholars who would adopt the style and bask in the freedom Miller and his compatriots had to fight for. The post-structuralist Miller ranged widely over literary, philosophical and historical sources. He became, in short, a more interesting (but not "interesting") critic, one who could now talk about "Cartesian doubt," "Husserlian 'bracketing,'' what "Jean-Paul Sartre has argued" and significantly—given his earlier, New Critical refusal to consult the non-literary writings of Dickens—what "Dickens often emphasized" in his letters.[21] These conflicting philosophical approaches are invoked, nay, *subsumed* by the larger, post-structuralist approach which authorizes their invocations, internal-coherence-be-damned. In light of the current status of Theory, the centrality of this authorization should not be underestimated. Nor, for that matter, can the importance of Part II of *Theory's Empire*: "Linguistic Turns."

Whatever it faults, the strength of *Theory's Empire* resides in its historicizing of the past 30 years of debates. Read in isolation, Louis Althusser's "Ideology and the State Apparatus," Paul De Man's "Semiology and Rhetoric," Jane Tompkin's "Me and My Shadow" and Lennard Davis' "Enforcing Normalcy" (all included in the *Norton*) don't speak *to* each other so much as *past* each other. It is possible to pluck a premise from all these essays, erect a formidable sounding philosophy framework and deploy it in the service of producing an "interesting" reading of a literary text. The isolation of these frameworks from the discourses in which they arose and the debates which accompanied their arrival creates a false impression of mutual compatibility. Miller, however, can pick and choose from whatever discourse he pleases, thanks to his commitment to what M.H. Abrams calls "the self-deconstructive revelation that in default of any possible origin, ground, presence, or end, [there is] an interminable free-play of indeterminable meanings" (205). Given this belief, Miller can justify his cherry-picking of philosophical and intellectual history and employ whatever interpretive scheme generates the most "interesting" reading of a particular passage. One need not worry the contradictions of unrelated discourses, after all, when self-contradiction is the definitive element of all discourses. Eschewing the law of non-contradiction allows "canny" critics, to use Miller's phrase, to connect anything to everything. Abrams again:

> Endowed *ex post facto* with the sedimented meanings accumulated over time, but stripped of any norms for selecting some of these and rejecting others, a key word—like the larger passage or total text of which the word is an element—becomes (in the phrase Miller cites from Mallarmé) a *suspens vibratoire*, a vibratory suspension of equally likely meanings, and these are bound to include "incompatible" or "irreconcilable" or "contradictory" meanings. (206)

If Miller wants to choose from these etymological traces the definitions of a Freudian or Marxist cant, he can justify his principle of selection on philosophical grounds: his anti-foundationalism authorizes whatever choice he wants to make because that choice, by virtue of the text's ultimate undecidability, is as valid as any other one he might make. This is not to say that he is a virtuoso critic, however; what he produces, in fact, are deconstructive curiosities able to pass for virtuoso readings. His anti-foundationalism allows for and encourages the practice of borrowing from other disciplines frameworks through which a work of literature can be read. But that doesn't mean the finished product will be something more than a theoretical curiosity. Deconstructive readings of literary texts bear the hallmark of their anti-foundationalism in the variety of their commitments, their flouting of Hegelian seriousness and their adoption of an eclecticism that, while liberating, has had a deleterious effect on the profession as a whole. I could call this effect "citational authority," but as it's conceptually identical to the "argument from authority" logical fallacy, introducing another term would be redundant. That said, the difference between the traditional argument from authority and what occurs in literary studies is so great it almost warrants the neologism.

Those who defend this eclecticism on the grounds that an interesting reading is justification enough for the application of a particular theoretical model seldom consider the difference between eclecticism in theory and eclecticism in practice. If I pick up my copy of Homi Bhabha's *The Location of Culture*, I can turn to almost any page and find sentences littered with clauses like "as Lacan reminds us" and "the work of Edward Said will not let us forget."[22] The sum total of these allusions to arguments is not, however, a deconstructive curiosity. Bhabha doesn't share Miller's commitment to deconstruction as a philosophical doctrine. What Bhabha produces—and what, I suggest, the current approach to Theory abets the production of—is not a curiosity but a philosophically incoherent panoply (in which "panoply" retains its strong sense of being a "complete suit of armor" with connotations of "brightness and splendor".) Bhabha's panoply is too eccentric to manifest a Jamesonian "rage for pattern and symmetry and the mirage of the meta-system." To the extent that it is systematic, it is meaninglessly so: Bhabha has borrowed injudiciously from too many mutually incompatible philosophical systems for his work to produce even the mirage of a meta-system. The problem for those who wish to challenge the legitimacy of Bhabha's thought, in Thomas Nagel's apt phrasing, is that "there is no direct way to refute a fogbank" (544).

Jameson's *virtuosi* could be refuted on their own terms; contemporary Theorists, indebted to Derridian thought but not themselves committed deconstructionists, lack philosophical and argumentative consistency and thus can't be refuted. If I were to disagree with the logic behind Bhabha's citation of Said, Bhabha could respond with another citation from another thinker who says much the same thing because the citation's felicity relies upon the authority granted Said by the academic star-system. An antique fallacy, I know, but in conjunction with the star-system, it has new legs. But in practice it also denies theorists the citational freedom conferred: it is no coincidence that when I flipped open *The Location of Culture*, I caught Bhabha citing Lacan and Said. Nor would it shock me if his index contains the requisite citations of Freud, Foucault, Benjamin, Bhaktin, Jameson, Spivak, &c. (It does.) An *ersatz* theoretical ecumenism channels critical works through the same limited set of thinkers, as is born out by the introduction to Bhabha in the *Norton*:

> Although "the wit and wisdom of Jacques Derrida" (as he calls it in another essay) is fundamental to his work, Bhabha draws on a wide array of twentieth-century theorists throughout "The Commitment to Theory". Building on the influential concept of nations set forth by Benedict Anderson in *Imagined Communities* (1983), Bhabha stresses how nationality is narratively produced, rather than arising from an intrinsic essence. From Mikhail Bakhtin, he takes the concept of dialogue to stress that colonialism is not a one-way street but entails an interaction between colonizer and colonized. Regarding identity, he draws on Frantz Fanon's psychoanalytic model of colonialism and Jacque Lacan's concepts of "mimicry" and the split subject, arguing that there is always an "excess" in the cultural imitation that the colonial subject is forced to produce.[23]

I could continue, but the unchallenged nature of the claims attributed to Bhabha here speaks volumes about the current state of Theory. My point is a simple one: the more debate about the fundamental claims of theoretical approaches the less likely the next generation of critics will be as philosophically incoherent as Bhabha. In the classroom, *Theory's Empire* could function as a simulation of the debates that created critics as rigorous and justifiably eclectic—i.e. the critic him- or herself can justify the applicability of a given theoretical approach to a given literary work—as Miller and Jameson. No one, I believe, advocates the return to New Criticism or to the production of philosophical and theoretical curiosities. But everyone, I believe, should desire the return to theoretical responsibility a collection like *Theory's Empire* can facilitate.

Originally posted on July 12, 2005

POSTSCRIPT:

Ideally, *Theory's Empire* would take the form of a traditional 'critical reader'. It is, after all, intended to overwhelm the traditional dikes, such that an army of little Dutch boys couldn't plug half the holes. The point is to introduce the basic arguments the conventional means of teaching Theory-qua-Theory neglects. Skim through the essays included in the *Norton* and you'll find one after another in which no argument occurs, or what does occur is by means of selective citation, i.e. the theories not addressed are the one with which a critic has problems. But omission isn't argument. Combine the notion that the collection may have been better named *Bad Applications of Theory's Empire* with a dash of Derrida criticizing Lévi-Strauss and my point will be clear: *Theory's Empire* should have been named *Refutations of Recent Bad Applications of Theory.*

My argument in "Ersatz Ecumenism" obtains here because the problem isn't with Theory but with a generation of unthinking and unargumentative theorists. Scan the last 700 pages of the *Norton* and examine the logic of citation. Most either 1) attack on acceptable targets (Freud, Bloom, &c.) or 2) cite unchallengeable Truth. Since no one will doubt the evidence supporting my first claim, I'll focus on the second:

I begin with one of the most infuriating quotations I've run across, from Monique Wittig's "One Is Not Born a Woman." Speaking of early 20th century feminists, Wittig notes "They went so far as to adopt the Darwinist theory of evolution. They did not believe like Darwin, however, 'that women were less evolved than men, but they did believe that male and female natures had diverged in the course of evolutionary development and that society at large reflected this polarization'" (2017). Can you believe Darwin said that? What an ass! Only, the rest of the sentence doesn't track, and what's this footnote at the bottom say? That Wittig's quotation is actually from Rosalind Rosenberg's "In Search of Woman's Nature"? Instead of consulting Darwin's work, Wittig dismisses Darwinian theory out-of-hand based on a quotation from a work which itself presupposes Darwinian misogyny?

That fit pitched, on to the mundane task of proving Wittig is no isolated incident:

Annette Kolodny:

> "as Geertz astutely observes" (2164)

Laura Mulvey:

> "psychoanalytic theory is thus appropriated here as a political weapon, demonstrating the way the unconscious of patriarchal society has structured film form" (2182, also note the monolith she calls "psychoanalytic theory".)
>
> "in his Three Essays on Sexuality, Freud isolated scopophilia" (2184)
>
> "Jacques Lacan has described" (2185)

Houston Baker (whose essay is attractive in that way that's "interesting" in the pejorative sense, in that he selects the texts that allow him to generate an "interesting" reading at the price of philosophical incoherence):

> "they are what Jacques Derrida might describe as the 'always already'" (2230)
>
> "Hegel speaks of a flux" (2232)
>
> "the absence of a content plane noted by Eco" (2234)

Donna Haraway:

> "Jameson points out" (2274)
>
> "Sandoval emphasizes the lack" (2276)
>
> "Kate King has emphasized the limits" (2277) [props accorded where due: she confronts MacKinnon (2279-80)]
>
> "the French theorist Julie Kristeva claimed" (2281)

Susan Bordo:

> "the body, as anthropologist Mary Douglas has argued" (2362)
>
> "it is also, as anthropologist Pierre Bordieu and philosopher Michel Foucault (among others) have argued" (2362)
>
> "Foucault constantly reminds us" (2362)
>
> "in the manner described by Erving Goffman" (2366)
>
> "agoraphobia, as I.G. Fodor has put it" (2367)
>
> "Helen Cixous speaks" (2369)

All of these come from the research for my original essay, but they all go to make the point I'm making now: the principle of selection is "what do I want to say and who will let me say it." Contemporary literary theorists need not confront arguments that 1) aren't convenient or 2) refute their position because they hold to a citational ethos of "use what you need, ignore what you don't." This highly personal principle of selection means that they're no longer talking about anything except the world they want to believe they live in. But they can't muster, and feel no desire to muster, proof that their desired world bears any relation to the one the rest of us live in. In truth, what they're producing are aesthetic objects, personal interpretations of the world based on trendy thought and idiosyncratic citation. They can speak of what "Foucault constantly reminds us" without presenting any evidence that Foucault's the sort of person whose reminders we ought to value. (Again: I'm not speaking about Derrida, Foucault et. al. but the logic behind citations which treat their thought as nuggets of unarguable truth.) There's a surplus of second-order theorizing in literary studies that is an affront to the philosophers, anthropologists, and, well, authorities whose works are mashed by literary scholars creating unattractive aesthetic objects.

NOTES

1 Responses still appear in *Critical Inquiry*, but no longer regularly or in a section devoted to them.

2 Frank Kermode, "A Reply to Denis Donoghue," *Critical Inquiry* 1:3 (1975), 699.

3 Walter Davis, "Offending the Profession (After Peter Handke)," *Critical*

Inquiry 10:4 (1984), 706.

4 "Hans Robert Jauss," in *The Norton Anthology of Theory and Criticism*, ed. Vincent Leitch (New York: Norton 2001), 1549.

5 Frederic Jameson, "The Symbolic Inference; Or, Kenneth Burke and Ideological Analysis," *Critical Inquiry* 4:3 (1978), 508, 509. Jameson's working definition of "theory" in this essay amounts to the "transcendence of the older academic specializations and the heightened appreciation of the inner logic and autonomy of language itself" (508).

6 Jameson, 508.

7 Jameson, 507.

8 Henry Fielding. *Tom Jones, X,* emphasis mine.

9 Jameson, 507.

10 An acknowledged problem with my argument is that Jameson speaks of the demise of naïve virtuoso readers precipitated by the rise of Theory.

11 Michel Foucault, *Archeology of Knowledge*, trans. A. M. Sheridan-Smith (New York: Pantheon, 1972), 55.

12 Louis Althusser, "Ideology and Ideological State Apparatuses," in *Literary Theory: An Anthology*, eds. Rivkin and Ryan (Malden: Blackwell, 1998), 299.

13 Foucault and Althusser aren't accidental selections.

14 Bradford A. Booth, "Review of *Charles Dickens: The World of His Novels*, by J. Hillis Miller," *Modern Philology* 57:1 (1959), 69.

15 Sylvere Monod, "Review of *Charles Dickens: The World of His Novels*, by J. Hillis Miller," *Nineteenth-Century Fiction* 13:4 (1959), 360.

16 Booth, 71.

17 Monod, 361.

18 Miller, J. Hillis. *Charles Dickens: The World of His Novels* (Cambridge: Harvard UP, 1958), 333.

19 Review of Hardy, by Irving Howe. *NOVEL: A Forum on Fiction* 2:3 (1969), 274.

20 J. Hillis Miller, "The Still Heart: Poetic Form in Wordsworth," *New Literary History* 2:2 (1971), 298.

21 J. Hillis Miller, "The Sources of Dickens's Comic Art: From American Notes to Martin Chuzzlewit," *Nineteenth-Century Fiction* 26:4 (1970), 467.

22 Homi Bhabha, *The Location of Culture*. (London: Routledge, 1994), 90.

23 "Homi Bhabha," in *The Norton Anthology of Theory and Criticism*, ed. Vincent Leitch (New York: Norton 2001), 2377-8.

6. Theory Tuesday

Michael Bérubé

Last week I posted a long reply to Mark Bauerlein's short essay on *Theory's Empire*; tomorrow I'm planning to post a more modest reply to his essay in that volume. (The issue is "social constructionism" and the claims made for and against it, if you're interested.) But I promised last week that I would also say a few words about my own take on the institutional status of "theory" in the humanities. The more I thought about it over the past few days, though, the more unwieldy the subject became (funny how that happens), so I've decided that I'll make this a mini-series—and keep each entry in the series at a reasonable length. So for the next few weeks, Tuesdays will be Theory Tuesdays, in which I'll offer you (at no cost!) a handful of the things I've taught to first-year graduate students at Penn State.

First, though, a hearty thank you to Kevin Drum for linking to last week's post. I couldn't help noticing, over the weekend, that some of Kevin's commenters have very little tolerance for any talk of "literary theory," and some of them were quite confident that the Alan Sokal hoax of 1996 proved to them that they need never bother to find out what any of the fuss in the past thirty or forty years has been about. I should be used to this kind of thing by now, but I'm not. I honestly don't think there's another field of intellectual endeavor that gets this kind of treatment from allegedly intelligent people. Yes, the Sokal hoax was bad, but it did not, in fact, demonstrate that all of interpretive theory is vacuous. A journal (*Social Text*—I've published in it twice, and I count some friends among the editors, too) accepted a hoax essay, full of nonsense, largely because the editors were so pleased and surprised to get a submission from a physicist. The journal isn't peer-reviewed, and they didn't send the essay out for a reading by someone who knew his or her physics. In other words, they done screwed the pooch—and, as I said in this essay, the response to the hoax was in some respects worse than the hoax itself. But over the past nine years, during which I've had a couple of pleasant and substantive exchanges with Sokal, I've found that his biggest fans can be a rather disappointing bunch. The conversations go something like this. I say, "what do you think of Jean-Francois Lyotard's insistence on 'incommensurability' and the 'heterogeneity of language-games'?" and they say, "I think that French stuff is bullshit." And I say, "OK, well, since I'm skeptical of Lyotard's dogmatism in some respects, what do you think of Habermas and his account of 'communicative action' and reciprocal recognition?" And they say, "yeah, whatever, it's all the same to me." And I say, "Uh, no, actually, Lyotard and Habermas are about as opposed as it's possible to be, and they even think of 'opposition' in different terms. And you might want to consider that some forms of opposition really are incommensurable—pick one, any one, from recent headlines—even as you consider that it's a good idea to try to create 'speech situtations' that are free of domination." And they say, "look, didn't Alan Sokal prove that all this was so much fashionable nonsense?" (Or, in the words of one Kevin Drum commenter, "The Sokal Hoax says all that needs to be said about lit crit folks. They're really no different from fundamentalists—they're both against the reality-based crowd." This position has been seconded by, among others, Noam Chomsky and Barbara Ehrenreich.)

Look, people screw up every once in a while. The physicists had their Pons-Fleischmann cold fusion scandal in 1989, the historians have had a few high-profile plagiarists in recent years, and we had the Sokal hoax. And yes, some of those French folk have provided pretty easy targets, especially the ones influenced by the late work of Jacques Lacan, many of whom apparently decided in the late 1960s and early 1970s that they should write bizarre and/or apocalyptic and/or ignorant things about math and science. But the Sokal hoax did not prove that language is a transparent vehicle onto the world, or that cultural practices don't change over time, or that interpretation is really a strikingly simple thing when you really look at it. It punctured a few balloons, and it insisted that humanists who write about science should, ideally, know what the hell they're talking about, but it didn't answer any of the questions about language and culture that constitute our stock in trade. (If it did, then literary theory really would be dead, and this facetious post wouldn't have been facetious at all.)

So, then, on with the first installment in the mini-series. Let's start with a particularly vexatious example: the question of deconstruction.

As I mentioned last week, during my initial attempt to teach "Introduction to Materials and Methods" to our first-year graduate students, one student informed me that one of her other professors had questioned why we were bothering with Derrida in an introductory course when three-quarters of the faculty in the English department know next to nothing about Derrida. I thought this was a reasonable question, so I tried to offer a thorough answer. First, I replied that the student's (or her professor's) estimate was probably a little low: there are only a couple of people in the department who really know their Derrida. I know a little Derrida here and there, just the basics, not a great deal—and the man did write a great deal. Many of my colleagues would say more or less the same. *Nous parlons Derrida un petit peu.*

It's in this sense that Mark Bauerlein is right to speak of the "decline" of theory. Once upon a time—some of my commenters say the late 1970s, some say the early 1980s, and I say think generally of the vast cultural period between the first appearance of the Ramones and the first appearance of Culture Club—deconstruction was so dominant, and its practitioners so confident that they and they alone were Doing Criticism, that you just couldn't avoid Derrida et al. if you were a curious or responsible member of the discipline. As I noted last week, many of the professors who dismissed Derrida in those days were not intellectually inspiring people; but on the other side, some of the professors who professed deconstruction did so with missionary zeal. The result, for graduate students like me (I started out in 1983), was that we very quickly got the impression that deconstruction was something we ought to know about, regardless of whether we would grow to live and breathe it. Derrida-Foucault-Barthes-Lacan took on the appearance of the Four French Horsemen of the Apocalypse, though Barthes fell out of favor precipitously after 1980, and Foucault took over whole districts of literary studies by the end of the decade. As Peter Brooks tells the story (in a fine essay, "Aesthetics and Ideology—What Happened to Poetics?"), the 1980s witnessed an entire division of literary scholars switching horses:

> At the moment when the media discovered "deconstruction," and accused professors of turning from the evaluative and normative function of criticism, another kind of swerve was in fact taking place, one which would turn even many of the deconstructionists into practitioners of ideological and cultural critique. It was as if what appeared as the triumphal entry through the porticos of American academia of such structuralist demigods as Saussure, Jakobson,

> Lévi-Strauss, and Barthes, and such useful attendant priests as Todorov, Genette, Greimas, had prepared, not the cult of Derrida and de Man that we began to celebrate, but the masked arrival of the cult of Foucault.[1]

Again, Bauerlein is right to suggest that no one theorist or school of theorists dominates the scene in quite that way today, and personally, I think this is a Good Thing. If, as Bauerlein writes, "the humanities are so splintered and compartmentalized that one can pursue a happy career without ever reading a word of Bhabha or Butler," then people like me have no business trying to re-create the days when the road to disciplinary relevance quite clearly ran through Derrida and deconstruction. (There's an ancillary point to be made here about the personalities of dissertation directors and the politics of discipleship, but I'll save that for a later installment.)

So, Student X, I said (not her real name—her real name was Z), you don't really need to know this or that text by Derrida in order to make your way through graduate school or the profession at large. *However*, and this is a seriously italic "however," you should be aware that deconstruction has seeped into the groundwater of the discipline, even as the term itself lost any distinct referent long ago. It has been "disseminated," in fact, in just the way that deconstruction itself suggests: the word is now floating around out there, and cannot be recalled to its point of origin. "To deconstruct" now seems to mean something like "to challenge and/or overturn" or even "to read carefully with a skeptical eye," as in the familiar warning, "don't sign your lease before you deconstruct it." But that's not what literary critics and theorists are doing when they "deconstruct" something. They're doing something more distinct and specific, *and you need to know what that is, so that you can recognize it in the future*. You don't need to be able to cite Derrida's *Dissemination* chapter and verse. But you do need to know what a deconstructive argument looks and sounds like, and you need to know what implicit and explicit claims are at stake in such an argument, because you will encounter these arguments in essays and books where they will not declare their names.

For example, when someone says that the opposition between A and B is not really an opposition between two different things but, rather, an opposition that is internal to A, that's a broadly deconstructive move. When someone says that the set of all correctly transmitted and understood messages is a subset of all imaginable messages that can be incorrectly transmitted or misunderstood, such that misunderstanding is the condition of possibility of understanding, that's a deconstructive move. (That one sounds weird, sure, but think of it this way: every letter is, in principle, capable of being delivered to the wrong address. The good people of the Postal Service correctly deliver the vast majority of letters that pass through their hands, true enough. Only rarely, and only in Chicago, do they throw thousands of letters into underground tunnels. But still, if you want to stress the precariousness of it all, you can think of every letter being haunted by the possibility of its loss or "misdelivery," just as you can think of every utterance, including this one, as being susceptible to distortion and incomprehension. It's in that sense that the priests of the cult of Derrida once chanted, as they fanned out across the country from New Haven, "all reading is misreading." And guess what? They were misunderstood.) And when someone says that a series of oppositions is being generated by a term that is actually part of one of those oppositions and hiding out amongst them, particularly if the term is "writing," well, then you get something like this passage from Derrida's "Plato's Pharmacy":

> It is not enough to say that writing is conceived out of this or that series of oppositions. Plato thinks of writing, and tries to comprehend it, to dominate it, on the basis of opposition as such. In order for these contrary values (good/ evil, true/ false, essence/ appearance, inside/ outside, etc.) to be in opposition, each of the terms must be simply external to the other, which means that one of these oppositions (the opposition between inside and outside) must already be accredited as the matrix of all possible opposition. And one of the elements of the system (or of the series) must also stand as the very possibility of systematicity or seriality in general.[2]

OK, take that in for a moment, and now, take a very deep breath and get ready for an inelegant sentence full of complicated "if" clauses. Keep in mind, too, that the *pharmakon* of which Derrida writes here (he's commenting on Plato's *Phaedrus*) means both "cure" and "poison," and that Plato writes of writing itself as such a *pharmakon*. (Just as Rousseau writes of writing—and masturbation, go figure—as a "dangerous supplement," where "supplement" means both "unnecessary appendage to a thing that is already complete and sufficient" and "absolutely essential element that fills up a thing and makes it complete and sufficient." I tell you, with Janus-faced words like *pharmakon* and "supplement," uneeda deconstructive reading—not to untangle the contradictions, but to render them palpable and strange.)

> And if one got to thinking that something like the *pharmakon*—or writing—far from being governed by these oppositions, opens up their very possibility without letting itself be comprehended by them; if one got to thinking that it can only be out of something like writing—or the *pharmakon*—that the strange difference between inside and outside can spring; if, consequently, one got to thinking that **writing as a *pharmakon* cannot simply be assigned a site within what it situates**, cannot be subsumed under concepts whose contours it draws, leaves only its ghost to a logic that can only seek to govern it insofar as logic arises from it—one would then have to bend into strange contortions what could no longer even simply be called logic or discourse. (My emphasis in boldface.)

The "then" clause is a bit of a letdown, I think; all the action is going on in those coy "if"s. And though the point may not, in the end, be a decisive contribution to the history of philosophy (as some philosophers have argued), it is nevertheless of some use to those of us who study language and literature: the attempt to create a string of oppositions, one of which is the opposition between speech and writing, has as its condition of possibility the existence of principles of opposition and of seriality. But if those principles of opposition and seriality exist within language (and it would be awfully hard to speak or write of them if they did not), then what Plato's doing in the *Phaedrus* involves some very deft sleight-of-hand, in which writing is assigned a site within which it situates.

And the reason why this kind of thing drew the attention of literary critics and theorists should be obvious: whereas philosophers tend to say, "never mind these petty details of Plato's language—it's the *concepts* that are important," we language-and-literature people look at this and say, "yes, but the concepts are expressed in language, and what's more, one of those central concepts has to do with the status of language as a vehicle for communication." We could add that Plato stages the quarrels between literature and philosophy by means of some of the most self-consciously "literary" philosophical texts ever written, *but we don't want to get into an argument, now, do we.*

But, as I told Student X, you don't have to memorize all this (although the *Phaedrus* also says some very interesting things about memory, which Derrida does not fail to notice.) You should simply take away from this the sense that whenever someone comes upon a series of oppositions and says, "hold on a second, one of these oppositions"—say, inside/ outside—"is not like the others, because it's the condition of possibility for the series itself," or "this opposition"—say, speech/ writing—"is built on the premise that thing A is unlike thing B even though both A and B share features that are occluded by the terms of the opposition", or "this opposition"—say, male/ female—"is predicated on the exclusion of everything that troubles or blurs the terms of opposition," then you're dealing with a deconstructive argument. And over the past thirty years, these arguments have been as common as rain, and they've seeped into the disciplinary groundwater. Whether you like them or not, you should be able to recognize them for what they are when you run into them.

Originally posted on July 12, 2005

NOTES

30 Peter Brooks, "Aesthetics and Ideology: What Happened to Poetics?," *Critical Inquiry* 20:3 (1994), 509.

31 Jacques Derrida, *Dissemination*, trans. Barbara Johnson (Chicago: U of Chicago, 1983), 103.

7. Theory's Empire—Wrestling the Fog Bank

Sean McCann

If you're even slightly simpatico, you've got to feel bad for the editors of *Theory's Empire*. There's no more basic feature of "theory" in the literary academy than its committed antiformalism and its hostility to definition of any kind. Despite John McGowan's suggestions to the contrary, there seems to be pretty universal agreement—among defenders as well as opponents—that for some decades now there has indeed been an identifiable fashion (marked by rhetorical style, ethos, and commonly invoked authorities, however eclectic) that all agree to call 'Theory'. But good luck getting its defenders to articulate core principles, methods, or topics. As Thomas Nagel says, arguing against Theory is like wrestling a fog bank. So putting together a critical anthology that would be both comprehensive and structurally coherent must have been quite a task for Daphne Patai and Will Corral.

I sympathize big time. But unfortunately, the effort shows. *Theory's Empire* is about as loose and baggy a monster as they come. And frankly a very uneven collection. There are many excellent and substantial essays. (I'd be grateful for being introduced to Stephen Adam Schwartz alone.) But there are also a lot of short book reviews, occasional lectures, and what seem simply like place markers. (E.g., Marks, Fromm, Spitzer, Harpham—whose other work I personally admire. Why is this stuff here?!) Alas, for a collection that means to land some devastating blows, a lot in the book is not really first rank stuff, leading to a collection that manages to seem both massive and thin. More importantly, the anthology doesn't really have a structure. Though it's divided into eight sections, few of their titles appear to correlate strongly with their contents, and almost every section bleeds uncontrollably into others.

As I say, you can't really blame Patai and Corral for this problem: "Theory as a profession"; "Identities"; "Theory as surrogate politics," to name but three of the sections—these are typically treated by Theory-heads as different faces of a single issue. So it's hopeless trying to separate out subproblems. But if you were looking for a lucid, comprehensive map, *Theory's Empire* can't provide it. Add to this the fact that the many voices in the collection inevitably have different interests and concerns, and the upshot is less the focused assault that one might have hoped for than, as McGowan notes, what often seems like a chorus of disgruntlement.

Are there major themes to be taken from that chorus? In my fantasies, I yearn for TE to convince its readers of what I think are two major conclusions toward which it leads: (1) Though they've been frequently, if not characteristically exaggerated to the point of absurdity, some of the widely shared beliefs made commonplace by Theory are, at least in some versions, perfectly reasonable—and at a certain point in the history of the literary academy may plausibly have seemed badly needed. (2) Criticism of Theory is not inevitably motivated by anti-intellectualism or political or cultural conservatism or characterized by intemperate bluster. (Indeed, if TE could convince the Theory stalwarts of that latter, simple and rightfully inarguable point, it would be a momentous accomplishment. Can it possibly be done? Doubtful, for reasons to which I'll return below.) If in fact both those conclusions are plausible, the major question is just why the Theory debate has been so strident so long, and with only a few hints of cooling down. A number of the pieces in TE (e.g., Donaghue, Schwartz, Appiah) have interesting suggestions to make on that front, only Schwartz really pursues it at any length. In my view, at the end of the day it's the major and unresolved question. I'll come back to it below.

But first, a quick thought on the question put front and center by McGowan and Michael Bérubé and sure to be emphasized by all hostile readers—motivation. Why did TE seem worth doing to Patai and Corral and worth discussing at length to Valvesters? For those of us who share Patai and Corral's conviction that the hegemony of Theory does in fact exist and is a genuine intellectual and institutional problem, there's not much to wonder about here, but as John M and Michael's responses suggest, it will be the first question to be raised by Theory's defenders—especially by voices less reasonable and humane than theirs. Both John and Michael all but directly say: hey, why get so worked up? Things aren't as bad as you think.

Most critics of Theory answer that challenge by turning first to the big guns—as say, Merquior, Goodhart, Jacoby do here. The anti-humanist dogmatism prevalent in much Theory talk, they suggest, is fundamentally threatening to our ability to think clearly, behave morally, act politically, and value art at all—leaving open the possibility for moderate voices like Michael and John to say: isn't this all a bit over the top? So, for the moment, let's just mention a less emphatic reason why it's well and good to criticize Theory and criticize it harshly indeed. Not first because it threatens humanity, or civilization, or art, or rationality but because it's there. Leave aside for the moment the question of whether Theory is an empire or whether it's dangerous to humanity. It exists, it's far from lacking in prominence, and in huge landmasses of sodden material, it is, as a number of the essays in this collection demonstrate, intellectually unimpressive indeed. Whether the stakes are high or low, whether the problem is big or small, it can't be a bad thing to indict sloppy argument, shoddy prose, and smug moralism. As Appiah says, "discriminating between what is and what isn't worthwhile is the purpose of intellectual judgment" (446).

It's also, of course, fundamental to professional self-governance. An intellectual community can't flourish if bad or just weak work goes regularly unchallenged—or is prominently rewarded—and, more pressingly, if both an ethos and an institutional pattern develop that discourage argument and challenge. I think Scott Kaufman is absolutely right, as is Mark Bauerlein in his essay in the collection, to suggest that a hallmark of the current literary academy is the strikingly low level of serious debate. (Here's a prediction. TE has already generated more extensive, vigorous, and fair discussion in the blogosphere than it ever will in the journals and conferences of literary academia.) Mark suggests that there are sociological as well as intellectual reasons for this phenomenon—on which, again, I hope more below. But Scott surely has an important point when he suggests that one consequence of the poststructuralist disdain for reason has been to license an indiscriminate theoretical eclecticism and one that encourages the sense that there's not much purpose to disagreement. It's not, as Michael puts it with arched brow, that Theory brooks no dissent, but that it makes argument seem unworthy, or unimportant, or just impossible.

How did this happen? John M. suggests we look to market causes. I think that makes a lot of sense and want to return to the point, but first let's consider some of the intellectual questions. As I say, reading over TE, I was struck by the way that so many of the ideas criticized by the book look like extreme exaggerations of reasonable intuitions. In different ways, Cunningham, Tallis, and Searle all make this point: poststructuralist theory takes plausible views of language or literature (or, it might be added, society) and, for reasons that still need clarification, extends or distorts them to an extraordinary degree. It occurred to me that it would probably be possible to list the core intuitions of Theory in abbreviated and basic form. Here's my shot at summarizing four that in highly elaborate fashion crop up throughout Theory talk:

> 1) Language is a complex and imperfect instrument of profound importance to our sense of what it means to be a self-conscious human being. Because communication makes use of conventional codes, it's always possible for a listener to misinterpret the intentions of a speaker or for a sentence to be given more or different meanings than a speaker intends (a matter which explicitly or not may become a reflexive resource and thematic concern of literary texts.) And the various possibilities for imperfect communication are comparable to, or perhaps consistent with or related to, the other senses in which individuals are less than fully autonomous, rational, self-directed beings.
>
> 2) Many commonplace beliefs, practices, and institutions owe far more to persistent habit, superstition, and ideology (in a word, culture) than to reason or evidence. These include once prevalent beliefs about the properties and boundaries of literature. They also include more fundamental matters—e.g., the social reproduction of race, gender, sexuality, and, to a degree, of class—whose role in shaping our individual and social lives may be of greater importance than explicit legal or governmental structures. Literature plays a role in establishing and legitimizing, as well as in revealing and challenging those tacit beliefs, practices, and institutions and in this way is connected to more extensive social problems.

> 3) The existence of those social conventions, and our understanding of them, is shaped by systematic social inequities. We have good reason, therefore, to be highly attuned to the way interest as well as culture affects belief.
>
> 4) Taking full cognizance of these matters could have emancipatory consequences.

A highly reductive list, no doubt. But I think it would be fair to say that a major portion of Theory talk amounts to extremely complicated and elaborate refinements on these basic intuitions. Summarizing them in this fashion is useful, I hope, for two reasons: because it makes clear why reasonable minds would find such notions perfectly acceptable; and because it illuminates the ways in which plausible—in fact, to some degree pretty much obvious—ideas have been taken by the Theory academy to implausible extremes. The deconstructive account of language in this respect is, say, not unlike the foucauldian account of a carceral society—a reductive, unidimensional, and melodramatic elaboration of perceptions that no reasonable mind would dispute.

If I'm right, and the habit of absurd exaggeration is a hallmark of Theory, the obvious question would be why the habit exists. To put it differently, why, virtually from the beginning, did both the advocacy for and opposition to Theory come cloaked in the language of culture war, and why to this day does it excite endless shouting matches in Crooked Timber threads?

Both Michael and John M. propose an historical explanation that emphasizes the stodgy unreceptiveness of the American literary academy in the seventies and eighties. No doubt there's something to that history. But it downplays the degree to which a highly confrontational language of ultimate ends was always a central rhetorical tactic of Theory-speak. *Of Grammatology* did look forward with anticipation to the apocalyptic end of an alleged western metaphysics. ("The future can only be anticipated in the form of an absolute danger. It is that which breaks absolutely with constituted normality and can only be proclaimed, presented as a sort of monstrosity.")[1] And as Mark Bauerlein, along with Harpham says, for those of us who fell under the sway, that millennial tone was thrilling. *The Order of Things* did look forward happily to the end of man. And, as Richard Levin's contribution to TE demonstrates with a long and in retrospect, I think, embarrassing list of quotations, the cultural materialist vanguard in Shakespeare scholarship did relentlessly call into question the *bona fides* of any criticism not taking the party line. Extremism, in other words, was not forced on Theory. It was part of the stance from the get-go. As Donaghue says in his contribution to TE, what distinguished Theory from less grandiose ideas about literature, language, and culture—Theory vs. theory in Holbonic terms—was precisely the way it claimed "total explanatory force" and in this way came to seem not something to argue over or consider, but a doctrine, or doctrines, that could either be accepted or resisted. Put differently, Theory promised not just to revise your ideas about language, or literature, or society, but to transform your life.

If so, what made the American literary academy so receptive to this grand style? Mark's argument that social constructionism is a "philosophy for the academic workplace," like John M.'s comments about market factors deserves to be taken very seriously indeed, I think. Both the employment market in literary academia and the social institutions of review and promotion may well encourage careless and rhetorically exaggerated work, while also undermining the professional institutions of academic community and peer review. (More on this later, I hope.) But that can't be the whole story. Take Mark's case: the "terms and principles" of social constructionism "fit the schedules and competitions of professional life," enabling young scholars under intense pressure to produce the quantity of scholarship they need to get by, while undermining their interest in its quality (349). There are two weak points to this argument as Mark frames it, I think. One is that his prime example, the need for young scholars to publish a book within six years to earn tenure, doesn't really suggest overwhelming pressure. Unless you're a *wunderkind* like Michael, it can feel awful indeed trying to write a decent book in six years, but it's not really a very onerous burden—and, of course, nothing that's not faced in other disciplines. The other is that professional burdens alone can't fully explain why any particular set of reductive ideas becomes more attractive than any other. As Nagel jokingly suggests in an offhand conclusion, evolutionary psychology would provide the same simple gratifications (big theory, easily applied to an endless range of material, gratifyingly counterintuitive results arrived at via circular argument, no particular need for evidence or careful reasoning) that Mark sees in social constructionism. Why have the particular, admittedly eclectic range of exaggerated ideas associated with Theory prospered in the literary academy?

Here, I think you have to begin by looking to ideology—professional ideology, that is. As a number of contributors to TE suggest without really pursuing the point, the professional discipline of literary study has traditionally defined itself, and cast itself in opposition to other fields (especially "science"), in ways that make it uniquely susceptible to the kinds of grand irrationalism propagated by Theory. Michael acknowledges this over in the comments at his blog when he says that it's an "occupational hazard" of literary academia to have "a very high tolerance level for things that don't seem to make any damn sense at first." My inclination, for which I think the Theory phenomenon gives warrant, is to drop the "at first" and probably for that reason to be a little more pained about this situation than Michael appears to be. Literary academia has not just a tolerance for things that don't make sense; it has a professional affinity for them. As John Guillory among others has shown, that attraction long precedes the arrival of Theory. It is, as John Holbo rightly says, a legacy of the late romantic ideology which, via the influence of the modernists and the new critics, was so important to the making of the postwar academic study of literature. Theory didn't create this situation. What it did was to provide a grand philosophy and a forbiddingly technical language for justifying and exacerbating it.

To my mind, the contribution to TE that best captures this phenomenon is, along with Raymond Tallis's careful rejoinder to the Derridean linguistic unconscious, Stephen Adam Schwartz's patient devastation of the epistemology and ethos of Cultural Studies. Schwartz does the mavens of Cultural Studies the service of reading their programmatically antiprogrammatic statements carefully, and (rightly, I think) discovers in the "antidiscipline" a latterday version of the historical *avant-garde.* (Ian Hunter makes a very similar argument, in an outlying contribution to the Cultural Studies tome itself.) Let me quote from Schwartz's excellent essay at length:

> In a sense, cultural studies represents less the sort of total politicization of the study of culture that it claims to be (and that its critics bemoan) than it does a generalized aestheticism: an extension of aesthetic—specifically Dada and surrealist—avant-gardism to intellectual work. The generalized call to transgression of all social norms; the sacralization of mundane and everyday cultural artifacts by a hyperarticulate and often arcane theoretical discourse; the formation of cadres on the basis of elective affinities; the radi-

> cal posturing and apocalyptic, vanguardist rhetoric; above all, the almost total absence of genuinely political aims and the almost complete political ineffectuality of the endeavor are all traits that cultural studies has in common with its surrealist precursors. Their aesthetics is essentially a romantic one. (373-74)

That's dead-on, I think. What is Theory? None of its defenders will define it, but Schwartz gives a good handle. It's the marriage of academic professionalism and aesthetic avant-gardism. It's an unlikely, awkward, and ultimately ugly marriage, and one whose consequences and implications deserve more consideration. Among other things, I think it raises some interesting implications about the culture of late capitalism, as the lingo goes. But more on that and other unresolved matters in another post.

Originally posted on July 13, 2005

NOTES

1 Jacques Derrida, Of Grammatology, trans. Gayatri Chrakravorty Spivak (Baltimore, MD: Johns Hopkins Univ. Press, 1976), 5.

8. Hostilities

Daniel Green

As the author of *Theory of Literature* (long considered the primary theoretical pillar supporting the New Criticism), René Wellek surely exemplifies the imperative to separate theory from Theory that John Holbo has been discussing. Wellek clearly believed in the efficacy of theory—which he defines as "concerned with the principles, categories, functions, and criteria of literature in general" (41)—but as early as 1982 he feared that literary theory was undermining the very assumptions on which literary study had been based. Were his fears (at least about the kind of theory then being promulgated) well founded? I think not.

His essay, "Destroying Literary Studies," reprinted in *Theory's Empire*, contends that Theory (primarily deconstruction and reader-response theory, but also extending as far back as Northrop Frye) was threatening "the whole edifice of literary study" in an "attempt to destroy literary studies from the inside" (42). In retrospect, this seems an absurd charge to have leveled against the likes of Derrida, Frye, Stanley Fish, and (!) Harold Bloom, and seems to vindicate the counter-charge that New Criticism was an especially narrow and insular movement. If even Frye and Bloom couldn't be countenanced as serious-minded rivals, wasn't it New Criticism that was doomed to destroy itself "from the inside"?

Probably so. Wellek is the only scholar associated with first-generation New Criticism to be represented in *Theory's Empire*, so perhaps it would be unfair to take his remarks as representative of the attitude to Theory of the New Critics as a whole. (The editors of TE seem to present it as such, however. There are only two references to Cleanth Brooks in the whole book, a few scattered references to W.K. Wimsatt—mostly summarizing "The Intentional Fallacy"—none at all to John Crowe Ransom.) And it is indeed disconcerting (to me) to come across such pronouncements as these from someone famous for having made the distinction between "extrinsic" and "intrinsic" approaches to literary criticism: that Theory "refuses to acknowledge that the relation of mind and world is more basic than language" (43); that Theorists "refuse to understand that words designate things and not only other words, as they argue"(45); that Theory represents "the rejection of the whole ancient enterprise of interpretation as a search for the true meaning of a text" (45).

This represents quite a retreat from, if not the letter, then certainly the spirit of New Critical practice. What other New Critic, faced with emerging methods somewhat more radical than his own but not finally that different in kind, would have resorted to the argument that interpetation is "a search for the true meaning of the text?" Did Wellek not read *The Well Wrought Urn*? In my opinion, Wellek finally comes off as a crotchety old man rejecting everything unfamiliar to him, which really does no good for an enterprise such as *Theory's Empire*, which presumably wants to reinforce the notion that some of the work done in literary study pre-Theory was valuable enough to be preserved.

Wellek's dismissals of Derrida and Fish seem especially peculiar to me. Derrida, writes Wellek, "argues that all philosophy is shot through by metaphors, ambiguities, 'undecidables,' as is all literature and criticism. This view was welcomed by some literary critics and students as a liberation, since it gives license to the arbitrary spinning of metaphors, to the stringing of puns, to mere language games" (44). This may indeed have happened among some of Derrida's followers, but that is no reason to throw out the deconstructive baby with the adulterated bathwater. Derrida's work should have been welcomed because it actually gave added credibility to the notion that all unitary, totalizing readings are mistaken and further undercut the view, still held even by some poets and novelists, that writing fiction and poetry is a matter of "saying something." The hysterical reaction to Derrida by people like Wellek only made deconstruction seem somehow relevant to the politicized varieties of academic criticism that followed, when in fact it was much closer to New Criticism itself, might even be seen as taking some of the assumptions of New Criticism to their logical conclusion.

Wellek's account of Fish and his version of reader-response theory is equally strange. "By absolutizing the power of [subjective] assumptions," according to Wellek, "he empties literature of all significance … Fish's theories encourage the view that there are no wrong interpretations, that there is no norm implied in a text, and hence that there is no knowledge of an object" (46). Fish has repeatedly defended himself against the charge that he encourages interpretive anarchy, and I can't improve on what he has said. (Interpretive communities do have norms, if the text itself does not.) Reading works of literature indeed does not produce "knowledge of an object" (not the kind of knowledge Wellek has in mind) but it does provide an experience from which knowledge can be derived (knowledge for interpretation). In some ways this is perfectly compatible with the New Critical precepts that would have us consider the reading of poetry to be a kind of dramatic experience rather than a process of gaining "knowledge of an object." Fish can be taken as giving this approach to reading a sturdier epistemological foundation.

(Wellek seems to have a particular animus towards an experiential account of reading. Elsewhere in the essay he claims that John Dewey's view of art "as the experience of heightened vitality" is part of an "attack on aesthetics." It is not. It merely relocates the source of aesthetic pleasure from the "object" to the act of perception.)

The "theories" of both Derrida and Fish could have co-existed comfortably with New Critical formalism if everyone concerned had not regarded the differences between them as so considerable that they justified critical and curricular warfare. Judging from René Wellek's essay (and many of the others included in *Theory's Empire*), the New Critics and other traditionalists were just as responsible for initiating hostilities as the Theorists who ultimately defeated them.

Originally posted on July 13, 2005

9. A Response to "The Deconstructive Angel"

Adam Kotsko

I WISH to take issue primarily with one sentence in M. H. Abrams' contribution to *Theory's Empire*, "The Deconstructive Angel"; it is exemplary of the register in which Abrams' misreading operates:

> What is distinctive about Derrida is first that, like other French structuralists, he shifts his inquiry from language to *écriture*, the written or printed text; and second that he conceives a text in an extraordinarily limited fashion. (202)

The second half of this sentence is just exactly wrong. If one is to object to Derrida's conception of "text"—and reasonable people can certainly do so—then one can only object that it is too expansive. The text becomes a metaphor, and more than a metaphor, for everything else, every other aspect of life that is accessible to human meaning. The text becomes exemplary precisely because philosophical texts are the repositories wherein the movement of a philosophical thought can be traced and tested for the coherence it seeks. The idea that an author intended something is not in question here, at all, whatever we might finally mean by "intend." Nor is there any trace of the idea that that intention is completely inaccessible to us (it is available—usually in another text, in the literal sense of the word).

The question is whether meaning escapes or overflows that intention and whether it necessarily does so. The answer to both questions seems to be yes, and it seems that Abrams would, if pressed, admit this: "I would agree that there is a diversity of sound (though not equally adequate) interpretations of the play *King Lear* ..." Why should they all be sound? How do we measure this soundness? Abrams says: "If it is sound, this interpretation approximates, closely enough for the purpose at hand, what the author meant" (200). But why "what the author meant"? For a historian of ideas, what the author meant may not be terribly relevant—we could all think of texts that have been widely misunderstood according to scholarly standards of reading and of reconstructing authorial intention, but were influential precisely insofar as they were misunderstood (for example, the Bible), or at least entered into public discussion only as they were misunderstood. Why is it that this should happen? Are not all texts made up of relatively simple units such as "Pray you undo this button," a sentence that Abrams claims, as do I, to understand in a rather precise way? What is it that keeps texts from being relatively transparent?

These are questions that Abrams is simply not asking. There is no particular reason that he has to be asking them, but there is also no particular reason to dismiss such questions out of hand in favor of a relatively unexamined "common sense" approach—an approach that is, in fact, "good enough" for the purpose at hand, but again, why is it good enough? Why is it self-evident that recovering the author's meaning is the goal of literary study, and if the goal of writing is to convey a more or less obvious meaning, then why is it that we elevate to the stature of literary monuments people who seem to do a very poor job of that (as evidenced by the fact that we need literary scholars at all)? And if it is the case that something like "one" meaning of the text is something we wish to uncover, why is it that we need a plurality of readings in order to surround and trap it? And why is it taking scholars so long to figure out that definitive meaning, even of relatively simple texts?

It seems to me that these are the kinds of questions that at least some literary scholars need to ask, and in fact that some were asking even before the advent of theory properly-so-called—as Abrams admits before the sentence to which I object above, with reference to the New Critics. Indeed, for the New Critics, something like meaning or authorial intention could very well be taken to be a textual effect ("What the master achieves is what he intended") and future writers or readers could retrospectively change the shape of the textual tradition (as in "Tradition and the Individual Talent"); they do not get to that conclusion by the precise route that Derrida takes, but there is room for a dialogue there.

And in fact, I think it would have been better had that dialogue taken place in a less adversarial way. That is, it would have been better if the advocates of what has become contemporary literary theory had not set themselves up as doing something qualitatively different from anyone before. First of all, it is a misrepresentation of what the (primarily) French scholars who inspired literary theorists were up to. Derrida is, in my opinion, the greatest and most exciting thinker of the 20th century, but he did not divide the history of the West in two with the mighty force of his intellect, or attempt to. In fact, he is great and exciting precisely insofar as he continues a tradition or intertwines several traditions—including primarily phenomenology, then also structuralism and psychoanalysis, adding others as his career progressed. Part of the problem is that he deploys argumentative strategies that sound very radical and reductive to Anglo-American ears but are in fact common currency in the continental European tradition. That is, he finds the marginal case and uses that to illustrate the normal; the best example of this in the twentieth century is Freud, for whom the study of neurotics comes to inform understandings of normal individuals, leading Lacan to say later that normal human behavior is a subspecies of neurosis. More generally, though, Derrida is in many respects a very conservative thinker, and one must start from that conservatism in order to measure the ways in which he is radical. But again, this conservatism can seem highly radical to thinkers who are attempting to graft Derrida into a tradition (or cover over a tradition using Derrida) in which many of Derrida's key reference points have historically been marginal at best.

So yes, it sounds wildly disproportionate to say that there is nothing outside of the text and that meaning is radically undetermined, but Derrida is not really talking about everyday situations. He is specifically talking about a very special class of texts (that is, philosophical texts) that make very special kinds of claims (that is, a degree of coherence and comprehensiveness to which *King Lear* does not aspire.) He doesn't think that those texts can make good on the claims they make for themselves, and he thinks he knows why. How much does that affect the way you read a sentence where someone asks to have a button undone? Probably not much. But it does help to clarify that (a) philosophical texts are written, and subject to the same vagaries as any other written text (even, and exemplarily, a written text reputed to have been inspired) and (b) there is a certain glory in being merely written—as is shown in Derrida's later work, where he makes continual, insistent reference precisely to literature as the result and condition of modern democracy, as "freedom of speech" in action, enabling and producing further speech/writing, further traces by which we continue to meet each other, often in quite disconcerting or pleasantly surprising ways.

To the extent that Abrams is right that deconstruction as deployed in literary studies "begins as an intentional, goal-oriented quest; and ... this quest is to end in an impasse" (207), then deconstruction has become not only boring but a caricature of itself. Coming to the conclusion that every literary text is a testament to the impossibility of meaning (or whatever cliché we want to put here) is precisely the kind of closed-off thinking that deconstruction hopes to find the conditions for avoiding. It is an abdication of the responsibility of the critic to find always the same meaning in a text, especially when inspired by a reader like Derrida who is always finding new and unexpected possibilities in texts—but then, I think it's also an abdication of the responsibility of the critic to find that every literary text in the canon is an indication of the greatness of its author, or of universal human values, or of whatever else.

In any case, it is clear that M. H. Abrams is a true scholar, and his intervention, rather early on in the history of theory, provides a model that one wishes were more often followed. First, it evinces none of the laziness that so often accompanies the sweeping dismissals of theory that have achieved—contrary to the persecution complex of many anti-theory advocates—a clear hegemony in the broader public sphere, and indeed, in many areas of academia outside of the humanities. Abrams tracked down and read two of the most challenging essays in *Margins of Philosophy*, before they were widely available in translation, often quoting the French text in addition to providing his own translation, the kind of scholarship that is nowhere present in the recent "take-downs" of theory, particularly of the "theorists don't understand science" variety that are universally cited as having discredited the enterprise of literary theory. Abrams knows he is dealing with serious thinkers in Derrida and Hillis Miller, and he shows them the respect due to serious thinkers. In addition, perhaps due to his wide erudition in Romantic literature, he displays a genuine admiration for the audacity of deconstructive thought. Who can imagine any contemporary opponent of literary theory quoting a passage like this—

> Derrida's vision is thus, as he puts it, of an "as yet unnamable something which cannot announce itself except... under the species of a non-species, under the formless form, mute, infant, and terrifying, of monstrosity"

—without the slightest hint of snark or derision?

That was, of course, a different time. Deconstruction was still new to the American scene (Paul de Man's *Blindness and Insight*, for example, was published only five years earlier); the Derrida translation industry had not yet kicked into full gear (*Writing and Difference* would not be published in English for two more years.) Perhaps then, a prominent scholar could afford an indulgent attitude toward the romantic young upstart, but when theory constitutes an Empire that is on the verge of collapse, then perhaps a decidedly more negative tone is appropriate, similar to the apocalyptic rhetoric of certain Jewish, then Christian, sects in that other Empire that was always-already decaying.

But I digress. My goal in this essay has been to show, first, that even given the information that Abrams had ready to hand, he was wrong about Derrida in a fairly decisive way. That is, I do not intend here to claim that Abrams should have had to read everything that Derrida has ever written, and then to request to review Derrida's notes for works that he had not yet written, in order to adequately understand what he read. I consent, as a practical matter, to the common-sense principles of reading that Abrams outlines in his essay and plan to argue merely that Abrams oversimplifies Derrida's work, in the shape it had taken by that early date, in ways that lead him ultimately into a match of shadow-boxing. Second, I wish to claim that this misunderstanding is not entirely Abrams' fault and that, if Derrida's exponents in the United States had corrected that misunderstanding at the time (which may well have been a misunderstanding they shared), then perhaps we could have avoided the shameful scene of American scholars writing eulogies of Derrida in which it is claimed that he was a bad person.

Originally posted on July 13, 2005

10. THEORY THURSDAY

John McGowan

BY ADDING a Theory Thursday to Michael's Theory Tuesday, we will quickly discover how many masochists we can count among this blog's faithful readers.

I had originally intended to use this post to fulminate against the following sentence in the "Introduction" to *Theory's Empire*: "Our chief aim is to provide students and interested readers with effective intellectual tools to help them redeem the study of literature as an activity worth pursuing in its own right." There are many, many reasons—about which I could go on at tedious length—why that sentence sticks in my craw. But, like any self-respecting English teacher, I'm going to ask the class what they think. Does the study of literature—and (surely it is implied) literature itself—need to be "redeemed"? And is the royal road to redemption to understand that study as "an activity worth pursuing in its own right"? Answers to be posted in the comments section.

I have been put off my polemical horse by the general reasonableness of the discussion of *Theory's Empire* over at THE VALVE. The number of participants is a bit disappointing, but the general quality of the conversation is good, and its tone is even better. This is not yet another round in the culture and theory wars, which have wearied hardier souls than mine long before our current late date in history. Is it possible that academics interested in such questions have won their way through to a place where they can be discussed and examined calmly? As someone whose most usual stance has been a plague on both your houses, I am hopeful. In any case, John Holbo is to be commended for using the blogosphere in this innovative and promising way. Even if this first conversation is a little halting, I hope this model proves, like so many other things on the web, a snowball, gathering more and more readers—and participants—as he stages similar events in the future.

I will confine myself today to thinking a bit about "criticism"—an activity that stands in uncertain relation to "theory". I'll start by saying that I am uninterested in whether or not every act of criticism relies on implicit, even if unexamined or unacknowledged, assumptions that a more self-conscious 'theory' would make explicit. I seldom agree with

Stanley Fish about anything, but I do think he is right that claims about the theoretical underpinnings of all practices are, whether true or not, without significant consequences. The theory/practice model offers us a highly dubious understanding of human behavior. Habits—both personal and social, and ossified in vocabularies as well as in various rituals and routines—are at least as crucially the background of our practices as any ideas or theories we might have about what we are or want to be doing. And habits are notoriously resistant to being changed by thinking. Habits are changed when you start doing something differently—and you need to do that different thing lots of times to undo the old settled ways.

Criticism as a practice, then, rests on the habits inculcated by training. We don't call them "disciplines" for nothing. And criticism is like playing the piano; you can't learn how to do it by reading an instruction manual. You learn how to do it by doing it under the tutelage of someone who is more adept and who criticizes your fledgling efforts and urges you to practice, practice, practice. "Theory," in this view, is not what underpins "criticism," but is simply another practice, one with different aims, stakes, and protocols. To be very crude about it, "criticism" is the practice of interpreting and judging specific texts, while "theory" is the practice of making wider claims about the characteristics of many texts (Aristotle on tragedy) or of a culture (Carlyle on "The Signs of the Times") or of a set of practices (Wittgenstein on "language games"). Which is my way of saying that the notion that "theory" and "criticism" are inimical to one another—or even in some kind of competition with one another—is mistaken.

As both Morris Dickstein and Marjorie Perloff indicate in their contributions to *Theory's Empire*, criticism is relatively rare in the tradition. The four elements of "poetics" identified by Perloff do not include interpretation of single texts. The ancients—Aristotle, Longinus, Quintillian—were closer to producing advice manuals for writers than to offering guides for readers. Interpretation enters from the Christian side, an outgrowth of Biblical hermeneutics. Dante was the first person to suggest that secular works might also require learned interpretation. But it is not until the late seventeenth century, with the French neoclassical writers and "the battle of the Ancients and the Moderns" in England, that literary criticism really arrives on the scene. And it does so in a policing and pedagogical function. Criticism—first as evaluation and only later as interpretation—is necessary because the insufficiently educated are making bad judgments. Their taste needs to be cultivated. We might prefer Addison's displays of how a gentleman reads, thinks, and behaves to Boileau's laying down the law of the unities, but both writers are engaged in the same enterprise. Growing literacy among relatively uneducated peoples calls forth teachers who will help them discern the good from the trash and to properly understand difficult works.

It is not surprising, then, that criticism moved into the classroom once compulsory schooling took hold in the nineteenth century. It was already a pedagogical enterprise. And it is not surprising that "English" as a school subject originated in the colonies, specifically India, because those to the manner born don't need these lessons. For all his commitment to education and to culture, Matthew Arnold rarely provides an interpretation of a literary work. He assumes that the audience of his essays is perfectly capable of understanding particular poems on their own. He is, of course, very worried that English readers have the wrong tastes, but he never imagines that they do not understand what they read. But democratic education soon produces that concern—and schoolboys and schoolgirls were set to producing "*explications du texte*" of various sorts in English, French, and American classrooms.

Just about the time that compulsory elementary education takes hold, we also get the creation of the modern research university. English as a "subject" had arisen for the pedagogical reasons I have suggested combined with nationalistic ones (inculcation into the national culture). Now, in the university, English needed to become a "discipline," not just a school subject. The two available models for the new American universities were the scholarly Germans (the philologists) and the quasi-amateur English "men of letters." (For reasons I do not know, French university practices had no influence at Hopkins and Chicago, the two original research universities.) At first, the Germans won the day handily, with Babbitt's "humanism" the only respectable alternative to full-bore scholarship. Criticism was something for the newspapers, the stuff of reviews not of serious academic work. It took the social upheavals of the 1920s, the tremendous influence and prestige of the Anglophile T. S. Eliot, and the scientistic trappings of New Criticism's account of its work and of the poetic object, to make criticism academically respectable. Dickstein tells this story well. Producing an interpretation of a literary text, after around 1930, counted as "research" in the modern university. So we got lots of such interpretations.

Is there a moral to this story? Not particularly. As many have noted, New Criticism was, and remains to some extent, a valuable pedagogical tool. As others—including Michael in THIS POST ON JUDITH HALBERSTAM'S ESSAY—have noted, the techniques of attentive reading developed by New Criticism are valuable aids to understanding. Criticism was—and remains—a worthy enterprise. Literacy can be enhanced by practicing criticism. That not all English professors are critics in their written work seems neither here nor there to me. That was always the case, since there were always professors who were textual editors, biographers, etymologists, and literary historians. Probably most English professors are critics at least some of the time in their classrooms. But there has never been a seamless connection between what we teachers do in the classroom and what we publish as scholars. Dissing criticism or recommending that all scholars be critics is as silly as dissing theory or insisting that all scholars be theorists.

Originally posted on Thursday, July 14, 2005

11. Book Notes: Theory's Empire

Tim Burke

So, OVER at The Valve, they're talking about the new anthology *Theory's Empire,* and I was asked to join in the fun. Beware of what you ask for: I may have achieved true Holbonian length here, at 3,000 words or so.

I'll start, like the book itself, with Jeff Reid's cartoon "Breakfast Theory: a Morning Methodology". ("Pretty dry and flavorless, isn't it?" "Your question is informed, or should I say misinformed, by the conventionalized bourgeois cereal paradigm ...") I was one of the thousands of academics in graduate school or newly hired in 1989 who cut that cartoon out and put it up on a bulletin board. I remember showing it to my wife, saying it was the funniest thing I'd seen. She read it attentively and smiled politely.

The cartoon stayed funny but it also started to become an emblem of something else for me, a growing awareness of distress. In 1989, I was well into graduate school. I'd actually had a lot of exposure to "critical theory" as an undergraduate major in history and English in the mid-1980s. I'd even had a class with Judith Butler on Foucault while she was at Wesleyan. I liked theory, even when I felt I didn't have the faintest idea what was going on, because if nothing else you could sense the energy behind it, that the theorists we read were urgently engaged by their work, the professors who taught the theorists were among the most exciting and skilled teachers at the college, because in the backwash of the 1960s and 1970s, many of us had a restless sense that the next intellectual and political step was waiting to be taken, but none of us knew what that might be. Theory made you feel almost like you were in the dream of the Enlightenment again, everyone speaking the same language with disciplines and specializations set aside.

The cartoon was funny for those of who spent time reading, thinking, speaking theory at a very particular moment in the institutional and intellectual history of American academia. For anyone who didn't, the cartoon is mildly amusing in another way: as a kind of pre-Sokal confirmation that the eggheads in the humanities had gone deep into the swamps of nonsense and pomposity. And this is how the cartoon wormed its way into my head: both as a funny satire of things I did and said and as a salvage operation dredging up an intellectual self already alienated by the distance between what I found myself doing as an academic-in-training and the underlying desires I'd brought with me when I signed up to get a Ph.D.

Which is still how I feel now about "theory" and its alleged overthrow. I warm to the talk that it was an empire, but I'm equally aware that my sense of it as such is a direct personal consequence of my individual experience of academic careerism. I warm to the various critiques and denunciations of theory in the volume but to some extent because I get both the insider and outsider version of them, the same way I could read the cartoon in two idioms—and for the same reason, the glee of some contributors can be a bit off-putting. This is why I tend to bristle on one hand at know-nothing denunciations of theory, like E.O. Wilson's in *Consilience*, but also at circle-the-wagons defenses of it, or even those defenses which argue that the problem with theory was only its occasional excesses and over-zealous acolytes.

The main point, and it is one made again and again throughout the anthology, is that theory was above all a professional consciousness, a way of feeling and being academic that was native to a past time and place (the 1980s and early 1990s). You can't just separate out some of the chief manifestations of the era of theory, like the star system, as unrelated epiphenomena, or insist that we just talk about the actual texts. (Though at the same time, the volume could really use an ethnographic retelling of a conference or conversation from the late 1980s or early 1990s. Anthony Appiah comes closest in his short essay, and maybe there's nothing that really fits the bill besides a David Lodge novel.)

This is not to say that theory's moment is done and gone, with no harm to anyone. There was lasting damage done in a variety of ways.

A number of contributors observe that one thing that the theoretical moment did which has had lasting effects on academic writing in general is not so much the feared disfigurations of jargon but the escalating grandiosity of scholarly claims, the overinflation of argument, the Kissinger-joke ramping up of the presumed stakes in scholarly writing and speaking. Theory, particularly but not solely in literary studies, withdrew from an imagined relation to public discourse which apportioned it a mostly modest role but in exact inverse proportion to that retreat developed a more and more exaggerated sense of the importance of its own discourse.

You cannot just make this a folly of the theorists, or talk about it in isolation from the economic and institutional changes in the academy itself. Academic literary critics in 1950, like most professors, made poor salaries while working for institutions which were still relatively distant from American mass society. Professors in 1989, particularly those employed by selective colleges and universities, were working for institutions which were relatively wealthy, paid good salaries and offered good benefits, and which were now a familiar component of the American dream. Most research university departments in the humanities and the social sciences at that time also had to confront the seismic shift in the internal budgeting of their institutions, that external grants not only kept the sciences going but also funded the whole institution in major ways. The scientists weren't usually being modest about the usefulness of their research in their grant applications, and a good deal of that spilled over as a pressure on the rest of the academy.

This inflation has a lot to do with explaining the relation between the first wave of high theory and its evolution into historicism and identity politics of the race/class/gender variety, much discussed in the anthology. (In many ways, this mutation is the central issue under discussion.) On paper, this relation is hard to explain: it is not an easy or natural evolution of argument from the initial round of continental postmodern or poststructuralist philosophy, much less so from the first wave of the high priests of deconstruction in the United States like Paul de Man. The contributors to the anthology hammer on this point again and again, but it's worth emphasizing: whatever "theory" began as, it quickly metastasized into a much vaguer way of being and acting that could be found in most corners and byways of the academic humanities, and a way of being and acting that was often a new and virulent practice of academic warfare which left a lot of casualties and fortifications in its wake.

It's true that a response to the volume that insists on reconfining theory to a properly constrained set of texts and authors has a valid point. If nothing else, it leads to taking the actual content of actual writing seriously, rather than just a marker of academic sociology. Saussure, Foucault, Derrida, Lacan, and even many of the various American academic superstars who dominated the era of theory like Fish, Jameson, or Spivak had important, substantive arguments to make that can't just be waved away or ignored. (Nor does this anthology: it collects some smart detailed ripostes to the substantive arguments of Derrida and many other theorists.) Still, I agree with many of *Theory's Empire*'s authors: the *Geist* and historical moment of theory is an equally important part of the subject.

Which may be best known experientially, by those of us who lived through the sometimes-subtle, sometimes-blatant transformations high theory brought to academic practice and consciousness. Many are right to say that is a perilous claim, not to mention a potentially narcissistic one: it's a short step from that insistence that "I lived it, so I know it", to blasting everything you don't like as "postmodernism", to ignoring the things that made various mutations and permutations of theory attractive and productive, to alienating your present intellectual self from the self that found it all very exciting and generative.

It's also dangerous because you begin to overread the theoretical moment as the causal agent behind every problem of the contemporary academy. Valentine Cunningham, for example, attributes almost every novelty in the vocabulary and practice of humanistic scholarship since 1960 to theory's conquest. There are deeper drivers here, and they not only survive theory, but predate it. Among them is academic careerism itself. Theory sharpened its knives, but aspirant scholars in the humanities and elsewhere must still today present an account of themselves as more brilliant, more original and more important than any others of their cohort while also pledging their fidelity to reigning orthodoxies in their discipline. Theory's overthrow hasn't changed any of that, nor did theory cause it to happen. Too many talented people chasing too few desirable jobs did. Cunningham argues that "criticism always claims newness", but really, all humanistic scholarship since modernism or so does, and in this, is really only following on the lead of literature itself, as Morris Dickstein notes in his essay in the volume.

This is not to underrate the particular forms of self-interest that theory serviced in very particular ways. J.G. Merquior's essay "*Theorrhea* and *Kulturkritik*" notes this by commenting: "That a deep cultural crisis is endemic to historical modernity seems to have been more eagerly assumed than properly demonstrated, no doubt because, more often than not, those who generally do the assuming—humanist intellectuals—have every interest in being perceived as soul doctors to a sick civilization" (245). In many ways, theory was the ultimate careerist maneuver, because its normal operations conferred upon the theorist a position of epistemologically unimpeachable, self-confirming authority (in part by claiming to abjure authority) while also freeing the theorist from having to know *anything but* theory in order to exert such authority. I can't be the only person who was subjected in graduate school (or later) to the peculiar spectacle of a dedicated, philosophically rigorous postmodernist proclaiming that only those who had thoroughly read the entire *corpus* of a particular theorist's work should be permitted to speak about it. Indeed, such gestures of intellectual hypocrisy—some of them more subtle, some less so—are a particular target of mockery and anger from the authors in *Theory's Empire*, and with some justification. It was hard not to see Derrida's infamous assertion of conventional authorial rights over his interview on Heidegger as one of many such moments of contradiction.

One of the other oddities of the anthology is that almost no one gives a convincing account of their own survival of colonial domination by theory (including those essays contemporaneous with theory's rise, which already adopt the posture of defeated defiance.) I suppose you could say that some paint themselves as autochthonous survivors who dug themselves into the institutional *maquis* for a long guerilla struggle and are now celebrating as the colonizer's regime collapses. Others set themselves up more as members of a lost Stone Age tribe who were never contaminated by the colonizer's modernity, or as archaeologists digging into layers of criticism that lie below the theory strata. A few are positioned as latter-day nativists reaching back to the precolonial era for renovation, and still others, as nationalists who worked with the empire, have assimilated the colonizer's ways but are now ready to renounce him and declare independence. (Pretty close to my self-presentation here.)

What's important in this regard is that because the anthology collects many older essays as well as recent ones, it gives rise to some suspicion that theory's empire was considerably less imperial than its most strident critics tend to claim, that it was always less influential and powerful than either the lords of theory or their enemies suggested. Perhaps I'm only inclined to think that because that's what I think about other empires, too, but I think many academics simply amiably went about their business in the era of high theory, borrowing a bit from such work here and there, but hardly worshipping at its altars or angrily burning its fetishes. Certainly that's the way Foucault was commonly appropriated by many historians, as a practical device for identifying new subjects to research (said historians then, as often as not, debunked Foucault's concrete historical claims in consequence.)

There are some other points that emerge along the way in the book that strike me as important. One is the amnesia of theory at its high-water mark, which I think was both a substantive feature of theoretical argument and sociological feature of the reproduction of the humanistic academy in those years. So when John Ellis observes of Stanley Fish's work that it ignored the past, that in Fish's work, "philosophy of science begins with Thomas Kuhn, serious questions about the idea of truth and the positivist theory of language begin with Derrida, jurisprudence begins with the radical Critical Legal Studies movement" (105). I think he's exactly right, and not just about Fish.

I think this became a feature of how many of us were trained and how we trained ourselves, a part of the ordinary discourse of conferences, reading groups, and so on. Theory began with the last person who was commonly authenticated as its progenitor, and that was good enough—largely because it helped younger academics frame themselves as making original gestures or "interventions" into various debates. I had a senior colleague in anthropology who used to fall into amusing rants every time he and I went to hear a presentation by a young anthropologist, and with some reason, because in the vast majority of such presentations, the author would proclaim, often citing critical theory, that they were beginning for the first time to reflexively consider the role of the anthropologist himself or herself in generating anthropological knowledge. He was right, this is a silly gesture: such concerns have haunted anthropology all the way back to its origins. The same affliction affected us all across a wide swath of disciplines: we reinvented wheels, fire, alphabets and chortled in satisfaction at our own cleverness. Theory dropped into our midst like commodities drop into a cargo cult, and our reaction was roughly the same, right up to eagerly scanning the skies for the next French thinker to drop down and inventing our own crude substitutes when the interval between drops grew too lengthy.

This makes me think that another issue which gets discussed here and there but whose importance is underappreciated is the role of theory in shaping the average or ordinary work of scholarship. Almost all the hue and cry in the essays is either about the foundational or canonical theorists or about various academic superstars. While I think it's true, as I suggested earlier, that many scholars only had a passing and pragmatic relation to theory, I also think theory was a kind of attractor that pulled a wave of "ordinary" scholarship towards it. I remember being paralyzed by one of the first scholarly book reviews I wrote, holding on to it for months, because I found when I had finished that I'd written a very hostile review, largely because of the way that a work which might have had some workaday, craftsmanlike value as a monograph about the history of European representations of African bodies had wrapped itself in a rigid Foucauldian straightjacket and used theory as a justification for its chaotic and empirically weak arguments. (I was paralyzed because I felt bad about roughing up the author so much, but I got over it and published it eventually.)

This would be one of my acute criticisms of the subspecies of theory that became postcolonialism, that the ordinary work of postcolonial scholarship takes the already deeply problematic arguments and style of the dominant superstars like Spivak, Prakash and Bhabha and operationalizes it as yeoman-level banality. There's a kind of missing generation of monographs as a result, an absence of substantive, minutely authoritative, carefully researched and highly specialized knowledge that serves as a foundation for more sweeping syntheses and broadly argued scholarship. As I look over my shelves, I spot numerous works in history, cultural anthropology, critical theory, literary studies, cultural studies, whose only major lasting usefulness is as a historical document of a theoretical moment, works that you literally wouldn't consult for any other purpose. As Erin O'Connor notes in her essay, the problem here in part is the dissemination of formulas, of totemic gestures, and more frustratingly, of a scholarship which is consumed by an understanding of its own impossibility, or as M.H. Abrams says of Hillis Miller, of a deliberate dedication not just to labyrinths but to dead ends within labyrinths.

Though once again, it's also important to remember that some of the deeper driver here is not the boogeyman of theory, but the whole of academic careerism. Our bookshelves still groan with books and articles that need not have been written, but they will continue to be written as long as they are the fetish which proves that the academic apprentice is now a worthy journeyman who can step onto the tenure track. But at least if we must write unnecessary books, it would be nice if those books might add minutely to knowledge of some specialized subject. In fact, one of the good things that came out of the moment of theory was the legitimate expansion of academic subject matter: I was pleasantly surprised to see that the bitching and moaning about cultural studies, popular culture and "trivial subjects" from scholars who superficially call for a return to a high literary canon as the proper subject of literary criticism was kept to a minimum in the volume, indeed, the longest specific criticism of cultural studies, by Stephen Adam Schwartz, never indulges in this vice. (I especially liked Schwartz' observation that cultural studies is actually governed by methodological individualism, and thus a form of ethnocentrism: my principal answer would be to say that for me that's a feature rather than a bug.)

It is a straightforwardly good thing that historians now write about a whole range of topics that were relatively unstudied in 1965; a straightforwardly good thing that literary critics read and think about a much wider range of texts than they once did. As Morris Dickstein notes, the era of high theory in the 1980s was not the first to discover the problem that there might not be a hell of a lot left to say about literary works that people had been reading and interpreting for centuries. This is why is makes me all the more regretful that theory dragged so much of the workaday business of academic writing towards its own forms of epistemological blockage and vacuity, because there were at least a great many new things to write about.

I suppose if I had one hope from this volume, it's that people who read it and take it seriously won't be the kind of lazy Sokolites that Michael Bérubé justifiably complains about, because nowhere in the volume does anyone claim that doing literary analysis or humanistic scholarship is easy or straightforward. If this is a roadmap to the future, it does not go from point A to point B, much to its credit.

Originally posted on July 13, 2005

12. Four Challenges to Postcolonial Theory

Amardeep Singh

Like other polemical academic anthologies, including *The Empire Writes Back* and *Fear of a Queer Planet, Theory's Empire: An Anthology of Dissent* is likely to be remembered, first and foremost, for its confrontational title, and for its editors' introduction. Some of the essays included are likely to be helpful and interesting at a general level for readers interested in the genealogy of the concept of "Theory," especially Stephen Adam Schwartz's "Everyman an Übermensch: the Culture of Cultural Studies," Kwame Anthony Appiah's "Battle of the *Bien-Pensant*," and Valentine Cunningham's "Theory? What Theory?" But in other ways the volume is limited by its commitment to only providing contributions that align with its anti-Theory orientation. It seems one-sided, for instance, to read M.H. Abrams's "The Deconstructive Angel" divorced from the essays by deconstructive critics it responds to, or by those who respond to it.

Big anthologies like the ones mentioned often mark turning points in academic discourse as a whole. But it's unclear what exactly is being positively expressed here by this collection of essays as a whole; they certainly don't *all* advocate going back to a pre-political or pre-linguistic theory New Criticism; no, the effects of various theoretical movements (poststructuralism, feminism, and postcolonial theory in particular) have been dispersed too widely for that to be feasible, even if it might be desirable for some. Some voices are advocating depoliticization, and some argue for less in the way of culture and identity, and more in the way of literature and literary forms. These are legitimate demands, though it might be that what is really needed—what would be productive for the academic humanities *as a scholarly community*—is not less politics, but a more balanced and thoughtful kind of politics; not less concern with culture, but a different kind of culture. With postcolonial theory in particular I agree with Jonathan Culler's suggestion in his recent book *The Literary in Theory* that the field would benefit from "good accounts of the literary norms against which postcolonial writers are said to be writing." As Culler puts it, "Lacking descriptions of such norms, the discourse of critics either swiftly becomes thematic, focusing on questions of identity and resistance to authority, rather than on artistic innovation; or else it takes theoretical arguments themselves as the norms, so that the literary works are used to challenge Homi Bhabha's account of hybridity or colonial mimicry or the appropriateness of Gayatri Spivak's question, "Can the Subaltern speak?" for the case under discussion."[1] It has to be admitted that the mainstream of postcolonial theory has fallen somewhat short of the mark with regard to incorporating ideas of literary form and language alongside political questions, and that far too many readings of contemporary African, Middle Eastern, and Asian fiction do exactly what Culler describes with regards to Bhabha and Spivak. But it's also not at all impossible to imagine the situation could be amended.

In the following essay I'll make detailed reference to four essays that challenge postcolonial theory. The essays by Erin O'Connor and Meera Nanda are included in *Theory's Empire*. In both of these essays, there is much that is genuine and productive—much to take quite seriously—though there are also troubling instances of rhetorical overreaching. A third essay is "The Postcolonial Aura" (1994) by Arif Dirlik, which is generally critical of the term "postcolonial," the kinds of people who study it, and the work they do.[2] Though Dirlik is probably one of the harshest general critics of postcolonial theory, by an unusual kind of irony he himself has been drawn into the fold; his work is widely assigned in postcolonial literature and theory courses as well as anthologized in Postcolonial Studies readers. Finally, the fourth essay I will refer to is actually a text that is on the surface quite sympathetic to the postcolonial project. It is Priya Joshi's introduction to her book, *In Another Country*, and it levels criticisms against some of the major voices in postcolonial theory that are as sharp as O'Connor's, without taking a confrontational tone. I also present her as an example of a kind of postcolonial scholarship that succeeds as a research project, avoids the pitfalls and traps often characteristic of "postcolonialism," and makes useful internal criticisms of the field.

1. Erin O'Connor

Erin O'Connor's "Preface to a Post-postcolonial Criticism", which first appeared in *Victorian Studies* 45.2 (Winter 2003), makes critiques that are apposite to both the problem of overreaching and the problem of rhetorical style and substance. It is an essay that makes some strikingly good points about the problems with a certain kind of theorizing, points which I think every graduate student interested in the field should probably consider. But it is also an essay that is guilty, sometimes egregiously, of over-assertion, and of a kind of polemical rhetorical aggressiveness that works against O'Connor's stated desire for a less politicized academic environment.

This particular essay has already inspired quite a number of responses, so perhaps it is sensible to address on two of the smaller aspects of O'Connor's "Preface," which neither PATRICK BRANTLINGER nor DIERDRE DAVID brought up in their respective responses in *Victorian Studies*.[3] One is O'Connor's claim that major figures in postcolonial theory—epitomized by Spivak—argue via epigrammatic generalizations rather than through empirical evidence or strong historical grounding. These overwhelming generalizations are demonstrably present, both in Edward Said's *Orientalism* and in much of Spivak's writing, especially in the text O'Connor singles out for critique, "Three Women's Texts and a Critique of Imperialism."[4] I am also inclined to accept O'Connor's characterization of the drift towards studies of Empire in Victorian Studies, though I speak as a non-Victorianist, and do not wish to trespass across period boundaries. I would not wish to be lumped in with the "Victorientalists" O'Connor accuses of launching a "hostile takeover" of her field, as follows:

> The end result of Spivak's hostile takeover of a genre, a history, and a criticism is thus finally to encourage territorial thinking within literary studies. My own response to the essay serves as a salient example. To this day I feel a personal affront when I read or teach Spivak's essay, an uncomfortable sense that someone from outside has dared to tread on my field with such infinite condescension, has dared to pass judgment on the critical practice of Victorian studies, and, moreover, has dared to do so with so little ultimate authority—the authority provided by a singularly skimpy and partial reading of a single novel that presumes to call itself a reading of an entire genre, culture, and politics; whose claim to cultural analysis is, in other words, that of sheer bravado alone. There is a majesty to it, one that can only be called imperial

> (calling Victorian literary studies imperialist is, after all, Spivak's own colonizing gesture). It is a move that casts the field as a fundamentally backward area, incapable of governing, or thinking, for itself, and hence in need of enlightenment from beyond. And it is a move whose power is revealed by the fact that we have yet to see it for what it is. (305-6)

There is a legitimate point here, but this is on the whole not a very admirable paragraph. O'Connor uses her enemy's tool exactly the way her enemy uses it. She gains no moral ground through this (perhaps, as Brantlinger suggests, it is meant as satire), and runs the risk of an unbecoming kind of proprietary isolationism ("my field," and "hostile takeover" are gatekeeper phrases, which sound strange coming from a younger scholar).

Having said that, we can go on to address O'Connor's substantial complaint about Spivak and Jane Eyre, which is the disproportionate impact of the essay on the scholarship that has followed:

> Spivak was right about what would happen if her "'facts'" were remembered. They have indeed not only been remembered, but have become the guiding premises for much subsequent work on *Jane Eyre*, which has tirelessly dedicated itself to filling in the gaps in Spivak's sweeping history. There are Spivak-inspired studies of *Jane Eyre*'s relationship to Jamaica, to India, to Ireland, and to Africa; to colonialism, to Orientalism, and to racism; to slavery and to sati. Together, they comprise a massive effort of retroactive documentation. Indeed, reading postcolonial readings of *Jane Eyre* since 1985 is virtually synonymous with watching Spivak's reading gradually get consolidated as scholars quietly assume the role of providing the context and the close reading Spivak left out. Committing themselves to supplying the evidence to uphold Spivak's broadest conjectures (to producing the narrative of literary history she desires), rather than to questioning the viability of an argument that is made without the benefit of evidence, scholars not

> surprisingly wind up producing readings that replicate Spivak's rather than generating substantially new ones. Indeed, what is most peculiar about postcolonial work on *Jane Eyre* is how uniformly it tends to bolster Spivak's argument, so much so that even critics who take issue with some of Spivak's premises do so in ways that enable her most basic claims to remain intact. Susan Meyer, for instance, argues that *Jane Eyre* questions the ideology of imperialism before finally upholding it, a thesis that differs from Spivak's only in order to fine-tune it. Building on Spivak's work rather than testing or challenging it, critics have set out to defend (by developing) a version of literary history that they have effectively accepted on faith. (301-2)

What exactly is it that has been accepted by these scholars 'on faith'? Is it the presence of the theme of Imperialism in nineteenth century literature? That does seem like a fact, though its *centrality* is both debatable and questionable; a recent book called *The Absent-Minded Imperialists* by Bernard Porter does just that. It is possible to address the meaning and historical experience of "centrality" narrowly, without lamenting the general politicization of literary study.

Contra O'Connor, one could interpret the work that's substantiated Spivak's "conjectures" as a positive development, rather than further evidence of the slavishness of academic taste. Some of that work may be second-rate in one way or another ("readings that replicate Spivak's"), but it might also be argued that the evidence that has been supplied, and the building that has followed have filled out the historical gaps. It would have been helpful if Spivak herself had done that work, but it is not inherently a weakness that "postcolonial" Victorian studies has, in the wake of Spivak's essay, amassed a sizeable volume of historically-minded scholarship focusing on the representation of Empire in the novels of the period.

More broadly, I question O'Connor's disdain for inductive reasoning, generalizations, and conjecture. As anyone who has ever struggled with arguments about literature must know, literary studies has never conformed to the modern scientific method. One generates viable arguments and new forms of literary knowledge via routes that are often tangled, using reasoning that may be equal parts inductive and deductive, as well as through conjectures (that are eventually substantiated), generalizations (that are hopefully true), and partial initial knowledge (that is later filled in).

2. Priya Joshi

In his otherwise surprisingly brief response to O'Connor's essay in a subsequent issue of *Victorian Studies*, Patrick Brantlinger nominates as counter-examples some scholars whose works are reviewed in the very same issue of *Victorian Studies* in which O'Connor's essay first appeared. One of those is Priya Joshi's *In Another Country* (Columbia, 2002), which responds to O'Connor's complaints, and even echoes some of them.

Joshi's book does everything that O'Connor says post-Spivakian "postcolonial" Victorian studies cannot do. It is based on a significant amount of empirical data describing a very particular historical phenomenon, the circulation of English books in colonial India in the second half of the nineteenth century. It tells us something new about reading practices and patterns of the consumption of English novels in India that shows some surprising patterns, which don't correspond to the broad generalizations about "mimicry" or "epistemic violence" that have been described by postcolonial theorists like Bhabha as characteristic of the colonial Indian encounter with the English Book.

Where O'Connor and others see a distressing uncritical tendency in postcolonial Victorian studies, Joshi shows herself to be ready and willing to criticize a famous postcolonial scholar (Gauri Viswanathan), whose *Masks of Conquest* might be said to follow some of the 'bad' rhetorical patterns O'Connor associates with postcolonial theory.[5] Here is Joshi:

> To an extent, Viswanathan is right in defining her inquiry as narrowly as she does. Indian responses are in fact complex and rich, requiring volumes to do them justice. Anything less would be irresponsible. However, her insistence that the story of British power and rule, beleaguered and paranoid though it may be, can be told on its own monochromatic terms without illumination, insight, or even reflection from the most direct source and recipient of its paranoia and rule is an awkward one. Perhaps recognizing this

> as she explains her refusal to include Indian voices in her study, Viswanathan's syntax with its repeated and contorted negatives suggests that she too is less than fully persuaded by her logic: 'to record the Indian response to ideology is no more an act of restoring the native's voice as not recording it is to render him mute.'[6]

Joshi sounds like she's being overly generous to Viswanathan here, but in fact the final sentences are pretty damning. Indeed, with more polemical phrasing she might be made to sound somewhat similar to O'Connor: Joshi sees Viswanathan as using an elaborate theoretical vocabulary to explain why she does in her scholarship what she says the British Empire did with language and literature. Though Viswanathan's *Masks of Conquest* is a much more substantial and historically committed work than Spivak's "Three Women's Texts" essay, it is nevertheless undeniably a book with a Big Argument about colonialism in the vein of both Said and Spivak:

> Drawing upon many of the insights and opportunities Viswanathan's important work has made available, this study differs from hers in both impulse and inclination in two significant ways. First, it resists the tempting and often easy Manicheanism that accounts for empire and its complex, clotted history with the disarming simplicity of ruler-ruled, colonizer-colonized. Insisting that each party inserted and imposed itself in unexpected quarters of the other's domain, I see each side of the colonial encounter illuminating the other in multiple and irrefutable ways. No account of colonial India can do it justice without taking into direct account the presence and practices of the British, much the way that a story of Britain in the nineteenth and twentieth centuries can never be complete or even fully accurate without acknowledging and addressing her colonies and their inadvertent and considerable presences within her. While this remark may appear a truism today in a world that has indigenized the dialectic of master and slave into a glib

> mantra, it is one worth restoring to status when reading arguments such as those Viswanathan advances in her meticulous study of British ideology that nonetheless ignores Indian responses altogether.[7]

After taking on Viswanathan's "easy manicheism," Joshi also marks the ways her empirical evidence tells a story that is sharply different from the broad generalizations about mimicry (Bhabha) or "imagined communities" (Benedict Anderson) that are so familiar to anyone who has read a little in the field. Mimicry has little to with the actual historical constitution of an Indian reading public, and much more was going on at the Calcutta Public Library than the straightforward establishment of a print-culture heralding the rise of "homogeneous" time and a generic nationalist movement fitting the European template

It's important to say that not everyone is as good as Joshi. But it's also worth remembering that we wouldn't have this excellent work of scholarship without the broad generalizations produced by the earlier generation of postcolonial intellectuals. It is true that Spivak is of limited utility as a close reader of 19th century texts, both in "Three Women's Texts" and in the expanded and updated version of the essay that appears as the "Literature" chapter in *A Critique of Postcolonial Reason*. I find Spivak to be every bit as opaque ("densely intriguing," as O'Connor sarcastically puts it) on Mary Shelley's *Frankenstein*—whose connection to imperialism never quite materializes in the *Critique of Postcolonial Reason*—as she is on *Jane Eyre*.

I cite Joshi primarily to show that postcolonial scholarship can be much more effectively self-critical than Erin O'Connor imagines. Joshi's work also represents the kind of scholarship on Empire in the Victorian period that might meet with the approval of someone like O'Connor. It makes small, limited claims, rather than sweeping ones. It is the product of a great deal of data collection, both in the British Library and in various libraries in India. And it makes an original argument about reading habits in India in the 19th century that call into question many received postcolonial 'generalizations' about relations between colonizer and colonized.

3. Arif Dirlik

What Joshi does not do, however, is challenge the field itself. But in a sense it's already been done: one of the most outspoken critics of "postcolonialism" as a field is the historian Arif Dirlik, whose 1994 essay, "The Postcolonial Aura," marked a kind of turning point in the field.

Among the many criticisms that strike home in Dirlik's essay, the harshest (or most effective, depending on one's perspective) has to be the one that suggests that postcolonialists see the world in ways that resemble the interests of the United States and the European powers much more than they do their peers at home:

> [T]he term postcolonial, understood in terms of its discursive thematics, excludes from its scope most of those who inhabit or hail from postcolonial societies. It does not account for the attractions of modernization and nationalism to vast numbers in Third World populations, let alone to those marginalized by national incorporation in the global economy. Prakash seems to acknowledge this when he observes that 'outside the first world, in India itself, the power of western discourses operates through its authorization and deployment by the nation state—the ideologies of modernization and instrumentalist science are so deeply sedimented in the national body politic that they neither manifest themselves no function exclusively as forms of imperial power'. It excludes the many ethnic groups in postcolonial societies (among others) that, obviously unaware of their hybridity, go on massacring one another.[8]

Of course, Dirlik's Marxism is every bit as unpopular among English-speaking Indian intellectuals as the writings of Bhabha and Partha Chatterjee. Dirlik's is hostility to free market capitalism in the rising era of post-Cold War globalization—in many ways, the true 'rhetorical moment' of his essay—goes against the dominant drift of policy making throughout the developing world. If Dirlik is delivering a devastating critique of out-of-touch expat-Indians in the American academy who question the "discourse of modernity" even as their former peers clamor for modernization at home, he is also in some sense out of step with the internal questioning of the socialist drift of

Nehruvian economics that has begun to emerge, even in the Indian left.

But Dirlik's most important point is that "postcolonial" may not have any denotative value at all. It is, instead, much more closely tied to a power-play within humanities departments (and English departments specifically) within the American academy that began in the late 1980s, and that continues today:

> What then may be the value of a term that includes so much beyond and excludes so much of its own postulated premise, the colonial? What it leaves us with is what I have already hinted at: "postcolonial," rather than a description of anything, is a discourse that seeks to constitute the world in the self-image of intellectuals who view themselves (or have come to view themselves) as postcolonial intellectuals. That is, to recall my initial statement concerning Third World intellectuals who have arrived in First World academe, postcolonial discourse is an expression not so much of agony over identity, as it often appears, but of new-found power.[9]

In short, "postcolonial" doesn't represent "third world" (i.e. historically post-colonial) interests so much as it does the interests of the scholars who advocate it. It isn't sufficiently descriptive of the current, evolving reality, which is for Dirlik rapidly evolving into a new "transnational division of labor" dominated not by the vestigial effects of European colonialism so much as by the present effects of Capital. "Postcolonial" is nothing more than a placeholder in the American academy.

Strong stuff; Dirlik makes one want to throw out the term "postcolonial" entirely. It's worth considering: why not? He's not discrediting the field of inquiry as a whole, but rather the terms on which it has heretofore been conducted. Following Dirlik, one might displace surveys of "postcolonial literature" with more narrowly defined courses, such as "Diasporic literature," "Literature of migration," "Literature of development," or, following Amitava Kumar, "World Bank Literature."[10] Such courses—which might in many cases wear their politics on their sleeves—probably wouldn't satisfy someone like O'Connor, who wants literary studies depoliticized. Indeed, what Dirlik wants from postcolonial theory is more overt, non-flip-floppy politicization, not less. Even if not everyone will share his aims, however, Dirlik's *non credo* is valuable because it reminds one how fragile, and possibly false, "postcolonialism" in fact is.

What is striking about Dirlik's essay at a general level is the way it has, over the years, been assimilated by the very field whose legitimacy it doubts. A number of my "postcolonialist" colleagues at other universities regularly teach the essay as a rejoinder to the standard "postcolonial theory" essays in classes on literary theory (or dedicated "postcolonial literature and theory" courses). And Dirlik's essay is included in a recent anthology called *Postcolonialisms: An Anthology of Cultural Theory and Criticism*, which by its title looks like a collection that believes in responding to contradictions by simply pluralizing everything ("Hybridities" "Differences" "Sexualities" etc). But it's a rather different—and better—kind of collection, which contains some important primary source materials alongside some more familiar voices (like Spivak's).

4. Meera Nanda

With the fourth essay we can return to *Theory's Empire*, with Meera Nanda's "Postcolonial Science Studies: Ending 'Epistemic Violence'". This is an excerpt from Nanda's recent book, *Prophets Facing Backwards: Postmodern Critiques of Science and Hindu Nationalism in India*, which frontally attacks the effect of postmodernist questioning of scientific values and methods in Indian society.

Two of Nanda's points here pose a significant challenge to postcolonial theory. One is the idea, widely substantiated in postcolonial scholarship (and not just by neo-nativists like Ashis Nandy) that western science is part of the apparatus of colonial dominance, which must therefore be questioned or even rejected in the interest of decolonization. Secondly, Nanda argues that the postcolonial challenge to the authority of "reason" is not merely an academic issue. The terms of the postcolonial critique are distressingly close to the rhetoric of the Hindu right as they attempt to broaden their presence and entrench themselves institutionally at Indian universities and in public life more generally.

Nanda can fairly be accused of a somewhat high-handed approach to postcolonial scholarship, but she makes some legitimate and very salient criticisms. Take the following paragraphs:

> 'Postcolonialism,' in the words of Dipesh Chakrabarty, is a project of 'provincializing Europe,' showing that what the West claims as universally valid categories are actually provincial ideas of Europe which have acquired the status of universal truths because of Europe's economic and military power. Universal truths, like language, Dipesh Chakrabarty argues, are only '[provincial] dialects backed by an army.' If truth does not represent a reality outside of discourse, alternative, non-Western truths, if backed by the required trappings of power, can become alternative universals.
>
> How is this task of provincializing and decolonization accomplished? The short answer is by deconstructing the universality of modern science. In this deconstruction, postcolonial theory joins hands (wittingly) with the social constructivist and feminist critiques of science, on the one hand, and (unwittingly) with the right-wing defenders of Hindu science, on the other. (577)

In the first paragraph, Nanda makes a point about Dipesh Chakrabarty that is indeed valid, but not without a certain amount of reductivism. For while her characterization of Chakrabarty's theoretical interest is correct, she neglects to mention that the project of "provincializing Europe" Chakrabarty envisions is also meant quite literally: what would it mean to think of world history without Europe at the center of the story? Nanda is right to zero in on Chakrabarty's dependence on Foucault, which leads Chakrabarty to make claims that I too find hard to swallow:

> Usually, or at least in South Asian studies, the Marxist or secular scholar who is translating the divine is in the place of the student who knows well only one of the two languages he is working with. It is all the

> more imperative, therefore, that we read our secular universals in such a way as to keep them open to their own finitude, so that the scandalous aspects of our unavoidable translations, instead of being made inaudible, actually reverberate through what we write in subaltern studies.[11]

Nanda, as a militant secularist, has no interest whatsoever in the "scandalous aspects of our unavoidable translations" (meaning, presumably, the traces of non-western logic or feeling that enter the work of secular South Asian scholars). Though the tone of my own response to Chakrabarty might be more measured, I too am somewhat skeptical about the prospect of introducing my "secular universals" to "their own finitude." Not all distant relatives need to know each other.

In the passage quoted above, Nanda also makes a jump from what is in effect a political point in Chakrabarty—about space and historiography—to "deconstructing the universality of modern science," which is not at all what Chakrabarty's book sets out to do. Admittedly, the slippage in this paragraph from the point about politics/Europe to the point about science might be a function of the redaction of Nanda's argument, but a similar discounting of the subtleties to be found in the works of writers like Chakrabarty and Partha Chatterjee is also unfortunately prevalent in the fully extended argument to be found in *Prophets Facing Backwards*.

This brings us to "Hindu science," where Nanda makes a point that is both accurate and quite necessary, and that is that the play of postmodernist science studies, which seems like a safe diversion in the relatively sedate and stable academic environment of the United States, is in fact quite dangerous when transplanted to India:

> The problem, however, is that what appears as marginal from the point of view of the modern West is not marginal at all in non-Western societies which haven't yet experience a significant secularization of their cultures. Local knowledges that Western critics assume to be standpoints of the 'oppressed' are, in fact, deeply embedded in the dominant religious/cultural idiom of non-Western societies. Using local knowledges to challenge Western science may, however, du-

> biously, illuminate the blind-spots of modern science in the West. But in non-Western societies themselves, such an affirmation of the scientificity of local knowledges ends up endorsing the power of the dominant cultural-religious institutions. Even worse, while the left-wing critics of science invoke local knowledges 'strategically' in order to fight what they see as the bigger evil, that is, the West, the right wing can use the same logic and invoke the same local knowledges much more 'authentically' and 'organically,' for it can mobilize all the traditional religious piety and cultural symbolism that go with local knowledges. (579)

Here Nanda is on sure footing. Indeed, this exact phenomenon in play in public statements by a prominent advocate of "Vedic science" named Rajiv Malhotra, by day a New Jersey businessman, but by night a TIRELESS CRITIC OF AMERICAN SCHOLARSHIP ON HINDUISM, as well as the chair of a foundation that offers grants to scholars interested in studying aspects of Indian Science/Vedic Science/Hindu Science/whatever. In some of his many essays published on the portal Sulekha, Malhotra has quoted postcolonial theorists like Edward Said and Homi Bhabha.

I don't at this point have a definitive response to this development. After all, no one is really responsible for how their works might be appropriated. If Malhotra finds Bhabha's discourse of 'hybridity' to be an asset to his idea that the principles of western science and the ancient Hindu scriptures ought to be blended together, why is that Bhabha's responsibility?

I can say, however, that both Spivak and Bhabha were surprisingly remiss in responding to the rise of communalism in India in the early 1990s. While Indian historians and social scientists have been speaking of nothing other than the problem of secularism for nearly a decade, Spivak and Bhabha seemed to wander a bit over the map, with essays about the Grameen Bank, UN concepts of Human Rights, and so on. To date, Spivak's engagement with questions of communalism has largely been limited to comments made in interviews; the topic is not discussed at length in her major published work.

On the other hand, the appropriation of discourses of "hybridity" and "strategic essentialism" by the Hindu right that Nanda refers to is surprisingly plausible and, as I have mentioned, real in at least one instance.

Conclusion—Some Thoughts on Thinking More Carefully.

Though four essays discussed here do not, taken together, provide any sort of definite blueprint for the future of postcolonial studies, they do suggest it may be time for postcolonial theory to reconsider its massive ambitions. In making huge claims about knowledge, epistemology, ontology, etc., it has written itself a ticket to academic superstardom. But it also risks overreaching and through overreaching, a severe vulnerability to the external criticisms of O'Connor, Nanda, and Dirlik (all fair), as well as possible misuse by people like Malhotra (foul).

In scholarship, it seems important to encourage thinking that is thoroughly historically grounded and richly textured. For studies that follow Joshi's in looking at patterns of consumption and other related cultural phenomena, it is important to rely on empirical evidence as much as possible. In parallel, there should also be greater emphasis on artful close readings, which are currently considerably under-valued (it is commonplace for postcolonialists to dismiss certain kinds of writing as "simple close-reading" as opposed to "Theory".)

Thirdly, I don't believe in depoliticization, but the postcolonial treatment of politics can be more balanced, more thoughtful, and above all, more in touch with current political realities. As Nanda's interventions suggest, there is more than one way to be a progressive Indian intellectual. Whether it's in the domain of an easy embrace of everything hybrid (there are reactionary hybridities, too), or in the uncritical acceptance of anti-science environmentalism (Arundhati Roy and the Narmada dam), substantial debate is often lacking. To actually work through these problems, very close and detailed study is required. Some (like the 'big dam' question) are going to have to remain beyond the scope of even the most adventurous literary scholar's range.

Finally, with these various ideas for more careful thinking, I would suggest taking greater care in pedagogy: courses on general topics such as "postcolonial literature" or "global literature" tend to end up almost comically thin. Courses that are more thematic and narrow ('diaspora') tend to work better, and afford greater intellectual coherence. Alternatively, one might move towards greater regional or sub-regional focus, even if that leads to an Area-Studies-esque marginalization.

Not everyone is going to be interested in something as narrow as the Nigerian Novel or Afro-Caribbean Poetry, but it's only at that level of geographic and generic specificity that we teachers of what is now called "postcolonial literature" can break the cycle of vast generalizations, insulting tokenism, and overstuffed syllabi, and give students something more serious to think about.

Originally posted on July 14, 2005

NOTES

1 Jonathan Culler, *The Literary in Theory* (Palo Alto: Stanford UP, 2007), 11.

2 Arif Dirlik, *The Postcolonial Aura: Third World Criticism in the Age of Global Capitalism* (Boulder: Westview Press, 1997).

3 Patrick Brantlinger, "Let's Post-Post-Post "Victorientalism": A Response to Erin O'connor," *Victorian Studies* 46, no. 1 (2003); Dierdre David, "She Who Must Be Obeyed: A Response to Erin O'Connor," *Victorian Studies* 46:1 (2003).

4 Gayatri Chakravorty Spivak, "Three Women's Texts and a Critique of Imperialism," *Critical Inquiry* 12:1 (1985).

5 Gauri Viswanathan, *Masks of Conquest* (Delhi: Oxford UP, 1998 [1990]).

6 Priya Joshi, *In Another Country* (New York: Columbia UP, 2002), 6.

7 Joshi, 6-7.

8 Gaurav Gajanan Desai and Supriya Nair, *Postcolonialisms: An Anthology of Cultural Theory* (New Brunswick: Rutgers UP, 2005), 568.

9 Desai and Nair, 569.

10 John Berger and Amitava Kumar, eds., *World Bank Literature* (Minneapolis: U of Minnesota, 2002).

11 Dipesh Chakrabarty, *Provincializing Europe* (Princeton: Princeton UP, 2000), 90.

13. Why I love theory / Why I hate theory

Jonathan Mayhew

Why I love theory

Theory is a large subject for me, because it has been a part of my intellectual life in the profession for more than twenty years. In graduate school I took several theory classes: narrative theory, theory of the lyric—even a course just on the work of Roland Barthes. I have been heavily influenced, at one time or another, by theorists like Barthes, Kenneth Burke, Maurice Blanchot, Walter Benjamin, Charles Bernstein. I have pondered the question of why so many theorists have last names starting with B. (Any ideas, Michael Bérubé?) I have taught courses in theory as well. I have spent many profitable hours with *Epistemology of the Closet*, a work inflected with Derridean interpretive modes and devoted to the close reading of canonical texts of literature. I think the story of the development of theory from Russian Formalism (which I love) to the present day is fascinating. It is the story of how intellectuals have incorporated the ideas of their time into the study of literature. I love watching how Kenneth Burke uses Freud and Marx to develop an idea of literature as symbolic action. How Barthes in his brilliantly dilettantish way tries to develop a "science" of literature from whatever intellectual currents were available to him. I love how current theorists use Wittgenstein or Gadamer to explain how we understand poetry.

So I love theory. How could anyone be against theory in general? *Il n'y a pas de hors théorie.*

Why I hate theory

Despite my love for theory, I hate many aspects of "theory" as academic practice. The decontextualized name-dropping, the arguments from authority, the intellectual stagnation that views Paris ca. 1968 as the "last word." Barthes at least was using the best ideas available to him at the time from structuralist linguistics and anthropology. The same could be said for Kenneth Burke in the 1930s. I am not attracted to the fashionable pastiches that mix Lacan, Said, Baudrillard, and whatever other convenient names occur to the writer, in pell-mell fashion, but ignore serious intellectual history since 1968. Theorists shouldn't just cite Freud as an authority without taking into account the biographical, historical, and theoretical critique of Freud of the past 20 or 30 years. Literary critics shouldn't sit down and translate Faulkner into a dull, Lacanian metalanguage. Derrida should be taken as an interesting avant-garde writer in a particular literary tradition, not as some authority who lays out the agenda for literary study for ever after.

Theory's Empire

This anthology throws the kitchen sink at theory. We have representatives of an older critical consensus like Abrams and Wellek. A proponent of Russian formalism and avant-garde poetics (Perloff). We have complaints about the spread of cultural studies, with its displacement of literature itself as object of study. I've always enjoyed Richard Levin's intricate take-downs of exaggerated claims and leftist pieties about literary studies. I like Searle's careful explication of principles of analytic philosophy that someone like Culler doesn't have a clue about. I am a Wittgensteinian at heart, but without enough real training in philosophy to do it right. My sympathy, generally, is with this camp, though I think they still need to bring up their game to the next level. (For example, that anthology that came out a while back, *Ordinary Language Criticism*, was a bit disappointing, although superior in some ways to *Theory's Empire.*)

I can applaud many "anti-theoretical" arguments, to the extent that they echo all the reasons I hate theory. At the same time I wouldn't trade Richard Levin for Eve Sedgwick. In other words, I still think there needs to be a way to preserve what I love about theory while working to solve some of the problems that make me hate theory. I don't know whether this is possible. I don't think this particular anthology is really the answer. Whatever the merits of the individual contributions they don't convince me as a global case against theory with a capital T, or much less against theory with a capital B. Isn't what we really need a return to theory, in the best sense? That is, knock-down-drag-out battles in the pages of *Critical Inquiry* about ideas? The end of sacred authorities, theoretical demi-gods?

Originally posted on July 14, 2005

14. On Mark Bauerlein's "Social Constructionism: Philosophy for the Academic Workplace"

Jonathan Goodwin

Bauerlein argues that social constructionism has gained prominence in the humanities (a too-general term he frequently uses, but at one point qualifies as mostly applying to literature and -studies departments) because its unquestioned assumptions allow for the mass-production of scholarship in an age of scholarly overabundance. I'm sympathetic to parts of his argument, puzzled by others.

I agree, along with everyone in scholarly publishing (and the official statements of the MLA as I recall) that the overemphasis on the quantity of scholarly production, particularly books, in English and affiliated departments is neither sustainable nor sane. (I should indicate here that I have rarely heard anyone, when observing the poor quality of today's books, include their own.) Bauerlein doesn't talk much about the cause of this problem, however. If he followed his materialist analysis to its conclusions, I suspect he would address academic labor conditions and status envy in more detail.

Few would disagree that, if people were able to take more time writing and researching their books, they would be better than they currently are. While uneasy with the specifics of Bauerlein's description of social constructionism, I agree that the canny will make intellectual choices that they might otherwise avoid if their entire future is at stake. There are two things to note here, however: 1) What Bauerlein calls "social constructionism" is thus only a symptom and 2) his analysis of institutional pressures applies even more accurately to the New Criticism.

GI Bill. Expansion of universities. Baby boom. Ready-made critical template. De-emphasized time-intensive contextual investigation. Superficially easy to teach. It's a familiar bit of institutional history.

And are the philosophical underpinnings of the New Criticism much different from social constructionism? One, perhaps, overemphasizes objectivity. The other, in Bauerlein's version, impatiently denies its existence. I don't think that's accurate or fair. But there's a more important problem.

What can be done to change institutional standards about scholarly publication? Bauerlein often speaks wistfully about times before the BFT. Did they exist at UCLA in the 80s? At Emory at any point since he's been teaching there? I'd guess not. I suspect the only solution is for the departments and institutions regarded as elite to unilaterally abolish the BFT (or B2FT). Though I have an estimate of the plausibility of this ever happening, I will first invite reader speculations.

I am reluctant to discuss "social constructionism" as presented in this essay because I don't think it's the main point. There's a brief mention of "science studies," but there isn't any analysis of the Edinburgh school, to take one important example out of many. An uncontextualized soundbite from Heidegger on Newton. Roger Kimball calls something "sophomoric." Ian Hacking has written lucidly on the topic. His *The Social Construction of What?* and the essays collected in *Historical Ontology* are both valuable and accessible resources for anyone interested in the philosophical issues too briefly treated here. But the essay addresses an important question about the social construction of academic standards. I wish that Bauerlein had spent less time with social constructionism and more investigating the history of the "quantification system" that "stands as the academic wisdom of the age."

Originally posted on July 14, 2005

15. Post-Post-Theory

Chris Cagle

My initial thought is: "Don't they realize that film studies has already had an attack on Theory"? David Bordwell and Noel Carroll put out the *Post-Theory* anthology about a decade ago.[1] And while respondents are trying to figure out which part of the moving target to discuss, Bordwell usefully REFERRED TO SLAB theory—an amalgam of Saussure-Lacan-Althusser-Barthes that guides the way film scholars approach film. However, for all of Bordwell's stature in the field, *Post-Theory* didn't topple theory; at best it was part of many critiques of 70s film theory and of cultural studies that led to the current methodological pluralism. Call it Post-Post-Theory. I've yet to read *Theory's Empire*, but I suspect their dissent may meet a similar fate.

Mind you, the traps critical theory often falls into (argument by reverential citation, over-abstraction from the object of study) strike me as far more excessive in literary studies than in film studies (my unbiased opinion). As usual, I find myself somewhere in between the anti-Theory crusades of the Valve and the defenses of the Theory camp, or halfway between John Holbo and Michael Bérubé. Despite Bérubé's rebuttal, Holbo is on to something when he diagnoses a tendency for critical theorists to treat anti-Theoretical arguments as anti-theoretical ones. At the same time, he should acknowledge that frequently the anti-Theory camp are anti-theoretical; they prefer a *belletristic* appreciation of Literature as is, without being sullied by rigorous academic study. As a defense of the ideas of theory, Bérubé's post is disingenuous to point out that the quality of the theoretical work of lesser known scholars obviates the larger argument of the anti-Theorists; presumably, these scholars might be doing excellent work in another theoretical frame. At the same time, he's right: once you stop taking umbrage at the philosophical assault that Theory represents and start looking at SLAB as an intellectual method that allows you to study cultural artefacts in productive ways, the issue is a little different. My defense of SLAB theory lies precisely along those lines; the very constitution of a "text" that can be subjected to non-thematic, non-normative interpretation is a heuristic device that's incredibly useful and is going to be hard to shake off. For all the excesses done in the name of Theory, I'm not sure why Barthes' *S/Z* or Christine Gledhill's essay on *Klute* can't continue to inform the practice of literary and film studies.

Perhaps I come closest to the sentiment of the Valve's Jonathan Mayhew, who writes,

> I can applaud many "anti-theoretical" arguments, to the extent that they echo all the reason I hate theory. At the same time I wouldn't trade Richard Levin for Eve Sedgwick. In other words, I still think there needs to be a way to preserve what I love about theory while working to solve some of the problems that make me hate theory. I don't know whether this is possible.

It is possible, if we try to clarify what Theory has done well (methodological reflection, constitution of the "text") while we open up to some valid criticisms.

Originally posted on July 14, 2005

NOTES

1 David Bordwell and Noel Carroll, eds., *Post-Theory: Reconstructing Film Studies* (Madison: U of Wisconsin, 1996).

16. Essentializing Theory: A Testimonial

Christopher Conway

In June of 2005, I did an independent study to help some of my graduate students meet the Modern Languages M.A. theory requirement at the University of Texas, Arlington. Although the department offers an "Introduction to Theory" core course taught by another faculty member, our students—most of whom are Latino school teachers with families—sometimes miss it because of scheduling conflicts. Some of them meet the requirement by taking a seminar on theory in the English department, but in this particular case, because of a series of misunderstandings with their professor, some them dropped the class. To help them graduate on time, I stepped in to help them meet the requirement.

By the time they showed up to my office, these students were pretty discouraged. Not only were they bewildered but fearful. Why couldn't someone just explain "it" to them? Why should they sit around a table, week after week, and listen to fellow graduate students dominate the discussion with half-baked, opaque or partial readings of the material? Why didn't the professor just lay "it" out and put them out of their misery?

I knew exactly what these students were talking about because I had experienced some of the same frustrations in my Cultural Studies Ph.D. program at the University of California, San Diego. A lot of us in the program were clueless and resentful, and the ones who understood theory (or acted like it, at least) used their classroom interventions to problematize what the rest of us did not fully understand in the first place. Later, as an assistant professor in the Department of Hispanic Studies at Brown University, I found that the graduate students were similarly afflicted. The Brown students had tools for reading "literature" by Miguel de Cervantes, Gabriel García Márquez and Elena Poniatowska, but they were often disarmed by theory and wanted someone to teach "it" to them.

In the seminars that I taught at Brown on nineteenth-century Latin American literature, I essentialized and justified theory. I wanted the students to begin to understand before expecting them to be creative interlocutors. It was also necessary for them to know that theory could help them in their literary studies, which meant returning again and again to the question "How can this help us read better?" In particular, I enjoyed challenging theory while teaching it. When teaching Queer Studies, I included conservative critiques of identity politics. When discussing Postmodernism(s), I set Marxist readings against Poststructuralist ones, essentialist arguments against decentered ones. Most importantly, I tried to communicate to my students that theory was not a hermetic sect, but a vital, historical debate with real and distinct positions. It was not a singular, coherent "it" but an ever-changing aggregate of historical discourses.

I won't mislead you: I am not a theoretician nor do I aspire to be one. My work has been praised and criticized by colleagues in my field for clarity, resistance to jargon or simplicity. My work tends to be historical. I enjoy "painting with words" more than self-consciously engaging theory in my work. I tire of drawn out theoretical debates because I need things to be still so that I can grasp them or put them into focus. And it's difficult for me to be passionate about theory. I don't believe in it enough. For me, theory is best utilized to guide scholarship to a different object, like scaffolding falling away from a structure when it begins to take shape and acquire stability. For these reasons, and most especially my difficulties in absorbing theory in graduate school, I have been able to "get into" theory when I've had to teach it. My students have forced me to discover and understand theory so that I could try to help them be less afraid of it.

My independent study on theory at the University of Texas, Arlington brought back memories of my days at Brown, and reminded me of how necessary it is for professors to actively guide their students through the labyrinths of theory. The problem with theory is not theory itself, but the refusal to assist in making it accessible to students. The inert, unfocussed discussions of a few graduate students among themselves in a theory seminar, with minimal intervention by the professor, propagates apathy, resistance or tremendous insecurity. Such pedagogy fosters the "impostor syndrome," a feeling of insecurity that can last for years, and sadly, turn people off of theory. And the continued dissemination of theory as a heavy, compact object (like those awful, expensive anthologies that are used in graduate seminars) rather than as a cacophony of voices best understood historically, in separate and often contradictory strands of thought, makes the teaching of theory more painful than it has to be.

For these reasons, I find the arrival of *Theory's Empire* on my bookshelf, and the bookshelves of my future students, to be an overdue contribution to a more critical and accessible construction of what we call "theory."

October, 2006

POSTSCRIPT: On July 14, 2005, a version of this essay, entitled "Not much of a theory-head, but..." appeared on the blog Academic Splat! (later: Camicao's Chamomile), under the pseudonym 'Camicao'.

17. Anthropological Theory, Siglo XXI

Kathleen Lowrey

This discussion has prompted me to reflect—not for the first time—on how glad I am that my time in grad school (1995-2003) came just after the high water mark of high theory. Some necessary battles were fought without my help, which suited me just fine, and I could approach the work of formerly outré scholars from the safe angle of necessity. I never had to shout at my scholarly seniors, "I'm stomping off to my room to read Derrida and Foucault and there's nothing you can do about it!" Instead, I read them because it was a given that one had to, and one could like or dislike them as one pleased without anybody getting too worked up about it.

A downside, however, was that the available paradigms felt a bit hoary. While writing my dissertation I got detoured in one chapter by my own critique of Bruno Latour's *We Have Never Been Modern* (Harvard UP, 1993), which consisted in part of chiding him for using the format of a self-help manual. Then it occurred to me that he probably meant it as a sort of joke; that, anyway, who was I to be so cranky when I'd found it so useful; that, somehow, the whole thing had become a decade old since I'd "discovered" it two or three years after its publication.

In the end … I just couldn't get too worked up about it. What excited me toward the end of my graduate career was perfectly straightforward work in political ecology and ecological economics. I still find that work very useful, and I am truly glad I'm not a battle-scarred veteran of the 80s. Still, I wonder: why hasn't a new generation of exhilarating theorists come along for my generation of scholars to fight about? Or have they, and I've just missed the boat?

Originally posted on July 14, 2005

18. Two Months Before the Mast of Post-Modernism

Brad DeLong

Over at The Valve, they are talking about the book *Theory's Empire*—and thus about the damage done by "Critical Theory" and its spawn on the American humanities over the past generation. But most of it is all too ... theoretical.[1] What work can you do with statements like:

> Derrida is... the greatest and most exciting thinker of the 20th century.... Derrida is in many respects... very conservative... one must start from that conservatism in order to measure the ways in which he is radical... can seem highly radical to thinkers who are attempting to graft Derrida into a tradition... in which many of Derrida's key reference points have historically been marginal.... How much does that affect the way you read a sentence where someone asks to have a button undone? Probably not much...
>
> This polarizing, personalizing rhetoric indicates that social constructionism has an institutional basis, not a philosophical, moral, or political one. It tramples on philosophical distinctions and practices an immoral mode of debate. Though it declares a political goal for criticism, it is not a political stance.... Herein lies the secret of constructionism's success... it is the school of thought most congenial to current professional workplace conditions of scholars in the humanities.
>
> I liked theory, even when I felt I didn't have the faintest idea what was going on, because if nothing else you could sense the energy behind it ...

The older philosophical critics, Jameson suggests, lacked Hegelian seriousness: in place of an aggressive commitment to the consequences of their premises, they were 'content' to 'simply' muse about literature 'in an occasional way'.... His sinecured dilettanti mass-produced 'curiosities of an existential or phenomenological criticism, or a Hegelian or a gestalt or indeed a Freudian criticism.' Burke, Empson et al. avoided indenture in the Curiosity Trade, Jameson argues, by processing literature in accordance with a personal interpretive ethos, one resonant with a nonsystemized theory nonetheless compulsively applied in a rage for symmetry. Jameson's notion of a virtuoso critic (of the good camp) can be summed up thus: a thinker of original temperament but suitable Hegelian seriousness whose passion for patterns generates interesting reading of literary works. His notion of a virtouso critic (of the bad): calicified mind, learned but unoriginal and philosophically fickle, whose passions for other people's patterns generates predictable readings of literary works...

I apologize for Heidegger's highly convoluted and neologistic prose. (I imagine that some readers are already thinking, 'come back, Derrida, all is forgiven').... In Heidegger's reading, we could say that the discovery of Neptune in 1846 could plausibly be described, from a strictly human vantage point, as the 'invention' of Neptune.... [B]efore we began to look for it, the planet 'Neptune' simply did not exist in any human consciousness.... And yet once humans had invented... Neptune, they understood [it]... as [a thing]... not susceptible to mere human invention...

[It] takes the already deeply problematic arguments and style of the dominant superstars like Spivak, Prakash and Bhabha and operationalizes it as yeoman-level banality

?

There is a certain bloodlessness here: the dry bones hop about and clatter, but there is no flesh on them: much too little is said about how High Critical Theory changed—for good and for ill—how "we" "read" "our" "texts".[2]

So let me get down and dirty: in the boiler room, at the contact point, before the mast. Let me recount the two months—November and December 1981—that I spent enthralled by the High Critical Theory of Michel Foucault.

By day I would rise late, eat a strange late breakfast of scrambled eggs mixed with cottage cheese (a kind of breakfast which I ate only from November 1981 through January 1982, never before, and never since), and then walk across the Charles River footbridge to the Kress Collection of the History of Economic Thought in Baker Library. I would read. I would hasten out into the lobby where I was allowed pens and note-taking. I would go back in and read some more. I would hasten out into the lobby. After dinner I would sit in my room, either staring at the wall, wondering what my thesis was going to be about or reading secondary works on the history of economic thought, hoping to spot a hole that I could fill with something sorta original.

It was Associate Professor of Social Studies Michael Donnelly's fault. He knew I was trying to write an undergradute thesis about the British Classical Economists and how they understood the economy of their time. He gave me a book by Keith Tribe, *Land, Labour, and Economic Discourse*. And Tribe had read and been hypnotized by Foucault—specifically *The Order of Things* and *The Archaeology of Knowledge*. I began to read Keith Tribe. He said very strange things. He said that *The Wealth of Nations* that economists read was not *The Wealth of Nations* that Adam Smith wrote. *The Wealth of Nations* that economists read was made up of two books: Book I on markets and Book II on capital. The *Wealth of Nations* that Adam Smith wrote was made up of five books: Book I on the "system of natural liberty," Book II on accumulation and the profits of stock, Book III on the economic history of Europe and why the empirical history of its economic development had diverged from its natural history, Book IV on the mercantile and physiocratic systems of political economy, and Book V on the proper management of the affairs of the public household by the statesman.

The Wealth of Nations, Tribe said, could not be a book of economics because a book of economics had to be about the economy. And there was no such thing as the economy in 1776 for a book of economics to be about. What was there? There was the undifferentiated stuff of the mixed social-cultural-political-trading system that governed production and distribution: material life. There was the study of the management of public finances. This was conceived in a manner analogous to the domestic-economic management of household finances. Just as—to Robert Filmer and others—the King was the father of the people, so the King's household—which became the state—had to be properly and prudently managed.

In the words of James Steuart, who wrote his *Principles of Political Oeconomy* nine years before *The Wealth of Nations*, in 1767: "Oeconomy, in general, is the art of providing for all the wants of a family, with prudence and frugality. What oeconomy is in a family, political oeconomy is in a state." It is managing affairs to make the people prosperous and the tax collections ample by governing "in such a manner as naturally to create the reciprocal relations and dependencies between [inhabitants], so as to make their several interests lead them to supply one another with their reciprocal wants."

There wasn't, Tribe argued, an *economy* that an economist could write a book of economics about until the 1820s or so.

Strip Tribe's (and Foucault's) arguments of their rhetoric of apparent contradiction and you can understand that within the mystical shell there is a rational kernel. It is—or, at least, I read them as—an injunction to analyze a school of thought in more-or-less the following way:

1. Read not just one or two important books, but a whole bunch of books that talk to or past each other and use the same or similar vocabulary in order to identify the school you will look at.
2. Strip your mind of what they must be talking about, and look with fresh eyes on what they are talking about.
3. Examine what rhetorical, conceptual, and intellectual moves are common within the examples you have of this "discursive formation."

4. Think hard about what rhetorical, conceptual, and intellectual moves you would think you would find in these books—but don't.
5. Think hard about what rhetorical, conceptual, and intellectual moves you do not expect to find prominently in these books—but that you nevertheless do find.
6. Present to the world, in as clear and straightforward a way as you can, what this particular form of discourse was—what it thought the world was like, what it saw as important, what its particular blindnesses were, what its particular sharp points of insight were.
7. Do not, ever, grade a discursive formation of the past by how much it falls away from the ideas of the *bien-pensant* of today. The past is another country.

And I became convinced that Tribe and Foucault were right. It was, indeed, only with Ricardo that the operation of what we now say is the economy—the production, exchange, and distribution of goods and services all mediated through market exchange—was seen as something that was important enough, or separate enough, or coherent enough to be something that it made sense to write books about, and, indeed, something that it made sense to be an expert in. David Ricardo was a political economist. Adam Smith was a moral philosopher. To try—as somebody like Joseph Schumpeter was—grading Adam Smith as if he were engaged in the same intellectual project as Schumpeter was somewhat absurd.

Tribe applied this methodology to Adam Smith, his predecessors, contemporaries, and successors. What they were doing, before Ricardo, was Political Oeconomy—writing manuals of tactics and policy as advice to statesmen, although manuals restricted to what Adam Smith would have called (did call) a subclass of *police*: how to keep public order and create public prosperity. Hence for Adam Smith Book V of *Wealth of Nations* is the payoff: it tells British statesmen what they ought to do in order to make the nation prosperous, their tax coffers full, and thus the state well-funded. Book IV is a necessary prequel to Book V: it tells the statesmen in the audience why the advice that they are being given in other books of Political Oeconomy—by Mercantilists and Physiocrats—is wrong. Book III is another necessary prequel: it teaches statesmen about the economic history of Europe and how political oeconomy of various kinds has been practiced in the past.

But Tribe's (and Foucault's) methodology collapses when we work back to Books II and I of *Wealth of Nations*. For Adam Smith is not the prisoner of the discursive formation of Political Oeconomy. He is not the simple bearer of currents of thought and ideas that he recombines as other authors do in more-or-less standard and repeated ways. Adam Smith is a genius. He is the prophet and the master of a new discipline. He is the founder of economics.

Adam Smith is the founder of economics because he has a great and extraordinary insight: that the competitive market system is a remarkably powerful social calculating and organizing mechanism, and that the sophisticated division of labor to which a competitive market system backed up by secure and honest enforcement of property rights gives rise is the key to the wealth of nations. Some others before had had this insight in part: Richard Cantillon, writing of how once you have specified demands the market does by itself all the heavy lifting that a central planner would need to do; Bernard de Mandeville, that dextrous management by a statesman can use the power of private greed to produce the benefit of public utility. But it is Smith who sees what the power of the "system of natural liberty" that is the market could be—and who follows the argument through to the conclusion that forever upsets and overturns the previous intellectual moves made in and conclusions reached by the discursive formation of Political Oeconomy.

And once I had worked my way through to this conclusion, I could start to write my own thesis. I had broken the thralldom. Foucault's ideas of "discourse" and "archaeology" were not my masters, but my tools. And as I wrote it became very clear to me that between David Ricardo and even the later John Stuart Mill the discursive formation that was Classical Economics did not produce anybody like Adam Smith. There was nobody who made the intellectual leap—produced the epistemological break—that Smith had done that shattered Political Oeconomy and enabled the birth of Classical Economics. I could write my thesis about how the British Classical Economists never understood the Industrial Revolution that they were living through.

- J. Bradford DeLong, B.A. in Social Studies
summa cum laude, June 1982.

Originallly posted on July 15, 2005

NOTES

1 Let me interject that the best contribution I have found so far is from Tim Burke—I think I like it the most because it is the meatiest and the bloodiest. But, as always, YMMV.

2 A second interjection: Sean McCann does attempt to put some sinews on what he is talking about: he lists six (he thinks four, but they are six) intellectual power-moves of High Critical Theory.

19. Theory's Empire—It's the Institution, Stupid

Sean McCann

A CONSENSUS appears to be developing among at least some of us talking about *Theory's Empire* that the major issues are institutional and sociological. The problem (to the extent we agree there is one) is not any ideas particular to Theory, in other words, but the academic celebrity system, the tenure review process, and/or the guild process of professional training.

If that is an emerging consensus, it's one I find both encouraging and disheartening.

Encouraging because I pretty much agree, institutional and professional constraints are the most salient factors in the existence of the alleged empire (and quite possibly, any set of bad and reductive ideas could flourish equally well among them.) Disheartening because no one seems to be much interested in talking about either Theory's big ideas—Michael's valiant attempts with Heidegger and Derrida aside—or the claims of its critics. To be cruel, you might call the situation symptomatic. Get a bunch of literary academics together and they'll be happy to talk about the institution of the profession till the cows come home. It's a topic whose powers of intoxication are only rivaled by the endlessly absorbing but-is-it-good-for-the-left discussion. Genuine argument about ideas or, um, literature, on the other hand, is harder to find.

Perhaps that's a sign that Theory's empire is truly crumbling, or, as Mark Bauerlein suggests, that it's become little more than routinized doctrine. That sounds right to me, though I also suspect that Theory concepts won't get much debate in the blogosphere because under scrutiny a good many are either uncontroversial or absurd. (Over at LONG SUNDAY, which as RAY SUGGESTS is an often interesting place where they really are eager to talk Theory, there's a DISCUSSION going on about whether Capital is Real. Resolved: "to assert that

Capital is Real is to embrace neoliberal ideology." This is a topic, may I suggest, that could only become a matter of debate after prolonged immersion in Slavoj Žižek.)

One downside of the emphasis on institutional factors is that it can easily turn into an alibi. It can be mighty convenient, in other words, to believe that the problem is with trustees, or administrators, or a professional norm for which trustees and administrators are ultimately responsible. Which is why I think it's important to try to keep the ideological and intellectual convictions that exist perhaps symbiotically with those factors at the forefront. That's what Mark's essay on "Social Constructionism" as a "Philosophy for the Workplace" (341-53) was trying to do, and whatever the limitations of the piece, the aim is an important one.

I think to the extent we're agreed about anything, we agree that what's at issue is in some way a reflection of the course of academic professionalism. (Anyone who hasn't yet seen Timothy Burke's beautiful essay on Theory's moment, should get there pronto. It's a blog masterpiece.) If so, it may be that while the academic humanities are distinctive in a number of crucial respects, they take part in a larger phenomenon. In many of the established professions (law, say) recent decades have seen an explosion of growth and competition, with a concomitant expansion of hyperspecialization and a relative decline in the once prominent legitimation of public service and self-regulation. (Or so says Steven Brint anyway.)[1] The history of Theory tracks that story well. The golden moment noted by Timothy, Scott, Mark and others coincided with a growth in the size and status of literary academia and a steep rise in the remuneration a humanities academic could expect to enjoy. You can sense the brio even in retrospect and see the pay-off that increased sophistication often brought to literary study. In subsequent decades, we've seen the effects of continued hyperspecialization (hat tip John Emerson) and, its underlying cause, a wildly irrational employment market. The consequences are, yes, the combination of inflated rhetoric and crippling intellectual caution. But also the decline of professional community, in its good as well as bad sides.

To return to ideological factors (and to beat a dead horse I've ridden before), my belief is that this situation is particularly toxic in literary academia because of a historic professional self-image that cast literature as the anti-disciplinary discipline. As a special kind of knowledge, or rather experience, literature was understood to rise above and cast into doubt the authority of other fields—especially mere "science." To look back over the grand moments of Theory—in its Deconstructive, or New Historicist, or Cult Stud moments—is, I think, to see renewed and intensified versions of that attitude. Not literature but Theory now is the special kind of expertise that challenges all other expertise, the unique kind of training that subverts all other discipline. In short, a professionalized assault on professionalism, one whose characteristic expression has been to turn expertise against the routine (and, to pick up on John Holbo's point, to thereby license an unviable synthesis of the Enlightenment and counter-Enlightenment).

No need to claim that the situation is utterly homogeneous, only to say that quite often the result has been the worst of both worlds. As Ben Alpers notes over at Michael's blog, mediocre work will always prevail in any academic discipline. But Timothy adds an important point when he says "there's a kind of missing generation of monographs . . . an absence of substantive, minutely authoritative, carefully researched and highly specialized knowledge that serves as a foundation for more sweeping syntheses and broadly argued scholarship." He's talking about postcolonial history in particular, but I think the description applies still more intensely to literary academia. The whole point of academic professionalism is to yoke mediocrity to a larger purpose. Theory's assault on routinized academic labor, combined with the institutional factors that encouraged it, freed some brilliant minds to become virtuosi. They became our celebrities. And, as Timothy notes, that assault also helped promote the undoubted good that the humanities now study far more than was once considered legitimate material. But it also undermined the structures that encourage useful mediocrity.

What should be done about that institutionally? I don't know, though I feel pretty certain that graduate programs in literature should cease overproducing Ph.Ds. (Easy for me to say, of course, since I've got a job and don't teach in a graduate program.) One side of me believes that the way to go is, as Timothy suggests, to try to follow out the logic of where things seem to be headed already and, say, use the blogosphere to try to break the hold of guild authority. (Heed the call of John Emerson! Deprofessionalize literary criticism!) Another thinks that what we need is actually more professional discipline. (Return to philology!) Ideally, I think they'll be some combination of the two—and perhaps it's inevitable, since as the saying in econ goes, situations that can't continue, won't.

Originally posted on July 15, 2005

NOTES

1 Steven Brint, *In An Age of Experts: The Changing Role of Professionals in Politics and Public Life* (Princeton: Princeton University Press, 1994).

20. Theorizing Novels

Matthew Greenfield

Proust, whom I have been reading on my family vacation, sometimes sounds like a contributor to *Theory's Empire.* In the final volume of *In Search of Lost Time*, Proust says things like, "I began to perceive that I should not have to trouble myself with the various literary theories which had at moments perplexed me;" "authentic art has no use for proclamations of this kind, it accomplishes its work in silence;" "and it is perhaps as much by the quality of his language as by the species of aesthetic theory which he advances that one may judge of the level to which a writer has attained in the moral and intellectual part of his work. Quality of language, however, is something the critical theorists think they can do without, and those who admire them are easily persuaded that it is no proof of intellectual merit, for this is a thing which they cannot infer from the beauty of an image but can recognize only when they see it directly expressed;" and "A work [of art] in which there are theories is like an object which still has its price tag on it." These are peculiar suggestions for Proust to make, since they come in the middle of sixty or so pages of literary theory. Inside the novel is a substantial work on the theory of the novel. The culmination of this sequence of novels, the telos of thousands of pages of fiction, is the moment when Proust at last realizes how a novel should be written.

There is also a lengthy theoretical digression in *War and Peace.* Toward the end of the book Tolstoy exits his fictional narrative and begins a treatise on historiography. He demonstrates that historians construct tidy narrative explanations that have nothing to do with the messy, infinitely complex unfolding of actual events. Tolstoy's discussion of historiography inspired Isaiah Berlin's great essay "The Fox and the Hedgehog". Similarly, many theorists of modernism have focused on Proust's explicit discussion of his theory of the novel.

Do these grand theoretical statements illuminate the other parts of the novels that contain them? Why insert a lengthy treatise in a novel? Are these novels great in spite of their treatises or because of them? Do Tolstoy and Proust somehow need the theoretical sections to counterbalance the moments when they tunnel into the consciousness of a single individual? Both authors try to discover the general laws governing human behavior. Is this a plausible ambition for a novelist? Or do the generalizations squeeze the juice out of the narrative? Does articulating general principles of sociology and narrative form break the reader's connection to the characters? Clearly literary critics cannot do without literary theory if great writers are so immersed in it. But we can also take an antithetical lesson away from Proust and Tolstoy: producing authentic theoretical insights often requires that one wound oneself or undermine one's projects.

How many literary works contain such lengthy theoretical insets? I have been trying and failing to think of any other examples quite so extreme. Melville inserts essays on cetology and whaling into *Moby Dick*, but these are quite modest in scope next to the theoretical sections of *War and Peace* and *In Search of Lost Time*. *Anna Karenina* of course contains a fair amount of social theory. There is a large georgic inset in *Paradise Lost*, but that is not disruptive in the same way: it is still narrative poetry, and its presence in an epic is justified by epic tradition.

Originally posted on July 15, 2005

21. Thinking About Theory's Empire

Morris Dickstein

Because of the impressive scope and seriousness of the essays in *Theory's Empire*, the book ultimately gives a devastating account of the academic literary culture of the last thirty years. To their credit, the editors excluded the many journalistic attacks on theory that came out in the 1980s and '90s. Most of them were based on little acquaintance with the work itself; instead they offered second-hand accounts of barbarisms of style, the preposterous titles of MLA papers, and the knee-jerk political bent of much of the writing itself. *Theory's Empire* also leaves out politically motivated attacks by neoconservatives, invariably arising out of a biased and superficial familiarity with theory. Once in a while such critiques made telling points, usually in a satirical vein, and they helped make English professors the laughingstock of both the larger public and serious professionals in other fields. But they contributed little to the debate within literary studies itself, which, despite its political turn, had effectively opted out of the public sphere, acknowledging criticism within its own frame of discourse. Theory-minded academics saw little but retrograde ignorance, willed malice, and anti-intellectualism in these tendentious accounts, and it had no public language of its own to respond in kind.

Instead of reprinting such attacks, *Theory's Empire* confines itself to serious academic critiques, some of them by distinguished students of earlier theory, including René Wellek and M. H. Abrams, along with many others by writers well versed in contemporary trends, beginning with knowledgeable older critics like Frank Kermode, Denis Donoghue, Eugene Goodheart, and Frederick Crews, who had strong roots in the literary life of an earlier era. The anthology reminds us that since 1970, the twists and turns of literary and cultural theory have been subjected to a steady stream of intelligent criticism, which was ignored by theorists in exactly the same way they mocked or disregarded the journalistic attacks. There have been exceptions. Since his early *Village Voice* piece on the p.c. controversy, Michael Bérubé has often responded both privately and publicly to critics of theory and occasionally even conceded them a few points, as he did recently in answering Mark Bauerlein. Stanley Fish has always been geared up for public debate. The earlier clash between Hillis Miller and Abrams showed how useful an exchange could be between supporters of poststructuralist theory and well-informed critics. But this could not happen as long as theorists saw criticism as a futile form of "resistance" by the aging dinosaurs of the old criticism.

Writers hostile to theory were sometimes guilty of the same closed-mindedness. My own book on criticism, *Double Agent* (Oxford, 1992), concluded with a dialogue between a critic of theory who was about my age and a younger colleague more sympathetic to it. It was a piece of writing in which I took some pride. It treated criticism as a subject for living conversation. (To my delight, one of the editors at Oxford took it for an actual conversation and asked me whether I'd secured permission to use it.) Few readers guessed that both points of view were entirely my own; I'd used the dialogue form to probe my own ambivalence. But the well-known British reviewer in the *New York Times Book Review* thundered that I was too soft on theory: this was a time for diatribe, not dialogue, as if there were ever a time when dialogue was out of bounds. I had also written far more polemical essays, but the editors of *Theory's Empire* surprised me by choosing something quite different: an argumentative but historical account of the growth of practical criticism from the Edinburgh reviewers and the New Criticism to Roland Barthes's structuralist narratology and Derrida's deconstruction. This was my first clue to the kind of anthology they had in mind, much more substantial and less rhetorical than the one I'd initially imagined.

Today the theory era is effectively ending and the public intellectual tradition is reasserting itself, along with a renewed attention in the aesthetic that many theorists dismissed as no more than an ideological formation. But thanks to tenure and the intellectual investments we make as graduate students, theory will have a long afterlife. It will also continue to inflect how many important issues are discussed, including the role of language in literature, the degree to which literary works reference the world outside the text, the role of social construction including class, race, and gender in forming our conventions of representation (as writers) and interpretation (as critics). Critical movements leave behind a residue of common sense after the dust of their polemics has settled and the most extreme positions have been abandoned. The New Criticism left its mark on how everyone reads, especially poetry, long after its assumptions about the organic unity of the text had been roundly rejected. Deconstruction terminated the notion, never entertained by any great critic in the past, that a literary text could be cracked open with a single definitive interpretation. Poststructuralism in general helped us question the belief that we could find a disinterested stance that would make some kind of definitive critical understanding possible, perhaps even objectively true. This I think is what Sean McCann means when he says that theorists have taken some reasonable positions to ridiculous extremes.

More and more, as Stephen Adam Schwartz argues in this volume, the evolution of theory fits the pattern of a classic twentieth-century *avant garde.* It pursued vast goals, such as the overthrow of Western metaphysics, with exaggerated confidence and in a sectarian spirit. Like many modernist movements, it ignored earlier traditions or appropriated them selectively. It tended to caricature its immediate predecessors and attack positions no one had ever held. The hostility it pursued only confirmed its sense of bringing light to a benighted world. We recall that Lacan came of age among the surrealists, that Barthes was an early exponent of Brecht and the *Nouveau Roman*, that Derrida's playful, punning language is deeply indebted to Joyce, especially in experimental works like *Glas.* Like so much of the work of early modernism, postructuralist writing flew in the face of older standards of beauty and coherence; its style drew the same kind of fire that had been directed *Les Demoiselles d'Avignon*, *The Rites of Spring*, *The Waste Land*, and *Ulysses*, a barrage of criticism and outrage that was as much moral as aesthetic.

But not every avant-garde movement has the same fate: some (like impressionism or mainstream modernism) leave behind an enduring body of work, others (like Dada) merely the memory of an ingenious course of provocative gestures, as evanescent as if written in sand. I suspect Theory will leave us more than that, if not in permanently readable works then in a handful of cautionary lessons. But it has also left us a legacy of pseudo-issues, such as the question of truth or objectivity in interpretation, that are more easily negotiated in practice than adjudicated in theory. The best essays in *Theory's Empire* all take a sensible middle ground on this issue. As Goodheart remarks,

> Criticism is not about the quest for a singular truth or a consensus view of its object. It presupposes a literary sensibility and its patient cultivation. It assumes a variety of critical temperaments and of personal, social, and historical experience in critics. The disagreements as well as agreements that occur among critics presuppose a common ground of intelligence, training, open-mindedness, flexibility, sophistication, and taste, ideals not often realized. (509)

Far from being elitist or old-fashioned, this notion of "a literary sensibility and its patient cultivation" is the *sine qua non* of any genuine critic, as shown in the quality of his or her engagement with actual works. This is an experiential test more than a conceptual one. This gut feeling for literature was a quality often dismissed by theorists, who associated it with the despised man-of-letters tradition and certainly did not cultivate it in their students. Yet when influential theorists like Barthes, Bloom, Said, Todorov, or Lentricchia veered sharply away from an earlier, more abstract approach, it was to some distinct notion of the literary—and the human within the literary—that they returned. For this reason, a sensuous, aphoristic critic like Barthes, a writer who is always right there on the page, whose work has a strong personal accent and an exceptional feeling for language, will survive when many of contemporaries are forgotten. This is not a quality often stressed in graduate school.

When an *avant garde* succeeds it is institutionalized, routinized, and finally trivialized, but this is not where recent theory most fell short. Nor should its major flaw be found in its obtuseness toward earlier theory, which John Ellis establishes so clearly in his essay. Such exuberant claims to novelty are a reflex of any *avant garde*, though they sit badly in anything that passes for scholarship. Theory respected no foundations but its own, which it rarely questioned. But its chief weakness lay in its hostile or neglectful dealings with literature itself. If we asked what made the critics of theory so incensed, it was this loss of the literary by those who should have been its most ardent guardians. Unlike the major critics in our tradition (but very much like earlier literary academics, philological, historical, even New Critical), they treated literature as material for knowledge rather than a source of personal power, affect, wisdom or beauty. As critics of humanism, they saw literature as symptom and ideology or as discourse in the service of power. They rejected its claims to autonomy or truth. Theory often raised important questions, some of which we are debating here today, but in its professionalized form it too readily fell into what Swift nicely called "the mechanical operation of the spirit." Perhaps prematurely, *Theory's Empire* writes a bittersweet obituary for the theory years but not one that's ungenerous or undeserved.

Originally posted on July 15, 2005

22. The Death & Discontents of Theory

Jeffrey Wallen

Reading through the very thoughtful posts about "theory" (with a capital T and/or a small t), about whether or not it exists (McGowan: "1) Theory with a capital T does not exist"), and whether or not it has been imperial and hegemonic, one irony keeps recurring to me. Most of the people I know, or at least most of the people I went to grad school with (the Humanities Center at Johns Hopkins, in the early and mid '80s), think that theory died, or rather was asphyxiated, some time shortly after the death of Paul de Man. The sorts of concerns and practices that seemed to be at the center of literary criticism in the late '70s and early '80s were now largely viewed as obsolete and tainted. The grand horizons for future deconstructive work projected by Paul de Man and Hillis Miller were mostly abandoned, and all of a sudden it became **very** difficult to get a job coming out of Yale in Comp. Lit.

So much depends on where one is located. What will appear to some as the hegemony of Theory, of [wildly varying] approaches that emphasize one's awareness of and adherence to some theoretical model, will appear to others as the decline in professional status of the practices that they're most inspired by and invested in. I don't think much is to be gained by trying to decide whether Theory really exists at such an abstract level, and whether it is a good or a bad thing. What would follow from such a conclusion, one way or another? Only in the journalistic denunciations of "theory" that one finds in *The New Criterion*, or *The New Republic*, or sometimes in *The New York Review of Books* is it necessary to jumble everything together into one easy narrative of professional idiocy. And I don't think that this question is central to most of the pieces in *Theory's Empire*. Rather, what's at stake in most of the contributions (and of course I haven't read all of them yet) is exploring the effects of different theories and theorists on academic (mostly literary) criticism. *Theory's Empire* could be also have borrowed a title from Freud (and Will and Daphne played around with several titles before settling on that one), *Das Unbehagen in der*

Kultur [Civilization and Its Discontents, but more accurately, "discomfort" or "unease" in culture]. The volume presents essays that express discomfort with the recent trends in literary theory and criticism, in marked contrast to anthologies such as the *Norton Anthology of Theory and Criticism* or MLA volumes such as *Redrawing the Boundaries* (from 1992), which embrace enthusiastically, almost as cheerleaders, all the trends that they document.

What I think needs to be explored then are the grounds for discomfort expressed in these essays. Do they have merit? And if so, what might be changed? As one who is uneasy in academic culture—and I guess that's why a piece of mine was included in *Theory's Empire*; I am certainly not "anti-theory" in some blanket way—I have been especially interested in describing some of the deleterious effects of certain theories. As everyone else seems to be doing, I'll also point to Mark Bauerlein's essay [in response to the question of why everyone is responding to him: he writes well, he's lucid, polemical, and fun to argue with, and he's engaged in the discussion and might respond—the same reasons that Michael Bérubé's posts receive a lot of attention], since it makes a point which I think is crucial (and not surprisingly, a point that is similar to my own arguments): the reigning standpoint ("social constructionism") shuts down rather than opens up debate. Bauerlein writes that those who adopt this position treat the most controversial contentions of their favorite theorists (e.g. Foucault) as "axiomatic" and "not open for debate." What should have been a wonderful opportunity for a vigorous discussion and rigorous investigation of fascinating questions instead leads to endless demonstrations that the text under discussion brilliantly encapsulates and "performs" all the high points of one's favorite theory, while placing these conclusions beyond dispute. This is one form of the empire of theory.

If I had to locate the moment in which a turn to theory leads to shutting down discussion and debate, I'd point to a passage from Fish's "Interpreting the Variorium" (and to get the full flavor of Stanley's efforts here to continually place himself one step ahead of everyone else, you need to look at the version in *Is There a Text in This Class?*, which also contains a preface to the essay, an essay responding to responses to the essay ["Interpreting 'Interpreting the Variorium'"], and a preface to this essay as well.) Fish writes: "The moral is clear: the choice is never between objectivity and interpretation but between interpretation that is unacknowledged as such and an interpretation that is *at least aware of itself. It is this awareness that I am claiming for myself,* although in doing so I must give up the claims implicitly made in the first part of this essay" (emphasis added).

So much smugness enters in here, in the guise of giving up the "superiority" of the earlier claim, of getting closer to what is "really happening." Fish's earlier version, of putting forth his own "good" model to replace the "bad model" which "had suppressed what was really happening," is less morally noxious and pious than the supposed doing away with "bad" and "good" as terms of criticism. Arguments about what is "really happening" can take seriously what the opponent says. There is the necessity to explain why one version is "closer" to the "real" than the other, and to explain why the opposing view is further away, missing something important, or off track. But when it is a matter of aware/unaware, there is no reason at all to take seriously the views of the opponent—they are by definition intellectually, and even morally (they prefer to remain in the cave) inferior. There is no need to argue any more except with others who are also "aware," others who also accept, buy into, to the whole set of interpretive assumptions (and interpretive strategies) that are part of this parcel of this particular set of critical practices.

Fish is no more "aware" than any of the critics he argues with. Each of them could explain the framework of their critical model (how it works, what it entails, and so on). The dispute here is between those who "acknowledge" that one is always only producing "just one more interpretation," and those who claim that their activity will (may, can) lead to some more conclusive interpretation, or one that gets one closer to the truth, etc. But the shift to aware/unaware, and giving up the earlier what really happens/not what really happens (closer or further away from the "real"), is a continual rhetorical trump card, in which every act of showing the "unawareness" in the work of another critique is a means to dismiss altogether the value of the interpretation. The new model—"just one more interpretation," nothing that exists prior to or independent of interpretive acts—is far more, rather than less, demanding. That is, rather than announcing a plurality of interpretations, rather than opening up and including in the field of interpretation much that had previously been excluded, we now get the disqualification in advance of any interpretive "strategy" that does not buy into this view.

I'll leave to others discussion of some of the other institutional effects of literary theory described in the essays in *Theory's Empire*. In closing I'll just add a few responses to some of the previous posts. John McGowan is certainly correct to point out Said's ambivalence in relation to "theory," and his hostility to de Man and Derrida, and in his larger point about the dangers of amalgamating sharply competing ideas under some general rubric. Said began a wonderful class I took with him on "The Role of the Intellectual" by spending 20 minutes making fun of de Man's writing (this was 1979), treating it as a symptom of abandoning any intellectual engagement with society. And in discussions during his office hours about Foucault and Derrida (I'd recently returned from studying in France) he was very dismissive of Derrida (and extremely knowledgeable about and interested in Foucault)—though this of course didn't prevent him from being kissy-kissy with Derrida when introducing him to give a speech in honor of the 100th anniversary of Columbia's graduate school. Said also made fun of "theory" courses that each week presented you with a different theory (if it's the week before Thanksgiving, it must be psychoanalysis, etc.). An overriding question here is what are (or what were) alternative possibilities for institutionalizing and teaching whatever one views as "theory."

In an earlier post Michael Bérubé takes Bauerlein to task for claiming that theory has been in decline for 30 years (Bauerlein actually wrote: "Because in the last 30 years, theory has undergone a paradoxical decline"—I don't think Bauerlein is arguing that theory has been declining continually since 1975), and stated that theory hadn't really even arrived in America by then: "In 1975, the hottest items in the theory store were reader-response criticism (Wolfgang Iser, *The Implied Reader*, 1974), and structuralism (Jonathan Culler, *Structuralist Poetics*, 1975)." As a sophomore at Stanford in 1974-75—and Stanford was hardly at the cutting edge!—I read Foucault's *The Order of Things* and Barthes's *Critical Essays* in one class, and Barthes's *Writing Degree Zero* and Lyotard's *Discours, Figure* in another. It was partly these courses that led me to switch my major to literary criticism (from mathematics), and to study in Paris the following year, where I took courses with Foucault, Barthes, and Todorov, among others. I think it was "French" theory, and not American (or German) syntheses, that was exciting people back in 1975.

Originally posted on July 15, 2005

23. Trilling's Taste, An Instance

Jonathan Goodwin

DAVID MARKSON, on trying to find someone to direct his master's thesis on *Under the Volcano*:

> As a matter of fact I had to wander around the English department knocking on doors looking for someone to approve the project. I remember Lionel Trilling's dismissal in particular: "What is all this drunkenness all about?" My whole object was to explain just that, obviously, but I decided to find less of a current to buck. Finally William York Tindall gave me a go-ahead.

I've written here before about the problem of seemingly inexplicable aesthetic judgments. You can't explain Trilling's failure to appreciate a work of such abundant genius as easily as the apparent motivation of the National Association of Scholar's litany recited by Valentine Cunningham in his "Theory, What Theory?" article: "modernism" and "Chomsky" being among the hieratic keywords infesting the academy in today's society (25-26). Szyslak's well-known rejoinder to Simpson captures what is wrong there: "A car-hole!" (2F21) (I should note that Cunningham doesn't exactly approve of the list.)

The Trilling case is more complex. If only very few readers can appreciate contemporary works which will later be acknowledged to be important, great, what have you, perhaps it is then maximally rational to choose books at random to champion. Though you can't know for sure what's going to be judged valuable, you do know that your own taste, constructed as it is by petrifying norms, is no reliable guide. But the value-judgments of the future are built on your own labor, complicating the matter even more.

Freedom is the recognition of the necessity of being wrong, of course, so *pecca fortiter* would be another worthy approach. Disputing the social construction of certain epistemological claims is one thing; who is willing to dispute the construction of evaluation? How relevant is evaluation to contemporary literary studies? John Ellis's contribution to the volume has some remarks about on the subject, and I hope to conclude my posts about the book with some comments on them and on how I imagine a volume like *Theory's Empire* might fare in the classroom.

Originally posted on July 17, 2005

24. Teaching Theory's Empire? ☙

Jonathan Goodwin

MANY ENGLISH Departments have an "Introduction to Graduate Study" course. The content of these classes varies depending on the school and who's teaching it. I believe it was once more common than it is now for the course to be devoted to research methodology. Perhaps over the last twenty years, it has been used more as an introduction to the theoretical debates that shape the field. *Theory's Empire* would have no place that I can imagine in the first type of course. Its essays are not exercises in literary theory or criticism; rather, they attempt to indicate the deficiencies of various contemporary approaches to these activities.

Supplemented by primary readings in the other texts being debated, TE would be useful in an introduction to the academic sociology of the English Department. I myself didn't pay much attention to this sort of thing as an undergraduate, preferring instead to cultivate my aesthetic (or hide under some blankets and hope that somehow everything would work out), and I had to learn a lot very quickly about the profession when I entered graduate school. My first two seminars comprised a survey of a major author and an exercise in the practical use of theory. The bullshitting among my colleagues was far more intense in the second, through no fault of the professor, a singularly creative theorist. His attitude towards the books we were reading was that they should be used to generate ideas you could apply in your own work—an exhaustive study of Lacan and Hegel to evaluate the claims of one of these books, as seemed necessary to me at the time, was not in fact necessary for the purpose of the course, which was not to evaluate but to use.

Ellis wouldn't approve: "Literary theorists find many useful ideas in adjacent fields, but to use them well they must master their meaning in the context of their origin. Because this mastery is rarely achieved, literary critics have always been prone to amateurish misuse of borrowed concepts" (95). One answer to this, and the one I received, is that the prospect of "mastery" is an illusion, one also fraught with considerable terminological baggage. There's little point in denying that standards of mastery are relative. I get the feeling that few critics/literary historians/theorists/philologists alive now would fare well in tests of comparative mastery with the average 19th C German philologist, for example. You could attribute this to the actual Flynn Effect, or, more plausibly, to the exponential growth of knowledge. The logical alternative then to the chimera of mastery is a generative pragmatism: take what you can use, and run with it.

Anyone who uses any ideas from anywhere is subject to the charge of "amateurish misuse of borrowed concepts." So much depends on the reader's perspective. The study of literature encompasses many things. Its theories and practices are only incidentally pyramidical, inverted or otherwise. A problem with discussing general theoretical trends is that so much depends on their use. The essays in TE don't deal with specific cases very often because they have been excised from longer works or larger debates. Some are content to evoke the snows of yesteryear.

Should then a class on academic sociology or professionalization be part of the required curriculum for any Ph.D program? An elective for undergraduate English majors who may be contemplating graduate school? If the choice is between that and a class heavy in bibliography and research methods, which is more important and why? I'm suggesting that the types of classes in which TE would be most logically taught would be just the very type that upset some of its traditionalist contributors.

Originally posted on July 22, 2005

25. Morally Sound

Daniel Green

In "Literary Aesthetics and the Aims of Criticism" (included in *Theory's Empire*), Paisley Livingston comes to this eminently reasonable conclusion about aesthetic experience:

> An aesthetic experience of literature, I suggest, is an intrinsically valued experience occasioned by the contemplation of the qualities of a literary work of art. Such contemplation is what is lacking in nonaesthetic modes of reading. In the latter, the work or its text is read in a purely and exclusively instrumental spirit, or the intrinsic value attached to the experience does not fine its basis in an attentive and apt attention to the features of the work. (661)

Livingston then renders his own description incoherent by sneaking "moral content" through the aesthetic back door:

> ... the moral content of a literary work should be acknowledged as being directly relevant to an appreciation of that work qua literary work, my principal reason being that in some contexts moral features directly influence the work's aesthetic function and value. Attempts to define the specificity of the artistic responses to works of fiction along purely formalist lines have been notoriously problematic . . . If, on the contrary, moral and political ideas are an intrinsic part of many literary works of art, their assessment would seem directly relevant to an evaluation of the works' overall merits. What is more, since it is reasonable to think that our emotional (or quasi-emotional) reactions to works of fiction are directly relevant to the aesthetic dimensions of these works, moral considerations should be recognized as of aesthetic relevance... (661-2)

It seems to me that in the second passage Livingston undoes all the good work he's done in the first to identify the distinctive features of an aesthetic experience of literature. How can it be that "nonaesthetic modes of reading"—which presumably would include reading experiences of such things as moral discourse or poltical analyses—lack a "basis in an attentive and apt attention to the features of the work," but nevertheless "moral and political ideas" ought to be assessed in an aesthetic mode of reading? Does Livingston mean that we ought to consider such ideas in their aesthetic dimension, whatever that might be? (A beautifully formed "political idea"?) Or in insisting that moral and political ideas be taken into account while evaluating a work's "overall merits," is he defining "merit" broadly, as something that goes beyond the merely aesthetic? (A given work has both aesthetic and "moral" merit?)

It would seem that Livingston thinks that "moral features" are somehow an "intrinsic" element of a literary work's aesthetic makeup—or at least of our "aesthetic response" to the work. "Aesthetic" includes both the formal and the moral. But how can this be? Dictionary definitions of the terms tell us that an aesthetic judgment applies criteria of "beauty"; a moral judgment applies criteria of "right behavior." It might be true that an obnoxious moral belief held by a particular artist or writer could lead to a flawed aesthetic choice, but ultimately our judgment of the work in question should be based on its subsequent aesthetic flaw, not on its moral repugnance (although we may feel moral disgust as well). If "aesthetic" and "moral" are as interchangeable and permeable as Livingston suggests, don't they become meaningless terms? They simply designate some vague and underdetermined "response" on the viewer's or reader's part.

Since human beings hold all kinds of beliefs, and give a higher priority to some than to others, it would be unreasonable to expect we could always neatly separate out our aesthetic sensibilities from our moral reactions from our political ideas. It does seem possible, however, that literary criticism could make an effort to "bracket" the aesthetic and the moral and not to deliberately conflate them. It could insist that while works of literature come loaded with moral implications that are well worth reflection and debate, moral considerations should not "be recognized as of aesthetic relevance" unless by "relevance" you mean "something to think about after you've located these considerations within the otherwise distinctive and qualifying context provided by the aesthetic." Moreover, it might be more specific about what a "moral consideration" properly might be other than to equate it with "emotional (or quasi-emotional) reactions to works of fiction." (I'm not sure I've ever had a quasi-emotional reaction to anything.) It might maintain, in fact, that both aesthetic and moral responses to literature are much more than just manifestations of "emotion" in the first place.

If the editors of this anthology want to return literature to the study of literature, the inclusion of Livingston's essay (its publication in the anthology marks its first appearance in print) suggests the editors of *Theory's Empire* don't want to exclude "content" from the consideration of "the literary." Neither do I, but I don't see how blurring distinctions between the aesthetic and the moral is going to set literary study back on a solid foundation. Ultimately, what's the difference between smuggling "moral content" into an account of the "aesthetic experience of literature" and smuggling in sociological analysis and political ideology, the sort of thing for which TE takes Theory's emperors to task? I don't say that the aesthetic counts for everything in the study of literature, only that it's where such study should begin. Let's "contemplate" for a little bit before we rush on to making moral arguments.

Originally posted on July 26, 2005

26. Literary Studies Without Literature ☙

John Emerson

I TEND TO READ everything I can find about topics of interest of me. The poets of the Chinese Han and Wei dynasties are among my favorites, so when I saw Christopher Leigh Connery's book *The Empire of the Text* (which *inter alia* covers the literary culture of that time) I bought it. But I didn't like the book and couldn't finish it, so I decided to use this opportunity to articulate my feelings about Theory (or perhaps Method), rather than just muttering and grumbling as per usual. (People tell me that Theory is passé and nothing to worry about any more, but in my opinion it isn't passé enough yet.)

The ideal audience for Connery's book would be someone who is able to read English and Classical Chinese, who has studied the history and literature of the Han and Wei, and who is pretty well on top of theory. I score something like 2.5 out of three, but this book was too theory-heavy for me. I'm not sure that the methodological and theoretical passages could have been of much use to anyone—they're too sketchy and basic to be valuable for someone who is sophisticated about methodology, but for the same reason they would not be helpful for someone ignorant of methodology. They seem like defensive writing, proving to people in the biz that the author has all his theoretical ducks in a row.

I suspect that there are only a few dozen people in the world capable of giving this book a better reading than mine, and what I especially fear is that the book will become a canned version of China for theory people, allowing them to pretend that they know what they're talking about when they don't. Connery actually cites two books which do just that—Kristeva and Barthes spent a couple weeks each in China and Japan respectively, and they came back to write fluffy books which were mostly just their impressions of the Oriental vibes, with little substantive content.

What is this book "about"? Well, it's not "about" "Chinese" "literature". It focuses especially on changes in the self-definition of the

Chinese elite and in the way they looked at what we call "literature". The author shows that, at the time when the poetic form was developed, during the late Han and the Wei, shi poetry did not have the enormous importance it was later given both by the Chinese themselves and by Western translators, but was just one among the many kinds of "literature" of the era (most of which have been forgotten).

Above all, however, this book seems to be about theory. Meta-statements, methodological discussions, and scare quotes stud the book like speed bumps. The book is remarkably argumentative, but one of the author's rules is that since his intervention (he uses no scare quotes on this term) attempts to replace the standard ways of talking about the era and about Chinese culture in general, he should therefore make no reference to, and use no concepts from, any of the standard interpretations except when he is refuting them.

As a result, the reader learns little about the collapse of the Han and of Han Confucianism, Cao Cao's unorthodox and perilous rise to power, or the lives and the works of the poets of the time. Since the Cao Wei dynasty and its poets have not been well covered in the English-language literature so far, non-Sinological readers will be somewhat at a loss reading this book—Connery is providing a revisionist view to an audience that is mostly unfamiliar with the received view. It would have been far better for the first substantial book in English discussing the literary world of Wei to have been more basic and inclusive. (Connery includes no Chinese texts, and only two translations of different versions of a single unexceptional poem.)

Theory is a jealous master, and Connery tends to slight the a-theoretical authors who have written about the origins of shi poetry. Diény's *Aux Origines de la Poesie Classique en Chine* and Birrell's *Popular Songs and Ballads of Han China* are not even listed in the bibliography, and the listed works by these authors are not discussed. He does mention Owen's *Traditional Chinese Poetry and Poetics*, but Connery ignores his most interesting points, limiting himself to the claim that that Owen is guilty of the subjective fallacy and the communication fallacy.

Connery makes a lawyer's case against the possibility of oral, folkish or non-elite antecedents of shi poetry, demanding that "minimum standards of evidence" be met. This amounts to begging the question, since the kinds of records he demands do not exist at all, one way or another—and even if they did, written records of oral poetry would no longer be oral any more. (On orality Connery seems to have relied on Finnegan's meticulously confusing *Oral Poetry*.)

The payoff from all this is slight. Anyone involved in the field at all already knew that the poetry of this time was produced by elite males for group events. How this proves that nothing subjective was expressed in these poems is not made clear, and the fact that a focus on subjectivity is characteristic of XIXc bourgeois criticism is pretty much irrelevant to the Chinese criticism of a thousand or more years earlier. (Furthermore, this sounds like "Tradition and the Individual Talent" all over again). Connery's stress on the bureaucratic nature of most Chinese writing of this time is valid and interesting, but I think that he takes the formal and official denigration and subordination of shi poetry too much at face value. (The Chinese official histories are famous for leaving out the things we would most want to know, while recording formalistic trivia and state fictions in enormous detail.)

Connery also misses some juicy stuff that he might have liked. For example Cao Cao, the warlord who presided over this era, was the grandson of a eunuch; it would seem that afficiondados of 'gender trouble' should have something to say about that. Connery also missed the avant-garde Confucians Kong Rong and Mi Heng, the first of whom was executed for sarcasm and impudence, and the second of whom once made his point in an argument by stripping himself naked while in attendance at one of Cao Cao's court functions. (Yes, Mi Heng also was eventually executed—but not by Cao Cao, and not for that).

I doubt that Connery is really the problem here. His book is obviously a recycled dissertation, and I imagine him chained to his carrel, pale and wan, flinching in fear every time he hears the door open, terrified that his dissertation adviser might catch him doing something bad. Connery has certainly done his homework, and we can hope for good work from him if he ever reaches free soil.

"Liberating potential" is supposedly crucial to theory, but in fact theory, like any other methodology in the methodologized university, has been imposed on a generation of scholars from above by standard bureaucratic processes—chiefly standards and procedures for the control of hiring, firing, and promotion. It would be interesting to see Connery apply the tools he has used to analyze text formation within the Chinese bureaucratized elite to the rules for text formation in the bureaucratized academic world of today.

October, 2006

POSTSCRIPT: An earlier version of this essay was published at idiocentrism.com as "Theory and Me", in July 2005.

Bibliography

Birrell, Anne, *Popular Songs and Ballads of Han China* (Honolulu:Hawaii UP, 1988).

Birrell, Anne, *New Songs from a Jade Terrace* (New York: Penguin, 1982.)

Cao Zhi, *Worlds of Dust and Jade*, George Kent, tr. (New York:Philosophical Library, 1969).

Diény, Jean-Pierre, *Aux Origines de la Poèsie Classique en Chine* (Leiden:Brill, 1968).

Diény, Jean-Pierre, *Les Poèmes de Cao Cao* (Paris:Collège de France, 2000).

Diény, Jean-Pierre, *Les Dix-neufs Poèmes Anciens* (Paris:P.U.F., 1963).

Goodman, H.L., *Ts'ao P'i Transcendant* (Seattle:Scripta Serica, 1998).

Owen, Stephen, *Traditional Chinese Poetry and Poetics*, (Madison:University of Wisconsin Press, 1985).

27. Theory Tuesday III

Michael Bérubé

I LEARNED OVER the weekend that the esteemed RJ ESKOW has called me the AL JACKSON JR. of literary theory. I am more honored and humbled than I can say, being a huge Al Jackson fan who still hasn't quite mastered the Master's playing on songs like Al Green's "Still in Love With You". But it raises the stakes considerably for Theory Tuesdays, which now, I suppose, are expected to be funky as well as informative. Sad to say, I'm just not up to funky today. Besides, we're doing structuralism, which is damn near guaranteed to de-funkify any atmosphere.

The early returns on Theory Tuesdays appear to be a mixed bag. The academics who read this blog tend to like these installments, even (or especially) when they take issue with them; everybody else seems willing (more or less) to wait them out in the hopes that someday this blog will be funny again. I should explain that these posts were originally meant (for those of who you believe in "intentionality") as an extended reply to the *Theory's Empire* challenge: because I teach Intro to Graduate Study with the help of the *Norton Anthology of Theory and Criticism* (I'm not one of the editors, as John McGowan is, but I did provide a big long blurb on the back cover, so you might as well consider this blog *Norton Central*), a couple of photocopied essays, and guest appearances from my colleagues (who come in to describe the past twenty years of work in their various fields), I thought it might be a good idea to offer some of my course notes on this blog.

The course itself—which, before I arrived at Penn State, some students disliked so much they called it "boot camp"—is also a mixed bag. (And that's why the department head asked me to teach it: I'm the Mixed Bag Guy.) The idea is to introduce first-year graduate students to the various workings of the profession, which means (a) research methods and materials, online resources, rare books, and the like; (b) learning about the recent histories of the various subfields, from medieval to postmodern; (c) acquiring the rudiments of what people call "theory"; and (d) learning how various conferences and scholarly journals work. I decided to approach (c) not by instructing students on What's Hot Now (which is, I fear, what theory-caricaturists tend to think) but by filling them in on the background that most theory-literate people take for granted. I've never forgotten the graduate student who once complained to me that no one explained Mikhail Bakhtin to her when she was an undergraduate, but nonetheless a number of her professors in graduate school assumed that she would be familiar with Bakhtin. "What, was I absent on Bakhtin Day?" she asked. "I think a lot of people were absent that day," I replied. Besides, I think that in order to "get" Bakhtin, you need to go back and replay those early debates between formalism and Marxism, just as you need to go back and catch up on your *ostranenie* in order to get a handle on literature since the Romantics and theory since the Russian Formalists.

So today I'm going to say a few words about structuralism, staying with the Old School for now before moving to Raymond Williams next Tuesday and American cultural studies the week after that. I know that Amardeep and Lance, LAST WEEK, asked me to talk about rhetorical hermeneutics and intentionality instead, but I think JOHN HOLBO has that one covered for now. But before I get to Roman Jakobson and (very briefly) Claude Lévi-Strauss, I want to bring up two side issues raised by the Valve crew.

The first one is minor: you would think, from reading the posts of the past month, that no one questioned people like Derrida until John Searle came along. That sounds strange to me, because when I read the 1985 *Against Theory* volume inspired by Walter Benn Michaels' and Steven Knapp's bizarrely reductive argument for a form of intentionalism that even intentionalists don't recognize, I came across Richard Rorty writing about how "Derrida looks bad whenever he attempts argument on his opponents' turf; those are the passages in which he becomes a patsy for John Searle" (135). I don't know why this doesn't count when Rorty says it, but it should. Or is it that, for some people, Rorty is too identified with the Theory camp? And likewise, I've gotten the impression once or twice that people imagine that all this Theory arrived to say nothing more complicated than "the sign is multivalent," to which the Theory-detractors can, of course, reply, "yes, we knew that already." Well, we knew that too, and we knew you knew it; even Robert Plant knew it, when he wrote, in *On Certainty*, "you know sometimes words have two meanings." I'll get back to this at the very end of this post, folks, but for now let it suffice to say that the devil is in the details: the real fun lies in finding out just how multivalent that sign can be, and what its multivalences can mean in various contexts. The current anti-Theory camp is quite right not to call for a return to a prelapsarian past or a faux-naif future (this just in: sign not multivalent after all!). But there's more to theory than a little ambiguity here and a little undecidability there, and again, the important thing lies in learning how "multivalence" and "multiaccentuality" (V. N. Volosinov's term, not mine) actually work.

The second side issue is more important, and I think was best represented by Sean McCann's complaint that some of the TE discussion was deflected onto the institutional status of theory rather than the merits of specific theories. Sean acknowledges that this was understandable and not entirely regrettable, either; but I still think the complaint misrecognizes its occasion. TE's publication is a response (as the editors say) not to theory but to its institutionalization in the form of the *Norton*, and it was meant to provide critiques of theories and theorists that the Norton does not. In other words, the discussion was always already institutional, which is why I considered it entirely within bounds to point out (at the very outset, in response to Mark Bauerlein's *Butterflies and Wheels* essay) that some of Theory got a free pass 20-30 years ago precisely because it seemed to be associated with the most exciting and prolific people in the humanities, whereas the anti-Theory crew seemed to be composed chiefly of cranks and curmudgeons. Theory acquired some of its authority for institutional reasons, and Sean's account of one of the consequences sounds about right to me: distinguishing theory-institutionalization from institutionalization in general, he writes,

> this situation is particularly toxic in literary academia because of a historic professional self-image that cast literature as the anti-disciplinary discipline. As a special kind of knowledge, or rather experience, literature was understood to rise above and cast into doubt the authority of other fields—especially mere "science." To look back over the grand moments of Theory—in its Deconstructive, or New Historicist, or Cult Stud moments—is, I think, to see renewed and intensified versions of that attitude. Not literature, but Theory

> now is the special kind of expertise that challenges all other expertise, the unique kind of training that subverts all other discipline.

Contrast this account of theory with BRAD DELONG'S NARRATIVE of How He Came to Grips with Foucault: for DeLong, a Foucauldian account of the history of economics brought him to see some things and take issue with others. And that's all I would ever ask a theory to do, myself. That's all I ever ask students to ask for, too.

As for the ancillary complaint (John Ellis', I believe) that theory has encouraged a kind of amnesia about intellectual history: this strikes me as precisely the kind of complaint that has more bearing on the institutional setting of theory than on theory itself. I mean, seriously, theory is responsible for quite a few revivals and recoveries here and there: the recent Spinoza boomlet is largely the doing of Gilles Deleuze, just as queer theory got some of us (belatedly) reading Sylvan Tompkins and Erving Goffman. The posthumous, three-decades-delayed explosions of interest in the idiosyncratic-Marxist work of Antonio Gramsci and Walter Benjamin? Those, too, were brought to you by Theory Productions Worldwide.

All of which reminds me of how very fortunate I was to have, as a theory mentor and dissertation director, Michael Levenson. At a time when the Theory Wings of some departments included a few poseurs and provocateurs and even flaneurs (!), Michael presented the theory division of the intellectual history of the twentieth century with real rigor—and without fanfare. Virginia wasn't a theory hotbed in those days; quite the contrary. When that *New York Times Magazine* piece on the Yale critics appeared in 1986, all of us in Charlottesville said "grrrrrrr" (and not much more), because we'd had a thing about Yale ever since they beat us 23-21 in the 1983 Aporia Bowl on de Man's last-second field goal. Likewise, just down south of us, Duke was amassing a queer theory/ cultural studies team that would win three consecutive NCAA championships; they were building toward the glory years of Bobby Hurley, Eve Sedgwick, Stanley Fish, and Christian Laettner. So dear old U.Va. sometimes behaved as if it had a kind of theory chip on its shoulder. But not Michael: Michael was all theory all the time, with no time for institutional politics. I don't think I've acknowledged my debt to him sufficiently in print, so—as I'm about to repeat much of what he taught me about Jakobson and Lévi-Strauss, and what I teach my students—here's to him. Thanks, Michael.

The Jakobson excerpts in the *Norton* are short but sufficient to the purpose. From "Linguistics and Poetics," we have the six functions of language, and the famous formula (which I suggest my students tattoo onto their arms), "the poetic function projects the principle of equivalence from the axis of selection into the axis of combination." If you've got the formula, the six functions, the distinction between metaphor and metonymy (in "Two Aspects of Language and Two Types of Aphasic Disturbances"), and the brief discussion of "Hiawatha" and "I Like Ike," you've got your Jakobson-in-a-nutshell. And if you have your Jakobson in a nutshell, you've got your structuralism in a nutshell; and (here's the best thing) if you've got your structuralism in a nutshell, then you could be bounded in that nutshell and count yourself a king of infinite space, were it not that you would have bad post-structuralist dreams. Because if there's one thing you can't say about structuralism, you can't charge it with being insufficiently ambitious.

OK, explanations are in order. Let's take the six functions of language first. Every message has six components: an addresser and an addressee, of course; a context, a message, a contact, and a code. The context is the setting, the contact is the physical or psychological channel of connection, the code is the shared language, and the message is the message. To each component there is a corresponding function:

> Messages that focus on the code—"what do you mean by that?"—are called *metalingual*;
>
> Messages that focus on the context—"the cat is on the mat" (a hypothetical sentence popular among philosophers, even though, curiously enough, no cat has ever been on a mat anywhere in the world)—are called *referential*;
>
> Messages that focus on the contact—"can you hear me?"—are called *phatic*;
>
> Messages that focus on the addressee—"please take that cat off the mat!"—are called *conative*;

Messages that focus on the addresser—"a slumber did my spirit seal"—are called *emotive*; and

Messages that focus on the message—"a slumber did my spirit seal"—are called *poetic*.

You can already see my thumb on the scales with those last two examples, but you get the idea. This really isn't a bad way to classify utterances, and what's even better, Jakobson insists that most utterances are mixtures, with one "dominant" feature among several. This gets him out of the Formalist Impasse, insofar as he's not required to adduce examples of utterances that are "purely" poetic and to distinguish them categorically from merely "practical" or "ordinary" speech. On the contrary, he insists that "any attempt to reduce the sphere of the poetic function to poetry or to confine poetry to the poetic function would be a delusive oversimplification. The poetic function is not the sole function of verbal art but only its dominant, determining function, whereas in all other verbal activities it acts as a subsidiary, accessory constituent." Jakobson thus deftly refigures the difference between the poetic and other modes of speech as a difference in degree rather than in kind, and disarms wiseguys like me who like to open class with poems like

Unbelted occupants
Are not able to resist
The tremendous forces of impact by holding tight
Or bracing themselves. Their impact
With the vehicle interior
Has all the energy they had
Just before the collision.

It is a compelling piece of work. I want particularly to draw your attention to the reiteration and personalization of "impact," as the impact is no longer that of "tremendous forces" but of the "occupants" themselves, and the way this process is repeated in line six, where we find that their impact "has all the energy they had." That abrupt modulation into the past tense is, I think, understated and powerful. We need not say any more about why these occupants are now spoken of only in terms of the energy they have lost. And that's why, if you want an account of a car crash that is at once clinically precise and strangely moving, I recommend the 2003 VW Passat owner's manual.

Jakobson's response to this (and all such Fishy endeavors) is simply, what did you expect? Of course you can find elements of the poetic even in the most utilitarian of utterances, even campaign slogans. Here's Roman on "I Like Ike": "both cola alliterate with each other, and the first of the two alliterating words is included in the second: /ay/ – /ayk/, a paronomastic image of the loving subject enveloped by the beloved object. The secondary, poetic function of this campaign slogan reinforces its impressiveness and efficacy" (1264).

And you thought jargon-laden overreading was invented in 1991!

Really, the notion of the "dominant" solves all kinds of problems . . . except one. How do you know that the emphasis on the message itself is the dominant feature of the utterance? Uh, because the utterance is poetic. OK, then how do you know the utterance is poetic? Uh, because the emphasis on the message itself is the dominant . . . oooooh (cue Yosemite Sam voice here), ya varmint, it's circularity all over again! What, after all, is the difference between citing Wordsworth's "A Slumber Did My Spirit Seal" as an emotive utterance and citing it as a poetic utterance? Aren't poetic utterances, particularly in lyric, likely to be emotive as well, whereas in epic (or pastoral, or georgic) they might be referential as well?

Yes, but (and here comes the bromide) it all depends on how you look at it. It all depends on who, or what historical epoch, or what cultural formation, is doing the looking. Where Jakobson goes wrong is just here: he insists that "Hiawatha" (for example) retains its dominant poetic function even when it's being read on the Senate floor by a filibustering senator, whereas I (because I'm of a more pragmatist bent) would suggest that any filibuster is at once phatic (a message about Senate procedure itself) and referential (in its attempt to forestall a vote), regardless of whether it involves a poem or a telephone book or a car owner's manual. Jakobson thus backs into one of two uncomfortable positions: either an utterance carries the designs of its utterer through all space and time, so that "Hiawatha"'s dominant is whatever Longfellow originally intended it to be, or certain utterances have intrinsic features that render them indelibly poetic, referential, metalingual, etc. Since Jakobson's inquiry set out partly to obviate the problems of postulating "intrinsic" features and original intentions, you can see that this makes for a bit of a mess. One is left with the conclusion that Jakobson has defined *not* six types of utterances but six ways of *attending* to utterances, and that the determination of which utterances have a dominant "poetic" function (and how, and why) is left profoundly up for grabs.

But, as I said above, that's where the real fun is.

Jakobson argues nonetheless that "the indispensable feature inherent in any piece of poetry" is that it messes with the principles of metaphor and metonymy. Metaphor, you know, expresses likeness or equivalence; metonymy expresses contiguity and/or combination. "My love is like a red red rose" is metaphor, "the White House said today" is metonymy. Now go back and plug this into that formula I mentioned above: *the poetic function projects the principle of equivalence from the axis of selection into the axis of combination.* Jakobson adds: "equivalence is promoted to the constitutive device of the sequence." Basically, the poetic function treats metonymic relations as if they were metaphoric. It sounds cool, and it is, particularly when you're trying to figure out why the only emperor is the emperor of ice cream. But this is a description of only certain kinds of poetry, and surely we want to escape the conclusion that very few poems contain a dominant poetic function. We also want to know just who is promoting equivalence to the constitutive device of the sequence: does the poet—or the poetic function—do this at the outset? Or do we (whoever "we" are) do it whenever we stop reading the owner's manual for content and start looking at the language *as language*?

Just to be clear about this: I don't teach Jakobson in order to trash him for not being pragmatist enough. Neither did Michael Levenson. Jakobson's work was hugely influential for quite some time, and for good reason: those six functions of language, together with the idea of metaphor and metonymy as "poles" corresponding to axes of selection (equivalence) and combination (continguity), will get you pretty far in the world. At one point in "Two Aspects of Language," Jakobson writes that, "Similarity connects a metaphorical term with the term for which it is substituted. Consequently, when constructing a metalanguage to interpret tropes, the researcher possesses more homogeneous means to handle metaphor, whereas metonymy, based on a different principle, easily defies interpretation. Therefore nothing comparable to the rich literature on metaphor can be cited for the theory of metonymy." Ha ha! I tell my students. We fixed that! If you root around in Lacan-inflected theory of the 1970s and 1980s, you'll find that *it's all about the metonymy*. In fact, the more intensely Lacanian you get, the more likely it is that you'll wind up speaking about metaphor as if it were the vehicle for Evil Incarnate (because it asserts a likeness between two things, a Dreaded Dyad) whereas metonymy disrupts all systems of likeness, initiates that exciting, never-ending Metonymic Skid, and ushers us into the way language (and therefore the world) really works. "The unconscious is structured like a language," said the Lacanians, and suddenly metaphor was out and metonymy was the shit. But if you take a step back, you'll realize that we were still working with the terms more or less as Jakobson left them to us.

Borrowing yet one more page from Michael Levenson, though, I hasten to point out to my students that there are two very annoying things about structuralism. One, it is constitutionally grandiose. No sooner does Jakobson discover two types of aphasia than he's off to the races, carving up genres (from lyric to epic), artistic schools, and even entire historical periods according to whether they are predominantly metaphorical or metonymic. (Romanticism and Symbolism are metaphorical; Realism is metonymic; Cubism is metonymic, but Surrealism is metaphorical. Bob, you and Kathy are metaphorical. . . .) And there's no reason to stop at literary and cultural history, oh no!

> A careful analysis and comparison of these phenomena with the whole syndrome of the corresponding type of aphasia is an imperative task for joint research by experts in psychopathology, psychology, linguistics, poetics, and semiotics, the general science of signs. The dichotomy discussed here *appears to be of primal significance and consequence for all verbal behavior and for human behavior in general*. (emphasis added.)

As Levenson paraphrased this twenty years ago: *today an investigation of two types of aphasic disturbances—tomorrow, ze universe*!

Two, even though (or, more precisely, because) structuralism wanted to be a theory of everything, it did not want to be a mere theory of "meaning"—especially in the hands of Lévi-Strauss, for whom meaning was "epiphenomenal." I'll spare you the full-dress analysis of Lévi-Strauss, since we're past the 3000-word mark, but basically, the man insisted that meaning is to structure as the taste of sugar is to the chemical composition of sugar. And Lévi-Strauss could not have cared less about the taste of sugar: he was after the structure, which was somehow "deeper" than mere meaning and antecedent to it. It is stunning, I think, how un- or anti-hermeneutic a position this really is. (That's one reason why Jonathan Culler's mid-70s structuralist dream of amassing all possible interpretive modes that can generate all possible textual interpretations was so mistaken. The other reason is that it was mad—mad, I say.) In his remarkable essay "Structure and Hermeneutics," Paul Ricoeur objected to the idea that structuralist interpretation could escape the boundaries of all human forms of interpretation (these would be the boundaries marked by the hermeneutic circle), and was willing to credit structuralist anthropology with being a kind of science while noting that "the passage from a structural science to a structuralist philosophy seems to me to be not very satisfying and not even very coherent." Suffice it to say, for now, that I'm with Ricoeur on this.

Originally posted on July 26, 2005

28. Bill the Butcher as Educator

John Holbo

In the latest issue of the *Chronincle of Higher Education* [July 29, 2005], there a piece about us by one William Pannapacker. This is very positive:

> Last March the ALSC launched the Valve, the name of which suggests a place for venting frustrations with the academic establishment. Its 14-member roster of contributors is headed by John Holbo, an assistant professor of philosophy at the National University of Singapore. The expressed aims of the Valve are identical to those of the ALSC: to serve as a "healthy" place for the expression of the love of literature that dare not speak its name. [that's not quite it regarding our stated aims, actually.]
>
> But no, this is a caricature [I hope of the ALSC as well], for the contributions to the Valve are usually much more complex than the black-and-white dualities of the so-called culture war. In fact, discussions on the Valve contain some of the most balanced, nuanced, and civil blogging on academic culture one is likely to find since the much lamented demise of the Invisible Adjunct last summer.

This is less positive:

> So *Theory's Empire*, along with organizations such as the ALSC, seems to provoke prophetic visions among some readers: Perhaps it will pave the way for a new generation of academics, gathering strength in exile, who will sweep away the Theory establishment, which had grown complacent in the wake of its triumph.

> Given this lively emotional back story, it is rather disappointing to report that the much-heralded, multiweek discussion of *Theory's Empire* on the Valve has turned out to be a dud instead of a blockbuster. I wanted to report that it was a signal event in the history of the blogosphere. Years from now we would look back on this as the moment when the void left by unread journals and joyless conferences would be filled by this new, youthful, unmediated forum for frank discussion of the real issues of the profession.
>
> If so, this is a case in which the world begins with a whimper instead of a bang. As the *über*-blogger Brad DeLong complains, the discussion has been all too civil and theoretical, rather than heated and cultural. Some readers, like me, were hoping for an academic donnybrook directly from *Gangs of New York* with Stanley Fish making a cameo appearance as Bill the Butcher. But, as of this writing, it looks like the Valve declared a war and nobody came.

Here's my response. I'm sure others will want to make theirs. First, thanks for the generally favorable vote of confidence about the form and its academic potential. But now, about those criticisms. You can want to see Stanley Fish as Bill the Butcher, and you can want frank, balanced, nuanced and civil blogging. You can welcome the substitution of complexity for the black-and-white of culture war, and you can lament the fact that someone redeclared culture war and no one came. But I fail to see how the Valve can be held responsible for not overcoming the severe mutual incompatibilities of these (independently understandable) objectives. You have to take your pick. We all recall that classic Bill the Butcher essay, "Is There A Fucking Knife In This Class?": "You see this knife?" Well, that's just the *question*, isn't it? "I'm gonna teach you to speak English with this fucking knife!" Perhaps Pannapacker has in mind some of Bill's other memorable lines: "I know your works. You are neither cold nor hot. So because you are lukewarm, I will spew you out of my mouth. You can build your filthy world without me." Well, spew or get off the pot. Can't have both.

This reminds me that I owe Michael Bérubé an apology for being the teensy tinsiest bit rude to him.

I owe a retraction, per his post HERE. In THIS POST I accused him of perpetrating what I called the T-to-t fallacy: investing 'Theory'—i.e. something recent and intellectually distinctive—with *ersatz* necessity, by conflating it with 'theory' in the generic sense of 'thinking at all'. Michael says he wasn't. He was just making the point that Theory's defenders are not necessarily so intellectually intractable. And Theory is not necessarily so monolithically exclusive as critics sometimes make out. Fair enough. I shouldn't have been so quick with the knife, thereby incidentally confirming Michael's point. The higher point to be made here ... concerns the dearth of things worth seeing at this very point. So let's scramble up for a better view of their absence.

Sean writes:

> In my fantasies, I yearn for TE to convince its readers of what I think are two major conclusions toward which it leads: (1) Though they've been frequently, if not characteristically exaggerated to the point of absurdity, some of the widely shared beliefs made commonplace by Theory are, at least in some versions, perfectly reasonable—and at a certain point in the history of the literary academy may plausibly have seemed badly needed. (2) Criticism of Theory is not inevitably motivated by anti-intellectualism or political or cultural conservatism or characterized by intemperate bluster.

But the comedy of it is that these 'major conclusions' are pretty trivial. Just not trivial enough that we can forego a 700+ page anthology, plus our humble book event, on their behalf. So the discussion is inevitably deformed. To keep it from being *even more* deformed than it has to be, you've got to distinguish *pointless* points that you've simply got to make from those you don't. My go-round with Michael is perhaps a case in point. Take TIM BURKE as a benchmark of balance: "I tend to bristle on one hand at know-nothing denunciations of theory ... but also at circle-the-wagons defenses of it, or even those defenses which argue that the problem with theory was only its occasional excesses and over-zealous acolytes." Now Michael and I can sign on to that, but doing so would mask real, deep disagreement. So it might seem we should haul all that into the light; but actually that would risk excavating a molehill. Because what do we disagree about? The degree of asymptotic approach to know-nothing? The diameter of the circle of defensiveness? The decibel level of over-zealotry? All very real, but hashing it out would basically amount to compiling dueling compendia of minor grievances, to see who has the bigger mountain. This is why debates about Theory tend to be either crude (if you don't bother to get all your points lined up very carefully) or peevish (if you do). The ideal way to advance the debate would be to get people to *grant* 1 & 2 as *obvious*, thereby obviating the need to solve for their truth to three significant decimal places; *then* we could actually get on with something complex and intellectually interesting on that basis.

It is always a good time to quote Nietzsche's "Bill the Butcher as Educator":

> They know, these solitaries, free in spirit, that they continually seem other than what they think: while they desire nothing but truth and honesty, they are encompassed by a net of misunderstandings; and however vehemently they may desire, they cannot prevent a cloud of false opinions, approximations, half-admissions, indulgent silence, erroneous interpretation from gathering about their actions. Because of this a cloud of melancholy gathers on their brows; for such as these it is more hateful than death itself to be forced to present a semblance to the world; and their perpetual bitter resentment of this constraint fills them with volcanic menace. From time to time they revenge themselves for their enforced concealment and compelled restraint. They emerge from their cave wearing a terrifying aspect; their words and deeds are then explosions and it is possible for them to perish by their own hand.[1]

We've all had days like that. Thankfully, we haven't had days like that for *days*, since—by general acclaim—this *Theory's Empire* event has been such a model of agreeable conversation. Taking an even longer view, as Hannapacker does ... well, *my* long view is different. One day it dawned on me that my polemical pieces were generally less intelligent than my mild-mannered ones. Also, I got tired of writing arch, high-handed polemical pieces, *then* having to apologize when my targets showed up in comments, complaining that I had been unfair; which was perfectly fair of them. Anyway, in the long run, in these sorts of fights, fighting *fair* is the best revenge. (If you've never tried it, the effects can be exquisite. People positively claw the walls when exposed to the stuff.)

I'm grateful to Pannapacker for writing a generally favorable piece about us. But it most definitely wasn't our intent to start a war. I think, in fact, it is one of the good features of *Theory's Empire* that it is so manifestly unsuitable as an implement of culture war. (This, of course, will not stop *some* people from pretending to regard it as such. But there is nothing I can do to *force* them to be philosophers.)

Originally posted on July 28, 2005

NOTES

1 Actually, it's from Friedrich Nietzsche, "Schopenhauer as Educator," in *Untimely Meditations* (Cambridge: Cambridge UP, 1983), trans. R.J. Hollingdale, 139.

29. T1 AND T2?

Mark Kaplan

I WAS FLICKING through a copy of *Theory's Empire* today (in a bookshop, that is), trying to get some sense of the 'Theory' that this anthology of dissent was dissenting from. One name I noticed in the anthology was Paisley Livingston. Now Livingston is by no means anti-Theory, or at least he wasn't when he wrote *Literary Knowledge*, in which we find, for example, this:

> Again and again, the supposedly nontheoretical approach amounts to a tacit reliance upon a complex host of invisible theories: the sedimented and unexamined theory of genres, a prejudicial nationalist parcelling out of 'literatures', an unreflective periodization, a Eurocentric and elitist canon mirroring a 'great man' view of history, a wholly idealist aesthetics, an arcane and incoherent semantics, colonial ethics, and so on.[1]

Livingston mentions also a 'pseudo-empirical' and 'immediate' approach to 'particular facts'. The scare quotes imply a false immediacy; the sense is that because certain conceptual distinctions, demarcations etc, are invisible, they allow an illusion of simply dealing with things 'as they are'.

Now, I'm not entirely sure I agree with that notion of 'invisible theory'. That is, when Livingston talks about 'invisible theories' isn't he talking about guiding assumptions, presuppositions and 'methodologies' that refuse to acknowledge themselves as such? The reason I'm not sure about calling these hidden assumptions etc. 'theories' is that, to me, one definition of theoretical activity is precisely the making conscious and reflecting on hitherto invisible frames and suppositions. Don't we speak of 'untheorized' assumptions?

Anyway, it was on the whole right and proper that these 'invisible theories' were dragged into the light and subjected to critical scrutiny. And part of what was experienced as exciting and liberating about (what is now called) Theory was precisely this working through, this objectification of what had been hidden. Such 'making visible', and the attendant and remorseless suspicion of 'self-evidence', of immediacy, are surely all constitutive delights of thinking as such, and the experience of freedom, of enlarged horizons, that comes with it.

Some time ago, my attention was drawn to a post in which THEORY was likened to a PUFFER FISH. The idea was that, when attacked, it inflated to twice its original size. To be honest I was a little baffled by this, as some of the actual examples given seemed to show the opposite: i.e., when attacked Theory 'deflates' to a position of false modesty. It says, in other words, 'I am simply critical or systematic thinking as such. How could you object to such a thing?' And indeed, no one surely could. Or Theory says, along with Coleridge, that to think at all involves 'theorizing'—you may imagine you're theory-free, but this is illusory. We're back to 'invisible theories'. Mr Holbo suggests we keep Theory separate from theory in this more modest sense. And doubtless we should.

Now all I want to do here is make an anecdotal point. You would expect people who are anti-Theory to at least to be perfectly happy with 'lower case' theory. But my experience has been that those opposed to Theory (roughly: 'a relatively modern trend within academia characterised by the hasty appropriation and employment of select post-modern thinkers') are also uncomfortable with theory as such, with a 'theoretical' approach to literature and literary texts. So, I tend not to meet people who say "It's so regrettable that literary theory has been hijacked by these 'Theory' people, or even "these Theory people just aren't doing good and rigorous theory." And I do often meet people who object forcefully to Theory in the name of an 'immediate', 'one-to-one' relation with the text. In other words, in the name of an anti-theory position. And indeed, there genuinely are, within literary studies, those opposed to the idea that there can be something called 'literary theory'. They are opposed to this in principle. Okay, so this is just anecdotal, and it's therefore up to the reader to agree or disagree based on his/her own experience. But I have certainly encountered such people.

And so as well as making the distinction, as Holbo suggests between Theory and theory, we might also distinguish those who oppose theory and those who object only to Theory, and let these two objections not be conflated. And let those who oppose Theory not use this opposition to smuggle in an anti-theoretical position.

Originally posted on August 4, 2005

NOTES

1 Paisley Livingston, *Literary Knowledge : Humanistic Inquiry & the Philosophy of Science*, (Ithaca, NY: Cornell University Press. 1988), 13.

30. There Be Monsters— or, Rosa Parks: Not Psychotic

Sean McCann

I HOPE THAT title grabbed you and will persuade you to ruminate for a second over a dry question or two: was Jacques Derrida an apocalyptic thinker? And, if so, why should we care?

I would have thought the obvious answer to the first question was: yes! I had my own spell of infatuation at the tail end of the high theory days, and my recollection is that Mark is right to say (as he does in his essay in TE) that, for many of us, a big part of the thrill was not just the fascination with what's difficult, but the closely related sense that the text was an *arcanum* that would put our hands on the very cockles of history. At the same time, even then some of it seemed a bit over the top. I remember querying readers more expert or devoted than myself about the Derridean tic of referring to monstrous births and event horizons and receiving embarrassed shrugs or expressions of confusion in reply.

Even when I was infatuated, I always thought this was one of the signal weaknesses of the Derridean *oeuvre*, but the TE event has brought to my attention the possibility that my impression might just be off. ADAM, who probably knows best, says, yeah, Derrida had that millennial thing in his early days, but he suggests that Derrida left it behind and that it was never really that important to the act anyway. (Closer to Pete Best than to Duane Allman is the implication, I take it.) GERALD GRAFF doubts even that much. Derrida rebuked the apocalyptic attitude strongly, he says. Claiming to see one in his work is just carelessness with the facts.

On reflection, I'm not convinced. First off, apocalyptic notes are sprinkled throughout Derrida's early writing and, in varying form, they appear to return with moderate consistency. (A quick, unscientific tour of the blogosphere suggests that the question is even a small matter of interpretation for some Derrideans. There appear to be conflicting schemes of periodization out there: he was apocalyptic early and then become something different—"perverformative," SOME claim;[1] he was apocalyptic, then he wasn't, then he was again, others say.) Second off, they seem pretty central to his view of things. Third off, I think they turn out to have a rather lasting legacy in American Theory, where they continue to exercise what seems to me a basic and unfortunate influence.

Here's the concluding paragraphs to the famous "Structure, Sign, and Play" essay, the critique of Lévi-Strauss that made Derrida's name at the epochal Johns Hopkins conference in '66 and launched the post-structural invasion.* (I've already posted this in the thread following Adam's comments, but here it is again.) The passage comes at the end of an analysis in which Derrida contends that Lévi-Strauss resisted the implications of his own structuralist theory and instead demonstrated a misguided "nostalgia for origins":

> There are thus two interpretations of interpretation, of structure, of sign, of freeplay. The one [i.e. that of Lévi-Strauss at his weakest] that seeks to decipher, dreams of deciphering, a truth or an origin which is free from freeplay and from the order of the sign, and lives like an exile the necessity of interpretation. The other [i.e., the repressed, good side of Lévi-Strauss's theory, discovered by Derrida], which is no longer turned toward the origin, affirms freeplay and tries to pass beyond man and humanism …
>
> For my part, although these two interpretations must acknowledge and accentuate their difference and define their irreducibility, I do not believe that today there is any question of choosing—in the first place because here we are in a region … where the category of choice seems particularly trivial; and in the second, because we must first try to conceive of the common ground, and the difference of this irreducible difference. Here there is a sort of question … of which we are only glimpsing today the conception, the formation, the gestation, the labor. I employ these words, I admit, with a glance toward the business of childbearing—but also with a glance toward those who, in a

> company from which I do not exclude myself, turn their eyes away in the face of the as yet unnameable which is proclaiming itself and which can do so, as is necessary whenever a birth is in the offing, only under the species of the non-species, in the formless, mute, infant, and terrifying form of monstrosity.[2]

By comparison to a lot of Derrida's writing, the meaning of this passage seems relatively straightforward. What's more, that meaning seems rather directly prophetic. Derrida's distinctive understanding of language has brought him to a unique pass. He stands amid a company of the sheepish, with whose timidity he can't help but empathize. At the same time, he (perhaps implicitly in an obstetric mode) has the wherewithal to perceive the dawning of a monstrous birth.

(As an aside, it is worth noting that there's a cleverness to this passage that could easily trip one up. SS&P criticizes Lévi-Strauss for his "Rousseauistic" attitude [292] and elevates deconstruction's awareness of the "free play" of the signifier—the insuppressible feature of language that undermines any hope of stable centers, origins, authority, what have you. But, while there's no doubt where his preferences lie, Derrida also clearly says that there's no chance of choosing between these two stances. They're both inevitable, and we stand on a terrain inhabited by both. Having made that point, however, Derrida then goes on to suggest that it's the full acknowledgment of this conflicted situation that portends monstrous births. "[W]e must first try to conceive of the common ground" of the "Rousseauistic" and deconstructive modes. In the challenge or "question" posed by that conception (get it?) we receive a glimpse of the monstrous. So, while you can't really choose Derrida over Lévi-Strauss, you can (by implicit contrast to Levi-Strauss) take full cognizance of the inevitability of each—in effect, that is, choose Derrida over Lévi-Strauss. Like the critique of Foucault, the essay is a masterpiece of one-upsmanship.)

Granted, you won't find many statements quite so direct as this in much else in the Derrida canon. It's not necessarily the wisest course to declare yourself a prophet, even if it played well at Hopkins or was the thing to do in the structuralist set circa '66. Derrida might well have regretted the romantic enthusiasm of this passage and come to decide that it reflected a naiveté (like the one he claimed to see in Foucault's *Madness and Civilization*) out of keeping with the strictures of his own thought. I don't know enough to say. But there are other statements of similar attitudes. Here, for example, is a passage from *Of Grammatology*.

> The future can only be anticipated in the form of an absolute danger. It is that which breaks absolutely with constituted normality and can only be proclaimed, presented, as a sort of monstrosity. For that future world and for that within it which will have put into question the values of sign, word, and writing, for that which guides our future anterior, there is as yet no exergue.[3]

In light of passages like these, I think it's a fair question to ask whether, even if he did rebuke the grand (almost Zarathustian) apocalypticism of SS & P, it would have been possible for Derrida to get beyond what seems the basically apocalyptic framework to his theory. Plenty of refinements and complications to that theory of course. (It really is a dizzying experience, at least for me, to look again over Derrida's work after long absence and to recognize the sheer candle power, the dazzling rhetorical display, the daunting erudition, as Scott might say, and the maddening, eelish ungraspability of so much of it. It's not that surprising that some of us were wowed.) But see if this doesn't capture one, perhaps vastly oversimplified version of the major argument:

> —The history of western metaphysics is a history of an effort, in the service of an inevitably doomed, but constantly re-erected illusion of presence, to exclude the fundamental, absolutely prior truth of writing—the truth, that is, that language is formal, conventional, iterable and thus the possession of no man.
>
> —The truth is there is no presence. Meaning is always shadowed by the inevitable meaninglessness built into language itself. Utterances are fated to escape the intentions of their speakers, etc.

> —What's more, the truth is that truth itself is a function of the gimcrack inventions (i.e., of standard language and western metaphysics: more or less the same thing) by which we conceal this reality from ourselves. "Difference, the disappearance of any originary presence, is at once the condition of possibility and the condition of impossibility of truth."[4]
>
> —Even to speak about language, or anything else, therefore is already to participate in a system that demands we obscure our awareness of language's underlying reality, while it also inevitably dooms our efforts to the failures we must nevertheless seek to repress.

This is involuted. (To be melodramatic, we might say that language is simultaneously demonic and angelic in the Derridean scheme—both the source of our illusions of meaning and the source of their bedevilment. And that combination produces all sorts of fascinatingly intricate complications.) But in fact, the fundamental scheme isn't *that* complex. Indeed, the combination of intricacy with a relatively straightforward, high intensity theory may account for a good deal of Derrida's popular success.

The more obvious point for this discussion, however, is that the argument has its own, fundamentally apocalyptic, metaphysics: 1) There is an ultimate truth. 2) It is hidden ordinarily from those who shield their eyes—is in fact incompatible with the normal structures of experience. 3) Its revelation comes only in terrible moments of annihilating, or at the least disorienting, exposure.

If I'm right to see things this way, Derrida might well have rebuked a naive kind of apocalypticism, but he couldn't have maintained his fundamental presuppositions without remaining apocalyptic nevertheless—that is, a philosopher basically oriented toward the revelation of otherworldly truths that are incompatible with and thus destructive to our current reality.

Graff cites as one of his prime exhibits *Positions*, an early book of interviews in which, as in the still earlier critique of Foucault, Derrida quite clearly says: look, there's no leaping beyond history, you can't just will your way past metaphysics, no horsemen are coming, and it doesn't even make sense to try to divide matters up cleanly so that the illusion of presence falls on one side of a divide and absence on the other. Such binary divisions are themselves the products of language and thus demonstrate their own inescapability, as well as their inevitable failure. In point of fact, the demonic always inheres in the angelic and vice versa. (Needless to say, Derrida wouldn't put things quite this way, but I think it's consistent with the argument.) To wit:

> We know what always have been the *practical* (particularly *political*) effects of *immediately* jumping *beyond* oppositions, and of protests in the simple form of *neither* this *nor* that . . . . [T]he hierarchy of dual oppositions always reestablishes itself.

So, Derrida, says: get ahold of yourself; no leaping into the ether. More particularly, before we can attend to the kind of monstrous births anticipated by SS&P, we have to engage in an "interval" of deconstructive analysis that will proceed by challenging our habit of accepting a condition in which we accept, say, the priority of speech over text, presence over absence, etc. All this deconstructive analysis, however, will be prefatory to:

> the irruptive emergence of a new 'concept,' a concept that can no longer be, and never could be, included in the previous regime. [5]

My knowledge is severely limited, but I think that this kind of move recurs regularly in Derrida. It's already anticipated in the ninja treatment he gives Lévi-Strauss. First the denial of naïve apocalypticism. Then the invocation of a sophisticated, tamped down version. (In fact, if I remember right, this is pretty directly the story told by Derrida's commentary on Kant's essay on "the apocalyptic tone in recent philosophy," which ends by invoking "an apocalypse without apocalypse, an apocalypse without vision, without truth, without revelation ... beyond good and evil.")[6] It's why there are such frequent references throughout the oeuvre to highly charged terms like trembling, trace, rupture, haunting, scar, fracture, secret, and so on. Each of those words, and many others like them, point to the thrilling divide between a this-worldly normality and an otherworldly revelation. We'll never get past that divide, of course. But it's at the point of trembling, the seam where the monstrous might appear, that all the excitement lies.

So, why should we care? As a matter of intellectual fashion, Derrida is so over. He has been for years now. (Yes, the true believers hang on, and there are still people like Adam who take a sober interest in some of Derrida's finer points, but deconstruction hasn't been cutting edge since the de Man debacle.) And, if I'm wrong and Adam's right, the apocalypticism was over even before that.

Well, I think we should care because, perhaps for understandable reasons, American intellectuals found Derrida's subtle apocalypticism quite attractive and certain aspects of it, or analogs to it, remain more or less staple features of contemporary discourse in the literary academy. I've run out steam, so I'm going to pause now and pick up this discussion in a subsequent post. But, here's a lame attempt at a cliffhanger.

One place I think we see the Derridean apocalypse alive and well—mutated and grafted with other influences, yes, but still recognizably there—is in the writing of Judith Butler. Butler's own devotion to the theory leads her to devise an argument which takes her to a position that comes quite close to saying, in effect, Rosa Parks was psychotic.[7] I find this quite an unappealing view myself, but also an illuminating one. A theory that leads you to that position, or one even near it, is not a good theory. Butler would in all likelihood both have a defense of her view and an account of why my understanding of is wrong. I think I can imagine how that defense would go and will try to explain in a follow-up why the argument remains misguided and of questionable coherence. More to come.

*Yes, I do know that poststructuralism is an American neologism and would make little sense in a French context. It does serve a useful purpose on these shores, though.

Originally posted on August 05, 2005

NOTES

1 Steven Helmling, "Historicizing Derrida," *Postmodern Culture*, 4.3 (May, 1994), http://www3.iath.virginia.edu/pmc/text-only/issue.594/helmling.594

2 Jacques Derrida, *Writing and Difference*, trans. Alan Bass (Chicago: Univ.

of Chicago Press, 1978), 292-93.

3 Jacques Derrida, *Of Grammatology* , trans. Gayatri Chakravorty Spivak (Baltimore: Johns Hopkins Univ. Press, 1976), 4-5

4 Jacques Derrida, *Dissemination*, trans. Barbara Johnson (Chicago: University of Chicago Press, 1981), 168,

5 Jacques Derrida, *Positions*, trans. Alan Bass (Chicago: Univ. of Chicago Press, 1981), 41-42, emphasis in original.

6 Jacques Derrida, "Of an Apocalyptic Tone Newly Adopted in Philosophy," D*errida and Negative Theology*, Eds. Harold Coward and Toby Foshay (Albany, NY: SUNY Press, 1992), 25-71.

7 In her *Excitable Speech: A Politics of the Performative* (New York: Routledge, 1997), Butler draws on Derrida (and others) to explain why conventional liberal complaints against censorship are too narrow:

> "The question is not what it is I will be able to say, but what will constitute the domain of the sayable. . . . [T]he question is not whether certain kinds of speech uttered by a subject are censored, but how a certain operation of censorship determines who will be a subject depending on whether the speech of such a candidate for subjecthood obeys certain norms governing what is speakable and what is not. *To move outside the domain of the speakability is to risk one's status as a subject. To embody the norms that govern speakability is one's speech is to consummate one's status as a subject of speech.* 'Impossible speech' would be precisely the ramblings of the asocial, the rantings of the 'psychotic' that the rules that govern the domain of speakability produce, and by which they are continually haunted" (133, emphasis in original).

Butler then draws on a mélange of J. L. Austin and Pierre Bourdieu to expand this account to virtually all kinds of social action, which in this view are governed by the same Derridean logic: normative subjects are distinguished from psychotic outsiders by their willingness and ability to reiterate conventional expressions. Like Derrida, in short, but still more strongly so, Butler elides the grammatical conditions of acceptable sentences *tout court* with the social and ethical restraints of particular historical communities so that unconventional social behavior appears to have the same status as ungrammatical utterances. (This picture is appropriately generalized by the combination of Austin with Bourdieu, a mixture that enables Butler to expand Austin's narrow definition of the performative to include all speech. For Butler, there is no point to distinguishing between performatives and other types of speech acts, since all "cultural practice" is "reiterative ritual" [123]). Butler draws further on Derrida to emphasize that non-normative speech or behavior is not merely an aberration, but integral to the structure of language itself. Thus,

> "The possibility of a resignification of . . . ritual is based on the prior possibility that a formula can break with its originary context, assuming meanings and functions form which it was never intended. By understanding the false or wrong invocations as *reiterations*, we see how the form of social institutions undergoes change and alteration and how an invocation that has no prior legitimacy can have the effect of challenging existing forms of legitimacy. When Rosa Parks sat in the front of the bus, she had no prior right to do so guaranteed by any of the segregationist conventions of the South. And yet in laying claim to the right for which she had no *prior* authorization, she endowed a certain authority on the act, and began the insurrectionary process of overthrowing those established codes of legitimacy" (147, emphasis in original).

From this perspective, then, Parks's non-legitimate action has the same status as the "ramblings of the asocial." It is the kind of non-normative action that exceeds "the domain of speakability," but whose possibility is created by the conditions of reiteration that are fundamental to speech and social action themselves. Among the other qualities highlighted by this striking parallel is precisely the apocalyptic tone of Butler's Derridean social theory, such that all "change and alteration" of "social institutions" must seem insurrectionary and an unprecedented break with the normative (i.e., without "prior right"). What this narrow (and necessarily intensely individualistic) view obscures, of course, is the extent to which Parks acted not as an individual subversive, but as a member of rich political and social communities, and the degree to which she and her associates were able to draw on a number of principles of "prior authorization" that ran counter to the norms of "the segregationist conventions of the South." From the Derridean perspective, valuable social change comes from the asocial ramblings of individualists rather than from considered, coordinated, and justified social action.

31. What's so Scary About Theory?

Jodi Dean

Matt Christie and Mark Kaplan have picked up a discussion of 'theory' that has been circulating over the past month or so. Both rightly take issue with the reductions (the elimination of an object, say—theory of what??—and the application of the term to particular thinkers thinking since 1965) necessarily part of the operation of the anti-theory polemic. Other than their posts, I haven't paid close attention to the blog discussion, although I have talked about *Theory's Empire* and the discussion around it with academic friends. From my vantage point as a political theorist in a political science department (as opposed to a scholar working in literature and the humanities), what appears to me as the reductive thinking about theory seems the result of displacing real anxieties over the academic job market onto a fantasied image of their cause (Theory!) and a recoding of tired critiques of so-called 'postmodernism' into the popular (and faux populist/read 'nationalist') terms of today's anti-intellectualism.

First, the academic job market is miserable. Over half of all Ph.Ds will not secure work in higher education. Over half of those who do, will not occupy a tenurable position. Graduate students, adjuncts, those of us low on the food chain will understandably be resentful and angry. Combine this economic insecurity with the generalized debasement and insecurity of academic life, and you have a seething cauldron of anger. Graduate school is a weird kind of hell: one feels stupid but has to present oneself as smart. Having an idea, saying something new, trying to think in different ways—all this is immeasurably difficult. One's very self seems at stake, and so easily shattered. No wonder that thinkers whose language challenges us, whose concepts are like nothing we've ever encountered, will be held up for particular vilification. It makes sense, then, that anger at the advisors and gatekeepers who think they are so smart when they say things the rest of us don't understand would take the typical form of debunking, exposure, saying the emperor has no clothes. That is much, much easier than learning the material (15 books by Žižek alone sit on a nearby table taunting me) and formulating a specific, engaged critique.

Similarly, trashing and overcoming those who have come before is a time honored intellectual tradition, the very mode of being of the academy. One of the ways many of us work is through critique and extension, identifying problems and trying to think about them and potentially even solve them in new ways. But this is not a matter specific to theory. And it is really not a matter specific to the French and French-influenced thinkers whose names are so readily and suspiciously easily inserted into attacks on theory. Within academic political theory, for example, volumes of lame scholarship has been produced on Rawls and liberalism. The liberal-communitarian debate dominated political theory for most of the 80s and 90s. Not surprisingly, it became boring, tedious, repetitive, uninteresting. Not surprisingly, graduate students became angry, resentful, tired of the way that this debate and the thinkers associated with it (Nozick, Sandel, Tayloy, Macintyre, Ackerman. Dworkin, Okin) seemed to hold the keys to entry into jobs and journals.

Now, to my second point on contemporary anti-intellectualism. Many on the left are tired and frustrated—our concepts seem trapped, perhaps even stagnant. Those few who are really beginning to think something new (Agamben, Ranciere, Badiou, Žižek, even Hardt and Negri) are difficult and much of their work is so out of tune with the dominant mind set (which is what makes them challenging) that its seems impossible, fanciful.

(I say this in part out of my own current frustration: I am desperately trying to present Žižek's account of enjoyment as a political concept in a clear, systematic way. Lately, I've been suffocating under the anxiety that there might not be anything there, that it isn't my failure but his. Then, little glimmers, little steps seems possible, so I keep going. No going back to Rawls, or in my case, Habermas, at this point. And, the case of Habermas is actually really interesting because for most of the 70s and 80s, Habermas was thrown in there with the 'hard' thinkers, as just another member of the Frankfurt school; these days, with the rapprochement between the liberals and the Habermasians via the categories of discourse and deliberative democracy (not to mention the notion of the public sphere from his early work), Habermas is positively mainstream, conventional, not really 'theory'.)

Anyway, I digress, back to anti-intellectualism: these days, there doesn't seem to be a lot of energy in left thought. The real energy, and power, comes from the Right. The Right seems to promise a kind of false courage—go against the academic grain! show who has the power! stand up to your masters! The Right promises a transgressive thrill of racism, sexism, nationalism: enjoy excluding! enjoy 'returning' to the true values, the true text, before it was corrupted by all these women and ethnically identified or figured people, when it was really English and American literature. Cut through the crap and speak authentically! It reminds me of growing up Southern Baptist: all you needed to preach the Gospel was the power of the Holy Spirit. Far from radical, this anti-theory mentality reiterates the dominate culture.

Originally posted on August 6, 2005

32. Prosthetic Thoughts ☙

Mark Kaplan

Whilst we're on the subject of Theory, I'd like to ask you about the curious locution 'doing theory'. It is as if thinking were replaced by 'doing thought'. Was George Lukacs 'doing theory' when he wrote *Theory of the Novel*? Is Adorno's "Lyric Poetry and Society" an instance of 'doing theory'? The answer is no, they were thinking in as rigorous and critical a way as possible, using the conceptual resources at their disposal, within the tradition in which they had been trained—i.e. Marxism and dialectical thought, now deeply ingrained in their sensibilities.

'Doing theory' on the other hand makes theory sound like a professional specialization, some kind of technical skill, perhaps, to be used at work, but basically optional and detachable from your personality. Thus whereas Adorno or Lukacs were engaged in an activity that was so intimate to them as to be, so to speak, inoperable, the 'theory' of 'doing theory' is more a prosthetic device, or a series thereof—A Deleuzian hand, a Foucauldian eye, a false Žižekian-beard.

Perhaps in some quarters this is indeed what thought has become, professionalized and prostheticised; something to be left on the desk on the way out of the office. And this through prudence, since to really live (& really to think) these ideas might be to change your life or, at least, render your existing situation unsustainable. But if this is the case, then what we need to be looking at are the economic and institutional factors responsible for this. Instead, what can happen is that the ideas themselves receive the criticism which should be directed at the institution that has distorted and reified them.

This, at any rate, was my first thought on the phrase. Second: 'Doing theory': the other thing about this is its intransitivity. To talk about 'doing theory' sounds like 'watching television', i.e., you're no longer watching a particular program; it's the activity itself which is now an object of enjoyment. Now here we are touching, I think, on how Theory is seen. Theory has become its own object, its practitioners caught in some kind of self-referential enjoyment. Theory simply loops back into and feeds itself, self-grounding and self-perpetuating with no social issue. Now while this may contain truth, we may at the same time be dealing with a version of that long-standing suspicion of theory as non-instrumental thought, as irresponsible, playful, insufficiently plugged in to social and economic reproduction.

Originally posted on August 7, 2005

33. Breaking News ❧

Mark Kaplan

THE THEORY MONSTER HAS ESCAPED

Its appearances mutate, it is amorphous yet threatening, its names are many. It sprouts a sinister Marxist head here, a sly post-modern smirk there, all the time waving an indignant Feminist finger at us and at itself. No sooner has it begun speaking the austere language of 'structures' than it is rejoicing in pre-rational intensities and bodily fluid. It is fatally attracted to systems and totalities yet does nothing more than cobble together half-assimilated ideas from miscellaneous sources. Here it's over-subjective, conflating meaning with reader-response; here it's reducing a text to a mere illustration of objective forces. Over lunch it celebrates the text's endless indeterminacy, by dinner it's imposing on it an alien, fixed meaning. When and where it was born remain uncertain, but it is certainly a mutant offspring, buggered into existence by the indiscriminate coupling of incompatible notions. Schools breed and multiply within it, and yet it remains One. Its poker-faced PC solemnity is forbidding, yet it is also a frivolous *homo ludens*, taking nothing seriously, forever playing and punning and putting the world in brackets. The rhetoric of hegemony and power pours from its mouth, but *jouissance* leaks from its arse. It is irrational, even as—and just because—it introduces into Literature the cold acids of conceptual thought and interpretation; it hates literature and is blind to literariness yet adopts a grotesque parody of literary style. It speaks in dry and boring jargon, yet lewdly seduces the young with an inexplicable sex-appeal. It is costive and hermetic and yet obsessed with changing the world. It is merely fashionable (and has been now for some thirty-odd years), yet stubborn or obtuse enough to survive its several publicized and prophesied deaths.

The Theory monster must be caught and grappled with. Reward: A prestigious academic career.

Originally posted on August 8, 2005

34. The Para-Costives ❧

Mark Kaplan

SUPPOSE WE invent a collective name for those people not 'doing theory' in Literature departments. Suppose we call them the Para-Costives. Yes, it's an arbitrary and possibly misleading name. We say: the name 'Para-Costives' refers to a cluster of related approaches to literature and other texts. And let us discuss the merits and demerits of Para-costive criticism. Let us say that Para-Costive criticism suffers from a lack of coherence and has failed to theorise it's assumptions adequately. We point out various contradictory Para-Costive claims, the inexplicable gaps in its canon of criticism. But wait. Let those impugned or hailed by the label Para-Costive rally together in self-defence. Let them, in so doing, discover things about what their methods have in common – analogies, themes, and shared assumptions. And so let them start saying things like 'Which way forward for the Para-Costives?', and editing new anthologies with titles like "The New Para-Costives". And eventually, as they become older and self-reflexive, conferences will spring up on "What is Para-Costivism?" Let them break away and form their own sub-department, with its own canon and terms of reference. They compile anthologies of Para-Costive criticism. And their enemies, who have lost much ground, will compile a counter-anthology; its cover shows a man shovelling horse dung and it is entitled 'Symbolic Ordure: Cleaning out the Para-Costives.'

Originally posted on August 12, 2005

35. Against My Better Judgment

Adam Kotsko

I haven't read all the comments ON THIS THREAD, but at the risk of repeating: if the anti-Theory crowd were to take John's advice and take on the best and most rigorous examples of theory, then there would be no grounds for dismissing the movement as such. Not everyone is going to like their style or agree with their arguments, but I would argue that a fair assessment would indeed conclude that Paul de Man, Jonathan Culler, Hillis Miller, Frederic Jameson, Judith Butler, Stanley Fish, Slavoj Žižek, etc., are "the real thing." It's not just for show—they are really developing real ideas, and simply dismissing them out of hand is a mistake. This is not to say that they are inevitable or that everyone will find their ideas useful or that it is morally wrong not to read these authors—just to say that people who value these thinkers are not *prima facie* trend-sucking dilettantes.

The problem, however, is that certain permutations of the anti-Theory argument address not "Theory" as such, but certain instinctive moves through which literary scholars produce tedious, bad impersonations of such scholars. Though particular Theorists may be objectionable, the real problem is the institutionalization of stylistic and argumentative moves that not everyone can really pull off. Thus, a certain glut of unreadable prose is produced. That's regrettable. It might be better if people were more inclined to write straightforward expository prose in most situations, simply trying to elucidate a piece of writing (or other cultural artifact). I would say that, by and large, that is actually what most literary scholars do, in my admittedly limited experience. *Modern Fiction Studies*, for instance, does not strike me as a journal that is glutted with Theory—the bulk of the essays are examples of straightforward literary criticism. (I could name other examples, but it's frankly been a while since I needed to draw upon lit journals.)

This is a point that Chun repeatedly made back when he was with us: the Theory-whores actually are not representative of the discipline as a whole. The "hottest" (i.e., hegemonic) work may still be Theory-based, and certainly there is now an expectation that any English program will deal with Theory (since it's, you know, part of the history of the discipline at this point)—but the kind of workaday literary criticism that John Holbo wants to see really does continue to go on. And although I'm not keeping up with the literature anymore, I'd be willing to be that English departments are still going to produce figures of the stature of a Jameson or Fish.

POSTSCRIPT:

I'd just like to note, in closing, that people generally seem to me to misunderstand the term "hegemonic." They seem to take it as meaning "dominant" in some straightforward way, when in fact, the entire point of the concept of "hegemony" is that one exercises power to a degree that is disproportionate to one's means. Thus, the United States is a "global hegemon" precisely insofar as it does not directly rule the world. Arguably, then, the way to deal with a hegemonic power is not to allow it to control the terms of the debate—hegemons thrive on attention!

So maybe the *Counter-Anthology of Good Literary Criticism* would be a better idea than, say, *Theory's Empire*.

Originally posted on August 13, 2005

36. On Theory and its Empire, 2: The Politics of Capitalization

Kenneth Rufo

Editor's note: inclusion of this post, without context, needs brief explanation: I wrote "YOU MUST TRY AGAIN TILL YOU GET IT RIGHT"*—which, on reflection, was not one bit righter than "Making Sense of The Theme", so I omitted it when the time came to make book. In it I linked, in passing, to* A POST BY JODI DEAN, *declaring that* A POST *by Ken Rufo, "clearly sets out the stakes of current discussion around theory." The key passage from Ken's post read as follows: "In a handful of years, colleges will be flush with undergraduates who have had even more limited exposure to critical thought. And yet, this is what theory does best, providing models for just the sort of critical thought sorely lacking in students already … With this situation in mind, there has never been more of a time to celebrate theory, to teach theory, to encourage philosophy and abstraction and practices that need not be tethered to some measure of their practicality. This isn't the time to celebrate theory's end; rather this is the time to work strenuously for its resurrection, or to sit down for a seance with the theory version of the Goddess. It is no coincidence that Derrida spent so much of his career working in GREPH to advance the high school curriculum by promoting a 'right to philosophy,' which in the context of the discussion of Theory's Empire might as well be renamed the "right to theory."*

I responded that this was 'just plain wrong', for reasons laid out in "Making Sense of the Theme", whose thesis is that really the one thing one absolutely must NOT do, on pain of failing to understand the stakes in the debate, is equate 'theory'—in the sense in which it is debated in books like Theory's Empire—with 'theory' in some more generic 'critical thinking' sense. Ken and I went at it in comments, it can't be denied. But I am pleased to report a more cordial correspondence eventually evolved out of all that. At any rate, what follows is Ken's response to my response to his post. It has an inclusion-worthy stand-alone quality (once one knows the backstory). And Ken has written a fresh postscript, containing second-thoughts.

Speaking of "the maelstrom that is The Valve," I got sucked in more than I expected recently, after John Holbo decided that my previous post was, shall we say, PLAIN WRONG. John seemed to take objection to the idea that "theory" provides a valuable bulwark against the empiricism and data-heavy model of education offered under No Child Left Behind. Seemed to, but he didn't really. His actual objection was to "Theory," a capitalized and more delimited version of theory, that is miraculously both very dangerous and very ineffectual at the same time.

I don't need to spend too much time on this, as my inclusion in the debate was for straw-person purposes only, and my responses to my inclusion are already available in the Valve's comments. But I do want to stress an argument I made there: the real political stakes have nothing to do with capitalized "Theory's" success or lack thereof; rather, they have everything to do with the authority and mechanisms by which Theory is homogenized and defined as something distinct from theory itself.

As a lower-case concept, theory is simply the name we assign to the practice of reflecting on our own practices, be they writing, or reading, or watching, or playing, or whatever. To write of a need for a definition, to proffer that definition, and then to castigate the object that you yourself have defined is precisely the sort of theoretical maneuver that should be subject to rigorous questioning. To dismiss the need for a definition, to negate or devalue some extant definitional claim, or to malign those that would attempt otherwise - these moves also demand interrogation. What makes theory so important, so essential, to pedagogy and to politics is precisely that it refuses to accept as a given the sorts of practices that obtain in everyday life. In so doing, theoretical investigation forces us to move, even if only to reaffirm our beliefs, rather than letting us sediment and presume the existence of fact when all we have is facticity.

Now, can theory be reified as something like an aggregate or a subject in ways that are maladaptive to the contexts in which theory is needed? Absolutely. But no one who does "theory" worth their salt would ever speak of "Theory" in this way, and so to read Holbo's constant anti-Theory rallying cry as a proactive defense against the imposition of oh-so tyrannical "Theory" is laughable, since he is himself producing the very gesture he finds so problematic. Instead, let us simply note, as Michael Bérubé did about Ward Churchill, that we can agree that we all have the ability to write and read what we want, just as we have the ability to dismiss what is written and read as being not worthy of our intellectual affirmation.

Originally posted on August 14, 2005

POSTSCRIPT (February, 2007):

Looking back over the debate generated by the Valve's reception of *Theory's Empire*, and doing so as a participant in subsequent debates that have followed similar trajectories, I think there might be—today—more common ground that there was over a year ago. Like it or not, the influx of (predominantly) French theory into the American academy carried with it a lot of unfortunate baggage and resulted in some rather glaringly missed opportunities. Not surprisingly, much of the scholarship that was produced along the lines of "theory" was, in a word, poor. Poor in quality, poor in insights, poor in spirit.

But it is a mistake, I think, to continue to locate the standards and histories by which the prolonged advent of theory can be known in a collection of the worst practices. That so-called theory had produced much posturing, and much confusion, goes without saying. It should be equally obvious that it has also contributed a great deal to thinking, pedagogy, and practice. At its best, the sorts of thoughts being grappled with under the rubric of theory force us to be more attentive to that wondrous capacity we have to see meaning, in what we or others say or write or do. To see, to theorize, to learn—I continued to believe that theorizing offers much, and costs us little; annoyance has rarely been reason for outright castigation.

That being said, if those concerned with the rise of Theory—and here that capital T denotes an institutional history of theoretical reception and promulgation, most typically in Anglo-based literature departments—want to continue to throw Theory from its pedestal, and to beat it while it scrambles along the ground, then in all seriousness, more power to them. Far be it from me, as a speech-communication trained rhetorician, to dip my toe into the rapids of another discipline's boundary work. And I would never suggest that efforts to offer the sort of disciplinary history that Holbo and others have offered lacks merit. Where I hesitate, and where the merit ends and my suspicion begins, is when that disciplinary history then provides the grounds by which to judge the reception of all that augurs under the name of 'theory' in other disciplines, all of which have their own agendas, grounds, and distinct histories. Theory with a capital-T is a particular and contingent phenomenon, and if there is anything like theory with a lower-case-t, then it is simply the attempt to think that which remains elusive to thought, and that in so doing, provides much of the motivation for thinking in the first place.

37. Conceptualization and Its Vague Contents ❧

John Holbo

A passage from John Searle, "Literary Theory and Its Discontents", in *Theory's Empire* (147-8):

> In a review of Jonathan Culler's book *On Deconstruction* (1982) that I wrote for the *New York Review of Books*, I pointed out that it is not necessarily an objection to a conceptual analysis, or to a distinction, that there are no rigorous or precise boundaries to the concept analyzed or the distinction begin drawn. It is not necessarily an objection even to theoretical concepts that they admit of application more or less. This is something of a cliché in analytic philosophy: most concepts and distinctions are rough at the edges and do not have sharp boundaries. The distinctions between fat and thin, rich and poor, democracy and authoritarianism, for example, do not have sharp boundaries. More important for our present discussion, the distinction between literal and metaphorical, serious and nonserious, fiction and nonfiction, and yes, even true and false, admit of degrees and all apply more or less. It is, in short, generally accepted that many, perhaps most, concepts do not have sharp boundaries, and since 1953, we have begun to develop theories to explain why they cannot. Indeed, in addition to examinations of the problem of vagueness, there have been quite extensive discussions of family resemblance, open texture, underdetermination, and indeterminacy. There has even developed a booming industry of fuzzy logic whose aim is to give a precise logic of vagueness.

When I pointed out that Derrida seemed to be unaware of these well-known facts, and that he seemed to be making the mistaken assumption that unless a distinction can be made rigorous and precise, with no marginal cases, it is not a distinction at all, he responded as follows: "Among all the accusations that shocked me coming from his pen, and which I will not even try to enumerate, why is it that this one is without doubt the most stupefying, the most unbelievable? And, I must confess, also the most incomprehensible to me." He goes on to expound his stupefaction further:

> What philosopher ever since there were philosophers, what logician ever since there were logicians, what theoretician ever renounced this axiom: in the order of concepts (for we are speaking of concepts and not of the colors of clouds or the taste of certain chewing gums), when a distinction cannot be rigorous or precise, it is not a distinction at all. If Searle declares explicitly, seriously, literally that this axiom must be renounced, that he renounces it (and I will wait for him to do it, a phrase in a newspaper is not enough), then, short of practicing deconstruction with some consistency and submitting the very rules and regulations of his project to an explicit reworking, his entire philosophical discourse on speech act will collapse even more rapidly. (123-3)[1]

Searle goes on to point out that it is impossible for him to renounce something he does not, has never, believed. Which is surely fair enough. Searle quotes another bit from *Limited Inc*: "I confirm it: for me, from the point of view of theory and of the concept, 'unless a distinction can be made rigorous and precise it isn't really a distinction.' Searle is entirely right, for once, in attributing this 'assumption' to me" (126). And: "I feel close to those who share it. I am sufficiently optimistic to believe that they are quite numerous and are not limited, as Searle declares, with rather uncommon condescension, to 'audiences of literary critics' before whom he has 'lectured'" (126). Searle concludes:

> It is clear from this discussion that Derrida has a conception of "concepts" according to which they have a crystalline purity that would exclude all marginal cases. It is also clear that on his view intentional states also have this feature, and they even have what he calls "ideal self-presence". (148)

Searle's foot definitely slips here. Derrida obviously does not *rest* with such a crystalline conception of concepts. The whole point is to *deconstruct* such stuff. But this slippage is easily repaired: it seems entirely correct to object to Derrida that the fluid dynamics of the deconstructive method or process (characterize it how you like) requires this starting point Searle is—quite rightly—too canny to concede. Searle's perfectly reasonable stance is a frustration to Derrida's dramatic ambitions. Let me illustrate this thought with a passage from J. Hillis Miller's 1976 essay, "Stevens' rock and criticism as cure, II":

> Already a clear distinction can be drawn, among critics influenced by these new developments, between what might be called ... Socratic, theoretical, or canny critics, on the one hand, and Apollonian/Dionysian, tragic, or uncanny critics, on the other. Socratic critics are those who are lulled by the promise of a rational ordering of literary study on the basis of solid advances in scientific knowledge about language. They are likely to speak of themselves as "scientists" and to group their collective enterprise under some term like "the human sciences" ... Such an enterprise is represented by the discipline called "semiotics," or by new work in the exploration and exploitation of rhetorical terms. Included would be aspects of the work of Gerard Genette, Roland Barthes, and Roman Jakobson ...
>
> For the most part these critics share the Socratic penchant, what Nietzsche defined as "the unshakable faith that thought, using the thread of logic, can pen-

> etrate the deepest abysses of being." ... The inheritors today of the Socratic faith would believe in the possibility of a structuralist-inspired criticism as a rational and rationalizable activity, with agreed-upon rules of procedure, given facts, and measurable results. This would be a discipline bringing literature out into the sunlight in a "happy positivism." ... Opposed to these are the critics who might be called "uncanny." Though they have been inspired by the same climate of thought as the Socratic critics and though their work would also be impossible without modern linguistics, the "feel" or atmosphere of their writing is quite different ... These critics are not tragic of Dionysian in the sense that their work is wildly orgiastic or irrational. No critic could be more rigorously sane and rational, Apollonian in his procedure, for example, than Paul de Man. One feature of Derrida's criticism is a patient and minutely philological "explication de texte." Nevertheless, the thread of logic leads in both cases into regions which are alogical, absurd ... Sooner or later there is the encounter with an "aporia" or impasse ... In fact the moment when logic fails in their work is the moment of their deepest penetration into the actual nature of literary language, or of language as such.[2]

What is happening in Derrida's encounter with Searle is, basically, refusal by the latter to read his lines from a rather Romantic—indeed, melodramatic—script Derrida is insistently pressing into his hands. Searle has been cast in the role of apparently sturdy, canny, happy positivist 'hail well met' Socratic man on the street, in the very heart of whose unshakable faith that thought (etc. etc.) shall open up the uncanny (etc. etc.) abysses (etc. etc.). Derrida himself is supposed to play at 'more reasonable than reason': that is, it is *only* by thinking *through* the rationalist position that we will deconstruct it. Dramatically, this set-up is promising. But, philosophically, it is sheer artificiality and staginess. What Searle's objections bring out, I think, is how what Hillis Miller thinks of as 'rigor' is really more commonly referred to as *rigging*. (This isn't what Searle *says*, obviously. I'm correcting him as to the proper conclusions to draw from Derrida's refusal to consider well-known possibilities, like vague concepts.)

The philosophic weakness of Derrida's dramatic impulse to see the metaphysical melodrama play out in the way Hillis Miller describes is that the players may choose not to play. To put it another way, there is a hazardous ambiguity in the notion that it is precisely the most rational position that reveals itself as irrational. Because it is hardly surprising that the most rational*istic* position will be irrational, i.e. imply contradictions. Because philosophical Rationalism—the doctrine that reason itself can give you all the answers—is an extreme and problematic view. The default rational expectation should be that pure Rationalism (System, certainty, self-presence) will produce contradictions because it's probably *wrong*. Simply put, it is not generally a good idea to assume that, to deconstruct a position, you need only deconstruct the *strongest* formulation of that position. Nuanced, qualified positions—i.e. *weaker* claims—are typically stronger, from the point of view of philosophic *defense*.

And so we end up with a sort of socratic counter-drama in which complacent uncanniness, lulled by the promise of impossibility of rational order, has its unshakeable faith in the shakeability of all canny faiths shaken by the rather uncanny inversion of Derridean uncanniness into a sort of elementary Wittgensteinian canniness, eerily immune to Derridean attack. Except Searle didn't play it quite that way, more's the pity. He just took a swipe.

So my question for you is this: is this fair? Or at least: is it fair to point out that Derrida needs an adversary to play against, and he needs his adversary *not* to play Searle's game? What Searle is pointing out, before he slips up in describing Derrida's position, is a problem for Derrida's procedure? Because allowing vague concepts—being healthily skeptical about dubious binaries and anything as extreme as a 'metaphysics of presence'—prevents the deconstructive game from getting underway? And there is really nothing wrong with this? (As to the plausibility of my counter-drama—I'm willing to waive any actual staging, if the philosophic point is granted. There's no accounting for taste.)

Originally posted on April 06, 2006

NOTES

1 Quotes are from Jacques Derrida, "Afterword: Toward an Ethic of Discussion," in *Limited Inc* (Evanston: Northwestern UP, 1988).

2 J. Hillis Miller, "Stevens Rock and Criticism as Cure, II," in *Theory, Now and Then* (Durham: Duke UP, 1991), pp. 121-2.

38. Nussbaum v. Butler, Round One

John McGowan

"The Professor of Parody",[1] Martha Nussbaum's essay on Judith Butler, captures rather perfectly why my usual response to assertions and counter-assertions in the theory wars is "a plague on both your houses." I'm mostly on Nussbaum's side substantively, but think she makes her argument in an incredibly unhelpful way. (Most important, I think, is Nussbaum's complaint that Butler avoids articulating the norms that underwrite her use of charged terms like "oppressive" and "injurious," and thus also avoids being specific about what political action should or might be aiming for. Vague, *ad hoc*, individualistic, and improvised resistance is Butler's substitute for any concerted or collective action that tries to change laws, institutions, practices, received beliefs, social hierarchies, or the distribution of material resources.)

In what, after all, is an intramural debate among writers and readers who are all sympathetic to feminist aims and who, more generally, are all left of center, Nussbaum cannot find it in herself to search for plausible reasons why Butler takes the positions she does or for why so many readers have found them convincing and attractive. Butler's followers just want a feminism that "is in many ways easier than the old feminism"(Nussbaum, Section VI) and choose to follow the "adversarial traditions of sophistry and rhetoric," spurning philosophy's commitment to "a discourse of equals who trade arguments and counter-arguments without any obscurantist sleight-of-hand" (Nussbaum, Section II). That's the best Nussbaum can do: laziness and intellectual dishonesty are the motives driving Butler and those who admire her work.

Barbara Herrnstein Smith, in her book *Belief and Resistance* (1997), offers something she calls the principle of symmetry. (She has derived this notion from the Edinburgh sociologists of knowledge, notably David Bloor and Barry Barnes.) The basic idea is very simple: when interpreting or evaluating any statement or any set of beliefs, I should begin from the premise that those who make that statement or hold that belief aim to be—and believe themselves to be—as committed to saying and believing what is reasonable and true as I am. The default position should not be that they are insincere, or that they have chosen to be sophists not philosophers, or that they don't want to believe what is true. I should instead assume their symmetry with me. If I am to question their sincerity or their intellectual honesty, I need to offer a plausible account of how they went wrong or why (what reasons they have) for being deceitful. We might also call this a principle of charity—and connect it to Donald Davidson's speculations about how we ever manage to make any sense of beliefs that are foreign, baffling, and even repugnant to ourselves.

Nussbaum's lack of charity means that she can only impute the worst motives to Butler—and to anyone inclined to view Butler's work positively. Butler wants the kind of fame and authority that comes from oracular charisma and obscurantist prose. Butler's readers want to indulge their American narcissism, "cultivating the self rather than thinking in a way that helps the material condition of others"(remember this line from Section VI because I want to come back to it in Part 2 on Sunday.) And both Butler and her admiring readers are borderline (at least) sexual perverts who sado-masochistically eroticize their relation to the powers that oppress them. Narcissistic sado-masochistic rhetoricians who can't write their way out of a paper bag. Ouch.

What would a more charitable reading of Butler offer in place of these nefarious motives? I think Nussbaum fails to recognize the power and appeal of psychoanalysis—and the fact that the Freudian perspective (filtered through Lacan) underlies Butler's whole approach to questions of sexual being and of the scene of socio-political action. (For the old-timers among you, think of Nussbaum versus Butler as a reprise of Herbert Marcuse versus Norman O. Brown.) I will admit at the outset to being as temperamentally hostile to psychoanalysis as Nussbaum—and I find it one of the great mysteries of our day why so many feminists are psychoanalytically inclined. But, probably because I come from literary studies and not from philosophy, I don't find Freudian thought just incomprehensible nonsense that only the willfully perverse could ever take seriously.

What Nussbaum misses in Butler is her Freudian mysticism. Butler takes from Foucault the notion that "identity" is as much a trap and burden as a source for the autonomous freedom with which liberalism seeks to invest each individual. And what Butler takes from Freud is the notion that prior to the formation of one's identity there is an amorphous, heterogeneous, primal chaos of unorganized feelings, impulses, and potentialities that are almost (but not quite) completely lost once "genital organization" and the "ego ideal" and "identification" with the parent of the same sex and "compulsory heterosexuality" do their work. Avoiding all the details of the Freudian narrative that describes the movement from polymorphous perversity and the undifferentiated "oceanic feeling" to an achieved identity, I suggest that Butler partakes of the romantic urge to resist the tendency of "identity" to cut off all contact with the varied contents of the unconscious. The convenient romantic name for everything that would swamp the categories and names within which the merely rational tries to confine the contents of the universe is "the sublime."

Butler's work, then, is trying to indicate how "the sublime" (lodged, for her, primarily in the Freudian unconscious) exceeds our given categories—categories like "male" and "female," or "heterosexual" and "homosexual." Identities, she insists, always impose a false coherence on a bodily and emotional reality that is heterogeneous. And her focus on parody reflects her attempt to think about techniques by which we can gain access to or provide expression for the repressed sublime, for exactly the stuff that reason, non-contradiction, and the clear use of standard vocabularies renders inexpressible. (Think of Freud on jokes.)

She also takes from Freudian thought a deep ambivalence toward the unconscious. Powerful forces of repression create the unconscious and keep its contents hidden; yet complete and utter repression is as impossible as no repression at all. Some return of the repressed will always happen, but Butler accepts Freud's conviction that a complete end to repression is neither desirable nor possible. Hence the tragic (or fatalistic) outlook that upsets Nussbaum so. In Butler's universe, we deeply desire the unconscious; we have intimations that the organized world and identities that repression builds for us are missing something vital; but we cannot simply embrace the unconscious. That way, quite literally, lies madness. We are caught between the rock of identity and the hard place of psychosis.

Given such a tragic view, it is hard to see how Butler could develop a hopeful politics. But she is in a position to rail against the rigid strictures of a repressive society. (Again, the parallel with Freud is exact.) No good can come, both she and Freud would argue, from trying to push all sexual desire into overly narrow channels. The chances for success are slim, and the costs of that forcing on psychic health are very high. Butler's politics, like Freud's, are necessarily therapeutic. The focus is on making individual lives easier to live and bear (which, I take it, accurately characterizes Nussbaum's aims as well. The difference comes in the means chosen—and in the diagnosis of what is causing the patient pain.) Social transformation in Butler as in Freud would be aimed at relaxing the rigidity of approved identity categories, in reducing guilt and anxiety.

As I have said, I'm with Nussbaum in finding the psychoanalytic focus both too individualistic and too fatalistic. But I think Nussbaum misses the fact that individuality has its strong discontents and the fact that some people have strong intimations of a trans-individual sublime to which they are attracted and into which they would like to submerge that burdensome self. Not just religion, but also much of the literature of the past two hundred years, witnesses to this recurrent longing. To rule such longings out of court as so much romantic, irrational nonsense is neither going to banish them from the earth or advance our ability to produce a better society. It is not even obviously true that a concern with adjusting one's individual relations with what one takes to be the wider forces at play in the universe is a luxury only the relatively well-off can afford. Plenty of extremely poor people put a lot of energy into and place a very high priority on their religious practices and beliefs. Nussbaum's self-congratulatory insistence that her brand of feminism deals with "material" necessities and "real" problems (as contrasted to the way Butler's feminism "complete[ly] turn[s] from the material side of life," providing "only the flimsiest of connections with the real situation of real women" [Section I]) is unrealistic in its narrowing of human concerns and commitments. If there is any empirical claim we can safely make about humans, it is that material concerns are not the only things that seem "real" to them. In fact, much of the philosophical tradition that Nussbaum claims to honor is devoted to explaining why material things are less real than other components of the universe.

Derrida seemed to acknowledge, in his later years, that he was a religious thinker. Freud, of course, went to his grave thinking of himself as a sworn enemy of religion even though early in his career he insisted that every dream contains a knot that resists all interpretation and late in his career he adopted the "mythology" (his term) of the two instincts, *Eros* and *Thanatos*, both of which lure the self to merger with forces beyond it. I suspect that Butler would understand the adjectives "religious" and "mystic" when applied to her thought as insults. Yet, for me, her monotheistic focus on the subject's relation "the Law" (a term and concept she takes uncritically from Lacan) as all-consuming and her corollary neglect of all inter-subjective relations in a mundane social field indicate how other-worldly her take on human existence is.

But the longing for contact with an ineffable that lies beyond the self need not take a very religious form. From Blake to the "language poets", the avant-garde has been interested in changing the terms of perception. Nussbaum simply fails to register Butler's argument about language. Butler points toward an experienced gap between the categories supplied by language and felt reality. Her work, quite simply, is for misfits, for people who have felt themselves to be square pegs that are constantly being pushed and prodded into round holes. The available categories are simply inadequate. They also carry normative force; they lay out everything that is deemed "normal." Misfits are abnormal—and subjected to a variety of practices aimed at changing them, quarantining them, or rendering them invisible. Butler's work—like "queer theory," generally—questions the legitimacy and inevitability of prevailing definitions of the normal. As such, it has proved enormously enlightening and liberating to those who suffer most from the stigma of abnormality.

Nussbaum's most egregious failure is her inability to recognize that Butler addresses a "real" source of pain felt by "real" people—and that Butler's work empowers such people by providing intellectual resources with which to cope with and respond to ungenerous norms. That failure undermines Nussbaum's taking the high ground as the one who is really attending to the needs of the oppressed. To ignore the suffering to which Butler's work is so clearly addressed, and thus to avoid considering if that work succeeds in any way to alleviate that suffering (as it clearly aims to do), is to refuse to assess the work fairly. No work—intellectual or otherwise—can set out to do everything. And we can even fault someone for taking up the wrong task, for fiddling while Rome burns. But, at least, we should correctly identify what that work sets out to do—and then explain why the worker should be doing something else or why the worker has failed at the task she has undertaken. Nussbaum misses the avant-garde aim of transforming the terms of thought and the forms of perception, and she misses the on-the-ground consequences of social categories that stigmatize.

Nussbaum clearly has no *avant-garde* intimations or yearnings toward the ineffable, so she cannot have any sympathy for a writing style that is trying to reach toward the "unthought," or the "inexpressible." Such styles are everywhere in romantic and modernist art—and they are built precisely on the premise that language is an imperfect tool, that our received vocabularies and categories are inadequate, and their inadequacy must be signaled even as we use the words we have inherited. Butler's work is perhaps best compared to Benjamin's. They are both figures who exist in some ill-defined space between avant-garde art and discursive, argumentative thought. (So here's another practice that defies easy categorization or location within neat disciplinary markers. To call Benjamin and Butler literary critics seems pretty lame, but they aren't quite philosophers or political theorists either. We end up with catch-all terms like "intellectual" or "man [sic] of letters" or "social critic." And I suggest that we see their obscurities as less a product of being "over-academic" and more akin to the obscurities of Mallarmé, Joyce, and Pound.)

Trying to push thought beyond received categories is frustrating—and certainly courts failure and incomprehension. But that doesn't justify rapid recuperation of *avant-garde* work back into received notions and terms. Nussbaum keeps assuring us that various things Butler has to say aren't at all new. Apparently, Nussbaum smugly assumes that the problems feminists are addressing are obvious: some individuals are not treated equally. We're past defining the problem; we just need to focus on solutions now. So she is deeply impatient with anyone who says, "Wait a minute; I'm not sure that's really what the problem is. I'd like to consider the nature of individuality and our investments in it, because I feel a deep urge to slough off my individuality, plus I also find the range of available individual identities oppressive." For Nussbaum, that's intellectual fiddling while Rome burns.

Nussbaum's lack of an *avant-garde* sensibility is not a major failing in my opinion, although it is a symptomatic one. But her blindness to the pain caused by received categories is more troubling. Avant-garde experimentation is not just a luxury for the comfortable sons and daughters of the professional classes. Even if it is play-acting in some cases, it is liberating and ennobling work in others. Nussbaum could only be so contemptuous of Butler's work if she "didn't get" the "gender trouble" felt by those who find it very difficult to be the "girl" or the "boy" that others expect them to be. And Nussbaum's very failure to "get it" reinforces Butler's argument that the categories of thought guide perception. Nussbaum's mind-set leads her to miss something. She assumes, way too confidently, that her vision of feminism is all-encompassing, that it has listed already all the harms done to women, and now just has to attend to alleviating them. Such close-mindedness in a thinker whose work I admire suggests the better course is to try to write as if de Man was on to something when he insisted that every insight is accompanied by a corresponding blindness. We would do well to suspect that the writers who most irritate us are the ones who have the most to tell us, are the ones most likely to lead us to see our own blind spots. If that thought is too close to Freudian ways of thinking about "resistance," I do recommend Herrnstein Smith's book to your attention because it considers the dynamic interplay between our "beliefs" and how we "resist" evidence and ideas that would threaten those beliefs in an entirely non-Freudian (and hence, for me at least, more plausible) register.

Thursday, August 11, 2005

NOTES

1 Martha Nussbaum, "The Professor of Parody," *The New Republic*, 02.22 1999.

39. Nussbaum v. Butler, Round Two

John McGowan

Just to keep you on your toes, this "theory Tuesday" post comes from John, not Michael, and is the promised discussion of the relation of theory (or "thinking"—to use Nussbaum's and Hannah Arendt's term) to politics.

Near the end of her essay on Butler, Nussbaum writes that it is no surprise that Butler's "hip quietism" has "caught on here [i.e. in America], where successful middle-class people focus on cultivating the self rather than thinking in a way that helps the material condition of others" (Section VI). This charge is connected to Nussbaum's opening gambit, the claim that, "for a long time, academic feminism in America has been closely allied to the practical struggle to achieve justice and equality for women. Feminist theory has been understood by theorists as not just fancy words on paper; theory is connected to proposals for social change."

There are any number of entangled issues here. For sanity and brevity's sake, I am only going to focus on what counts as "political" and what does not. Nussbaum is obviously outraged by the fact that Butler and her readers think that her work is radical and has significant, even if not immediate, political consequences. At most, Nussbaum is willing to grant that, "in its small way, [Butler's work offers] a hopeful politics. It instructs people that they can, right now, without compromising their security, do something bold." Except that whatever "small" concession these two sentences offer is completely withdrawn in the next sentence: "But the boldness is entirely gestural, and insofar as Butler's ideal suggests that these symbolic gestures are political change, it offers only a false hope." And Nussbaum returns to her basic "get real" position: "Hungry women are not fed by this …" (Section VI, penultimate paragraph).

If our criteria for true or real politics is that the formerly hungry now get fed, what academic work will meet the test? I want to highlight just how weird Nussbaum's formula is. Truly feminist academics, she says, should be "thinking in a way that helps the material condition of others." What could that possibly mean? Even at the most concrete level—a nutritionist in a university's School of Public Health who thinks about how to improve school lunches—thinking is still at least one step away from helping the material condition of others. Thinking is not politics.

Hannah Arendt was admirably clear about this distinction, one that much current academic work seems to have abandoned in favor of some magical faith in the "omnipotence of thoughts." Arendt distinguishes sharply in *The Human Condition* between the *vita activa*, which is the very stuff of politics, and the *vita contemplativa*, which much of Western philosophy and many of the world's religions have extolled as superior to action. And she knew that her own work was about politics, but that it wasn't politics. "You know," she said in a 1972 interview, "all the modern philosophers have somewhere in their thought a rather apologetic sentence which says, 'Thinking is also acting.' Oh no, it is not! And to say that is rather dishonest. I mean, let's face the music: it is not the same! On the contrary, I have to keep back to a large extent from participating, from commitment … And I think I understood something of action precisely because I looked at it from the outside, more or less."[1]

Thinking can have political implications. But politics involves the realm of action and thoughts are not political until they are put into action. What one chooses to think about is a good indication of one's interests and commitments; that fundamental choice may be (but is not necessarily) a clue to the thinker's political beliefs and priorities. But none of that thinking is political until it undertakes to translate itself into action (with all the complications, difficulties, and frustrations that such translation always entails, not least of all because unilateral action is impossible, whereas unilateral thought is all too common.) And, finally, we should recognize that some thinking neither desires nor attempts to connect to action—and we should be happy that such is the case. Freedom from politics is as important as freedom within the political realm.

My proposal, then, is straightforward. 1) Thinking in ways to help the material conditions of others may prove useful indirectly. But there are crucial and complicated intermediary steps between the thinking and the helping. Someone who just thinks a lot about the hunger of others is not morally superior to or more politically involved than someone who thinks a lot about his red car. 2) Therefore, any thinking that is going to qualify as even potentially political needs to articulate its political implications clearly and suggest some ways to act upon those implications in the world. 3) But political action per se only begins when one leaves the library or the study. Even the rhetorical urging of others to embrace this or that political cause is preliminary to political action itself.

So: are some thoughts more useful politically than others? Undoubtedly. But it is not so easy to judge that usefulness from just hearing or reading the thoughts. Who is doing more useful work on health care at the moment? Someone who is trying to think about extending health coverage within our current system of mixed governmental and employer-provided benefits, or someone who is developing a model of a single-payer system? The second proposal may be completely unfeasible politically (i.e. within the current alignment of social forces.) So that thinker may be very far from helping anyone concretely, no matter what her intentions are. But do we really want to say that such utopian or radical thinking should be barred—or should not think of itself as having any political interest because it doesn't have any way to put its proposals into action?

There are other ways to judge usefulness and relevance besides feasibility. The range of human interests is remarkably wide, as is the range of actions taken to promote and live out those interests. Thinking and the ideas it introduces into the world play a large role in the formation and extension of that possible range. Richard Rorty has proposed that we distinguish between intellectual work that aims primarily to imagine the forms our collective life together should take (and perhaps even how to act to develop and maintain different forms) and intellectual work that has a more perfectionist slant, focusing on the forms an individual life can or should take. (He develops this distinction most fully in his book, *Contingency, Irony and Solidarity* (1989).) As with a disconcertingly large number of Rorty's ideas, my original response was vehement disagreement, only to find myself as the years roll by slowly coming to think that he was on to something important and probably even right about how to think about that something.) Rorty's distinction was introduced in part to suggest that much post-structuralist work is best understood as perfectionist. It is work that is aimed more at personal transformation than at social transformation, which accords with its *avant-garde* and Freudian heritage. Foucault's final work on "the care of the self" explicitly forefronts this focus on the person.

Butler, of course, believes her work is political because she presents the subject as formed by social processes that include an insidious, oppressive power. As I said in my last post, there seems good reason to accept Butler's insistence that certain selves suffer very real pain as a result of not fitting within certain social norms. Thus, her thinking, while not addressed to hunger, can plausibly claim to be addressed to suffering that it urges us to alleviate. Can her thinking aid in that political work of alleviation? Yes, insofar as it alerts people to the existence of a problem, gives them a vocabulary and concepts for the articulation of the problem, and suggests some forms of action that would remedy the problem.

Nussbaum objects that the action Butler suggests is vague, non-collective, and likely to be ineffective. Those are possible objections, but the only proof is going to be in the pudding. Thinking about what is possible or effective is never going to be an adequate substitute for doing something and seeing if it works—where works is defined as getting approximately what you aimed for. Better to try things than to argue ourselves out of it. It's not like we are flooded with proposals, or that what we are currently doing is working all that well. Much of what we do is habitual and follows well-traveled paths. Suggestions—and actual instantiations—of something different should be encouraged. Nussbaum comes across as the old fogey who lodges in every institution, the one who meets any proposed change with the pronouncement: "we tried that already in 1935 and it didn't work."

Nussbaum's more important point, it seems to me, is that Butler's proposals for action are so under-developed because Butler in fact believes that action is most likely going to be futile. Or, to put this in a slightly different way, Butler works on the personal, therapeutic, perfectionist side of the pitch because she believes the social forces she describes are ineluctable. I think Nussbaum is right in this analysis. Many radicals of what we can call the "cultural left," like Butler, have adopted the notion that "liberalism," or "capitalism," or "patriarchy" or whatever other name you want to give to the overarching "system" within which we live has gotten so deeply inside our heads and has developed such subtle ways of co-opting all opposition, that collective political action on social conditions is hopeless. So, instead, they emphasize work upon the self. They believe more hope rests in the utopias that can be projected in art than in the nitty-gritty of political work within the terms and institutions of the present. They are impatient with the compromises and far-from-perfect results of mundane politics, in which progress is piecemeal at best, preferring instead the visions of complete transformation expressed in various cultural artifacts. Not surprisingly, those engaged in mundane politics will often be annoyed by such pie-in-the-sky dreamers, especially when the dreamers criticize some concrete accomplishment as trivial or deeply flawed. But does that really mean we want to stop all dreaming, that thinkers should not articulate ideals that extend far beyond what we can currently achieve? Be careful what you ask for.

Rorty has it more right than Nussbaum. Perfectionist concerns and recommendations have a crucial and honorable place in our intellectual traditions and in our daily lives, as do utopian visions. It is quite simply misguided to insist that "real" feminist work or the only useful thinking must be directed toward the social rather than toward the personal, and to what can be feasibly accomplished in a relatively short time frame. Not only are self and society intertwined (remember "the personal is political?"), but each involves matters of ultimate concern for every self. We should fully expect that intellectual work will engage these two realms with different intensity—just as such work will offer different understandings of how they are related to one another. And we should fully expect that intellectual work will continue to articulate ideals that are far from realization and remote from the difficulties of providing basic material resources to all. In both cases, these various intellectual musings and modelings will be distinct from the political work of putting thoughts into action, even if they do suggest motives for such action and a map (an understanding) of the world in which such action will transpire.

Originally posted on August 23, 2005

NOTES

1 Hannah Arendt, "On Hannah Arendt," in *Hannah Arendt: The Recovery of the Public World*, ed. Melvyn A. Hill (New York: St Martin's Press, 1979), 304.

40. Nussbaum v. Butler, Footnotes

John Holbo

John McGowan calls the match for Nussbaum on points but takes off for low blows. Nussbaum is uncharitable not to acknowledge Butler's "Freudian mysticism". (He says he knows Butler won't thank him for applying that tag, but I agree with him it seems apt.) McGowan is at pains to make clear he doesn't mean you should *like* Freudian mysticism, let alone subscribe, only that it is wrong to trace its effects on Butler's prose to more *cynical* motives:

> Nussbaum clearly has no *avant-garde* intimations or yearnings toward the ineffable, so she cannot have any sympathy for a writing style that is trying to reach toward the "unthought," or the "inexpressible." Such styles are everywhere in romantic and modernist art—and they are built precisely on the premise that language is an imperfect tool, that our received vocabularies and categories are inadequate, and their inadequacy must be signaled even as we use the words we have inherited.

I think this is possibly right about Nussbaum. She is a *rationalist*, with a lower case r. (This is complicated, not contradicted, by her interests in literature.) Still, it overlooks the rather large possibility that someone could say almost exactly what Nussbaum says because she regards Butler's ineffable yearnings as not of the better sort, as ineffable yearnings go. Or, even more likely: Nussbaum could be saying that Butler wants to have her canny cake, and eat it too uncannily (or vice versa). A passage McGowan does not much discuss:

> It is difficult to come to grips with Butler's ideas, because it is difficult to figure out what they are. Butler is a very smart person. In public discussions, she proves that she can speak clearly and has a quick

> grasp of what is said to her. Her written style, however, is ponderous and obscure. It is dense with allusions to other theorists, drawn from a wide range of different theoretical traditions. In addition to Foucault, and to a more recent focus on Freud, Butler's work relies heavily on the thought of Louis Althusser, the French lesbian theorist Monique Wittig, the American anthropologist Gayle Rubin, Jacques Lacan, J.L. Austin, and the American philosopher of language Saul Kripke. These figures do not all agree with one another, to say the least; so an initial problem in reading Butler is that one is bewildered to find her arguments buttressed by appeal to so many contradictory concepts and doctrines, usually without any account of how the apparent contradictions will be resolved.
>
> A further problem lies in Butler's casual mode of allusion. The ideas of these thinkers are never described in enough detail to include the uninitiated (if you are not familiar with the Althusserian concept of "interpellation," you are lost for chapters) or to explain to the initiated how, precisely, the difficult ideas are being understood. Of course, much academic writing is allusive in some way: it presupposes prior knowledge of certain doctrines and positions. But in both the continental and the Anglo-American philosophical traditions, academic writers for a specialist audience standardly acknowledge that the figures they mention are complicated, and the object of many different interpretations. They therefore typically assume the responsibility of advancing a definite interpretation among the contested ones, and of showing by argument why they have interpreted the figure as they have, and why their own interpretation is better than others.

Nussbaum's characterization of Butler's style seems to me fair. (Does it seem fair to you? This is an important premise. I am not going to argue for it, but the argument will depend on it. It seems to me the sort of assumption which, should it be denied, could be debated, should Butler's defenders chose to take that tack.) Nussbaum is obviously most concerned with what she sees as *intellectual* failings. But it would be possible to marshal the same evidence on behalf of an *aesthetic* complaint. The suspicion is that Butler writes, if you will, philosophical *kitsch*. A quote from the musicologist, Carl Dahlhaus:

> Kitsch in music has hybrid ambitions which far outreach the capabilities of its actual structures and sounds, and are manifested in effects without cause, empty attitudinizing, and titles and instructions for performance which are not justified by the musical results. Instead of being content with modest achievements within its reach, musical kitsch has pretensions to big emotions, to "significance."

More specifically: "by side-stepping the dialectic of form and content in music, extracting from it a topic or subject matter (mistaken for the work's contents) and withdrawing from the acoustic phenomenon into the listener's own frame of mind. In this way the music, instead of constituting an aesthetic object, degenerates into a vehicle for associations and for edifying or melancholy self-indulgence."[1]

Nussbaum sees Butler sidestepping *philosophic* dialectic in favor of associations and self-indulgence. Butler's writings do not lead you into the ideas and arguments of the figures she references: the impressionism of the presentation precludes it. Rather, a fleeting, and highly aestheticized *sense* of these figures chases after a pathos of 'significance'. Butler provides a sense of what it would be like if she really were making Saul Kripke and Monique Wittig do a dionysian dance to ineffable pipings. But she isn't *actually* making them do this. (How could she be?)

To put the point another way, I think what bothers Nussbaum (what perfectly well *could be* bothering her) is not the ineffability of Butler's Freudian mysticism but the impropriety of ineffability that approaches us pseudo-armored in scholarly apparatus. *Sublime* is sublime. Sublime, footnoted, is sublime to ridiculous in one doozy step. A scholar, like Nussbaum, will emphasize that this *scholarship* seems unacceptable. A different sort of thinker—Kierkegaard, say—will perhaps emphasize that this has all the hallmarks of *bad art*. From *Concluding Unscientific Postscript*, criticizing Hegel's *Logic*.

> The reduplication of the content in the form is essential to all artistry, and it is particularly important to refrain from referring to the same content in an inadequate form. But as it is now, the Logic with its collection of notes makes as droll an impression on the mind as if a man were to show a letter purporting to have come from heaven, but having a blotter enclosed which only too clearly reveals its mundane origin ... Imagine Socrates in conversation with Hegel. With the help of the notes he will soon have Hegel on the hip; and as he was not accustomed to being put off by the assurance that everything will be made clear at the end, not even permitting a continuous speech lasting five minutes, to say nothing of a continuous development lasting through seventeen volumes of print, he would put on the brakes with all his might—merely to tease Hegel.[2]

Let's step back and talk to McGowan again:

> But I think Nussbaum misses the fact that individuality has its strong discontents and the fact that some people have strong intimations of a trans-individual sublime to which they are attracted and into which they would like to submerge that burdensome self. Not just religion, but also much of the literature of the past two hundred years, witnesses to this recurrent longing. To rule such longings out of court as so much romantic, irrational nonsense is neither going to banish them from the earth or advance our ability to produce a better society.

I think this is right—then again, taking Kierkegaard to heart, it is wrong. (Kierkegaard was hardly tone-deaf to individuality and its discontents. But he was sensitive to the point past which footnotes became silly.) Nussbaum should not lump Butler with the "adversarial traditions of sophistry and rhetoric," without at least nodding to the potentially distinct attractions of her romanticism (mysticism: call it what you will.) On the other hand, acknowledging these attractions simply makes fresh trouble.

McGowan's defense of Butler has two legs:

1) "When interpreting or evaluating any statement or any set of beliefs, I should begin from the premise that those who make that statement or hold that belief aim to be—and believe themselves to be—as committed to saying and believing what is reasonable and true as I am."

2) So, rather than simply assuming Butler is lazy and dishonest, consider her *positive motive* to be, as McGowan says, Freudian mysticism.

But the fancy footwork of 2) kicks away 1). The fact that many people are attracted by mysticism goes to show that *not* everyone is committed to being 'reasonable'.

POSTSCRIPT (January 8, 2007): This short piece was extracted from a much longer—approximately five times as long—POST, concerned with broader questions. It seems to work better as a narrow-bore response to McGowan.

NOTES

1 Carl Dahlhaus, *Between Romanticism and Modernism*, trans. M. Whittall (Berkeley: California UP, 1980), 12.

2 Søren Kierkegaard, *Concluding Unscientific Postscript*, trans. D. F. Swenson and W. Lowrie (Princeton: Princeton UP, 1968), 297.

41. Afterword

Daphne Patai &
Will H. Corral

I. The Project and the Process

Mark Bauerlein, in his essay with which this volume opens, asks: why another door-stopper of a book about theory? We are pleased to let him and the other contributors to the present volume argue about the appropriate responses to that question, and wish, here, merely to assure Bauerlein and others that *Theory's Empire* could easily have been twice its size. In fact, when we initially started compiling a list of substantive early pieces that were critical of Theory and its *maîtres*, we soon found ourselves with an entirely unmanageable list of essays (or chapters in books) that we considered very useful. This led to a bi-coastal email dialogue (Patai is in Massachusetts, Corral in California) as we engaged in contrapuntal readings and communications about those readings.

We recognized that a large volume of essays doing something other than celebrating or further explicating-and-legitimizing today's Theorists would be a hard sell to most publishers and indigestible to the type of readers we suspected would be our public. So from early in our project we had in mind the need to select very carefully and judiciously. We were aiming not only at breadth but also at depth, variety, and above all durability. In his first blog entry John Holbo addresses the end result of our intent, and in "Theory's Empire—Wrestling the Fog Bank," Sean McCann predicts that our book "has already generated more extensive, vigorous, and fair discussion in the blogosphere than it ever will in the journals and conferences of literary academia." We are of course grateful for these posts, and suspect McCann is right about the journals (though we've had generally positive reviews in the few academic journals that, thus far, have taken notice of the book).

As we worked on the book between about 2001 and 2004, key criteria in our selection from the works of well-known scholars became our own reactions to all that we read and re-read: Were the essays compelling? Were they still fresh and necessary? Had their arguments been incorporated into the discourse of the field so that their inclusion would be superfluous or too familiar? Did we find those arguments and critiques acknowledged and incorporated into recent anthologies of theory? Naturally, each essay led to others, and as a result we found ourselves with an ever-expanding corpus, going back more than four decades. And so we began to try out these essays in our own classes and by recommending them to our graduate students and inviting their responses.

Certainly there had always been disagreements, even acrimonious attacks and counterattacks, between and among theorists. What concerned us, however, was the failure of these debates to have an influence on the second and third generations of scholars, whose generally uncritical use of the maîtres' terms and concepts are what created the orthodoxy we refer to as Theory with a capital T. We also noticed that, if one really wanted to demonstrate one's theory credentials, the standard expectation involved the obligation to adopt politically engaged rhetoric (on the left, it need hardly be said), even though until the early nineties some major theorists, such as Derrida, had little to say about radical politics. We were concerned that where arguments had taken place, they were often couched as fights over political commitment and utility (Foucault vs. Derrida) rather than over scholarly depth.

As our list of contrarian essays grew, our initial reactions were of delight at the scope and subtlety of work challenging and demystifying the theorists who, from the early 1960s on, were becoming the lords of Theory. Soon, however (and partially reiterating an argument we make in our general introduction), we realized with profound dismay that one after another of the standard anthologies we carefully read through failed to take account of this body of work, often to the point of simply not mentioning that such critiques had ever been voiced. Similarly, as we looked at the types of secondary or complementary sources available for use in theory classrooms, we were astonished that so rarely was there any mention of critics and criticisms of Theory – other than the occasional facile dismissal typically accompanied by slurs about challengers' politics. Thus students were being exposed to one side of a conversation, which no doubt helped explain the familiar monologues constantly heard to this day in literature departments, where merely dropping the right name or phrase became a sufficient token of membership in a club that was increasingly hermetic even as its rhetoric became more and more commonplace in the academy.

Moreover, the concept of theory had obviously undergone a tremendous conceptual shift since the end of the sixties, and there was really no way to circumvent that development, as our general introduction summarizes. We noticed that students born in the seventies or eighties were distancing themselves from the activism of the sixties while progressing toward merely verbal stances justified by postmodernist relativism, as we have also outlined. We did not want to lament the depoliticization of theory, so our quandary was how to negotiate shifting values and perceptions while recovering what we deemed to be sensible and just readings, not the typical re-reading of a re-reading. The actual reading of theories and theorists that our book was designed to put in perspective has been replaced by many "guides for the perplexed," just as today there are numerous introductions to introductions to theory. It was hard to avoid skepticism as we noted that at the time Empson, Trilling, and others were theorizing there were no guides to their writing, nor a need to have "accessible" accounts of the inter-relationships between theory and students. As Cynthia Ozick laments in the April 2007 issue of *Harper's*, we are now missing the entire infrastructure of the serious criticism of previous decades. Thus, Ozick writes:

> (Academic theorists equipped with advanced degrees, who make up yet another species of limited reviewers, are worthy only of a parenthesis. Their confining ideologies, heavily politicized and rendered in a kind of multisyllabic pidgin, have for decades marinated literature in dogma. Of these inflated dons and doctors it is futile to speak, since, unlike the hardier customer reviewers, they are destined to vanish like the fog they evoke.)

When we began looking for a publisher for our book, we first contacted Norton, which had just brought out its famous theory anthology. We hoped they might be an equal-opportunity publisher, but we were not unduly surprised when William Germano quickly responded to our query with a letter saying he doubted there was a market for our sort of book. Next we contacted editor X, at prominent academic press Y, who was cautiously interested in our project. After considering it for about two months, he declined our proposal, telling us he had elicited "more than twenty reviews," and, even after eliminating the obviously biased negative reports, he could commit to such a project only if its market was clearly defined and if it had been, "in principle, embraced by the community." We were amused by the latter phrase, since of course what is "embraced by the community" is precisely what our book was challenging, and the clearly defined market may not emerge until the work is available and publicized. Still, we understood his concerns. What we did not readily understand was that, although X had initially assured us he would "of course" send all reports to us, we were never allowed to read them—unprecedented in our experience. Our request to see at least some of them, so that we might benefit from the criticisms of our peers, was met with silence.

This tale has an interesting postscript. A year ago, a colleague forwarded to us the letter he had initially received from X. In 2002, X had written as follows to this potential reader (and to how many others? we wondered): "I have received the proposal below and I should be very grateful to have your advice on it. You will see that it is a reactionary project, that might be timely or not, or might be a spasm in the moribund body politic of those who never liked theory ..." The dismissive and prejudicial tone of this request strikes us as further evidence of the institutional hold of Theory, well beyond the academy. As for X, he has gone on to greater things at still more prestigious academic press Z.

Still, though we received half a dozen other rejections of our proposal over the next year, in late 2003 we found ourselves with two offers: from Columbia University Press and from Palgrave. When we contacted Jennifer Crewe at Columbia University Press, we were well aware that Columbia had published anthologies of the kind we criticize, as well as a considerable number of translations of work by theorists based in France. But Crewe surprised us with her enthusiasm. She made it clear she thought the timing was right for a project such as ours, and after receiving several positive reports (which were sent to us), debated with us at some length about the appropriate size and range of such a book. Just before Columbia finally accepted our project we received an offer of publication from Palgrave, but its contract required us—and this was the first we'd heard about this demand—to turn an 800-page text into a 300-page book. We both knew that a 300-page book critical of Theory would be pointless. As discussed in our introduction to *Theory's Empire*, a few such works exist and have proven easy to ignore, despite the high quality of their contents. From this reality we had taken the lesson that critical mass was important, as was the breadth and depth that a large book allowed us to achieve. Nonetheless, we understood that size is always an issue and so we reached a compromise with Crewe, forced ourselves to delete quite a number of essays, and the new, reduced version produced a 700-page book containing 47 essays by 50 scholars.

II. Reactions to Theory's Empire

For the past two years, we have regularly received letters and emails from professors and graduate students (and some general readers as well), thanking us for having published our book. We are also aware of the many comments, blurbs, and reviews on internet bookstores stressing the timeliness and utility of our work. Almost all of the email messages sent to us about our book make the same point: Any criticism of Theory or preference for a different approach to literature meets with intolerance or dismissal in the writers' academic milieu. Four examples—three of them received during March 2007—well represent these responses.

A British colleague, Brigid Lowe, who is a Research Fellow at Trinity College, Cambridge, wrote to us:

> I am part of a generation who, as students, were subjected to the Theory canon as revealed truth. In my first job I had to teach a Literary Theory course, with the capital letters. It would all have been much easier to survive if your volume had existed back then.
>
> . . .
>
> Theory is becoming accepted as common sense in English departments, and hence acquiring an invisibility that makes it hard to combat. I was quite shocked to find how hard a time I had getting my book published—presses couldn't seem to find two non-Theory readers to send it to, so I kept getting one good reader's report and one scandalized one. With typical inconsistency, the hostile readers at once claimed that Theory was all over, and that I was fighting paper tigers, and at the same time said things about it being impossible to "go back" to before Theory, and were openly outraged by my "insup-

> portably negative" approach to Theoretical critics. I was shaken by their dismissiveness—they explicitly declined to engage with my argument, one on the grounds that she found it difficult to believe I would not change my opinion if I just re-read my opponents more carefully.

In response to our request for more details about her experiences, Lowe wrote as follows:

> My education in Theory as revealed truth began in 1997. My discontent dates to a lecture in an introductory course in my first semester, in which the lecturer gave a "feminist reading" of *Adam Bede*. I was moved to put my hand up and point out that she was what I, in my naïvete, called "misreading" the novel. I remember thinking she must really not have read it, and it seemed important to point out the facts before she embarrassed herself any further- but she told me no questions were allowed in lectures, and afterwards told me I would understand that hers was not a misreading once I'd read *The Madwoman in the Attic*. I did my BA in a small but quite well-regarded and traditional department, but by the time I left they had drawn up guidelines for students telling you what you would need to do to get each grade, in which it was explicitly stated that you could not get over 70% in an essay unless you showed awareness of the ultimate opacity of language and the decentering of human agency, etc. …
>
> To me the "Theory is over" argument is so unconvincing as to seem disingenuous. If you replied "right, so we can carry on with humanist criticism where we left off?" you would not get assent. What it really meant is that the argument is supposed to stop and that we all have to live with an apparatus of slightly washed-out and mechanical Theoretical premises and moves as our starting points. If Theory was really over, I don't think people would use that as a criticism of

> your book; history suggests that people don't usually have any problem dancing on the graves of cultural moments when they are genuinely over. No one criticized Lytton Strachey for ridiculing the Victorians on the grounds that the queen was already dead.
>
> In this country, almost all English departments have at least one, and generally two, compulsory theory modules on their undergraduate programmes—and these always cover Althusser, Foucault and Lacan, and very seldom cover any recent "theorists" of literature who are not also Theorists. This is even true at those supposed bastions of traditional literary scholarship, Oxford and Cambridge. …

Because there is a generational frustration regarding the state of theory from the mid- nineties right up to the time we published our book, as attested by the brief testimonials in the entries by Christopher Conway and Kathleen Lowrey in this volume, it is worth continuing with Lowe's observations:

> I think in this country grad students are writing fewer really silly pure Theory dissertations these days—some "serious" study of primary texts is pretty much required in the better grad schools. But Theory has left a lot of that study a bit joyless - there's usually a thin pseudo-political Theory-ish argument used to pull together a lot of research on rather dry non-literary texts, and all the work gets done in the horribly predictable areas you mention in your intro ("constructions of national identity," for example). Everyone, but especially grads, are terrified of conveying any pleasure in or admiration for "literary' texts," and they certainly aren't looking to theorize or understand the workings of pleasure or greatness.
>
> This joylessness gets passed on in teaching—I'm shocked to see so many students utterly unenthusiastic about literature, and I do think Theory is greatly to blame.

> Over here some bits of literary studies are worse hit than others. The few people who study poetry have a pretty good time, because it's harder to do that without some acknowledgment of pleasure and aesthetics, albeit implicit (I think Ricks is only able to say Theory is not worth arguing about because he works mainly on poetry rather than prose). The study of texts of the past is always more irritatingly self-righteous and accusatory than study of more recent stuff. And personally, I think the work done in my area—Victorian fiction—is worst of all.

Lowe's comments exemplify the very real and practical consequences our book sought to explore, for it is also obvious from other contributions published in the present volume (such as those by Burke and McCann) that any problem surrounding theory is now institutionally based. We are thus delighted that Lowe's story has a happy ending. Her book, *Victorian Fiction and the Insights of Sympathy: An Alternative to the Hermeneutics of Suspicion*, was indeed published, in early 2007.

A second email we received recently was from Charlie Wesley, a PhD student in English at Binghamton University, who describes himself as having "an uneasy relationship with theory."

> For a long time I have enjoyed theory, but of late I've experienced a discomfort with it that I couldn't quite articulate (this is often a problem for many students of postmodernism). Heck, I have even used theory dogmatically from time to time, partly because my passion for it was great. But when a few friends of mine (who are MA students quite into theory themselves) saw an advertisement for *Theory's Empire*, they rolled their eyes and instantly labeled the text a "conservative" rant against "people who are trying to change the world." The dogma of their statements—a dogma I had been participating in for quite a while—stuck with me, and has caused me to become more and more critical of the almost fanatically religious overtones that many "theory heads" espouse. That was a few years ago. A few weeks ago, I finally started

> reading *Theory's Empire*, and I was shocked that so many of my own feelings about the uncritical, overly political, contradictory, twisted logic of the "theory folks" were articulated in this collection. … Thank you for helping to give me a new insight into the English literature field, a new openness, and a sense of possibility.

Yet another graduate student, Matthew Goodwin, now at the University of Massachusetts Amherst, by chance spoke to one of us recently of how relieved he was to come across *Theory's Empire*, whose introduction confirmed many of his own observations. We then asked him if he'd be inclined to set in writing an account of his experiences. He responded that not only would he be glad to do so, but that it was something he'd been wanting and needing to do for some time. To our surprise, he then sent us a brief essay, from which we've extracted a few paragraphs. Goodwin has a BA and MA in philosophy, had worked for some years in non-profit organizations dealing with immigrant communities, and had returned to school out of a love of literature. What he found were courses heavy in Theory and disinclined both to wonder why some theories become fashionable and others do not, and to take a critical look at the very institutionalization of Theory that such courses presupposed. "The central tenet of Theory," he wrote, "is that literature should be examined critically using some particular theorist. And this tenet shapes undergraduate composition classes up to the highest levels of graduate study." Generally, he continued,

> the particular theorist being used has written the theory in another context such as philosophy or one of the social sciences. The theory is often taken for granted and left unquestioned. For example, I studied Wittgenstein as a philosophy graduate student and when I entered the field of literature I was amazed at how just a couple of his popular sentences were used to prove some point in an argument. Those who used him in this way generally did not understand his place in the history of philosophy or that there were alternative views. This is a problem if the theorist is taken as the *only* authority in a particular field, in this

> case, the philosophy of language (and there are philosophers who are guilty of the same thing). When the theory is not taken for granted and is questioned, it is done so from a perspective outside of the discipline from which it arose. This is not an absolute problem. However, it makes the arguments highly limited and normally they cannot attain to the claims made by the literary theorist.
>
> When I entered a Comparative Literature department as a Masters student, I took an introduction to Comparative Literature course. In addition to discussions about the field of Comparative Literature, a large part of the content of the course was an overview of literary theory and its application. The class was engaging, and the professor was interested in debate, yet the class took various philosophical texts out of their context in terms of the debate surrounding the theorist and the philosophical history leading up to the theorist. In my eyes this was a problem for some of the students who did not have this philosophical background. Similarly I knew that my understanding of, say, Freudian Theory was limited, as it was taken out of context of the vibrant debate among psychoanalysts. I later took Literary Theory with a professor, a Marxist critic, who generally gave a fair reading of all the major literary theorists. The class consisted of lectures and discussion was not encouraged, and the students were asked to mimic this style with their own presentations. What was clearly not criticized was Theory itself and its place in the study of literature.

Nevertheless Goodwin persisted, with the following results:

> When I started the PhD at another university, I again took an introduction to Comparative Literature course. Similar problems arose as students struggled to debate Derrida, but here the fashionable nature of the field was stressed and current trends were valued sim-

> ply as current trends. One major concern in the class, and in the anthology of comparativists used, was to search for what Comparative Literature consisted of or what it should be, a kind of theodicy of comparative literature: how to justify our ways to the academy. My perspective was that we did not need to justify our field, and to find out what we are, we would only need to look around and see what we are in fact doing. Thinking about this issue in Comparative Literature now, I think that behind this anxiety is the desire to find the next fashion first, or at least to be on the bandwagon at its start. And of course there are budget or job concerns.
>
> The benefits of these theory classes are many, and I certainly read many texts I would not have in a basic literature class or a normal philosophy department. However, I always felt that the classes relied too heavily on the assumed authority of the theorists. And when these theorists were questioned, they were questioned clumsily and without real dialogue since not every student could have experience in every discipline.

Once again, as with Lowe, the consequences of challenging the received wisdom about Theory were not good:

> [Early in my PhD program] I said to another graduate student that I was skeptical of the arbitrary use of theory. Eventually this discussion got around the department, and I ended up being labeled as anti-theory. This result was strange to me for a variety of reasons, the biggest being that I have been, in my opinion, very theoretically-oriented my whole life. Nevertheless, it seems to be the case that in the current situation, where Theory is the status quo, to question Theory is to not do Theory at all. But it does not need to be so.

In many ways the concerns of the younger scholars we have quoted at length mirror those expressed in some of the blogs collected in this volume, and together they are additional proof of the need to have similar forums widely disseminated. What these individuals experience is group-thought that reinforces the view that one has to stake out an already well-established political and rhetorical posture if one wants to succeed in literature departments today. Self-congratulatory professions of commitment from teachers of theory make it impossible to divorce theory from its purported radicalism and from its role in carving out a career for oneself, since the goal is to see oneself as a powerful agent of political advocacy all the while enjoying the considerable perks of the academic life. Nor is this merely a current defect of literature departments. As should be obvious to anyone in the academy, though with a bit of a lag, the same assumptions have found their way beyond language and literature departments. It is now no surprise to meet historians and colleagues in other fields who tell us that their kind of work is disdained by colleagues who are "into Theory."

Several years ago, before our book came out, we received an unexpected email from a professor in the Midwest, recounting his own recollections of graduate school in the 1980s:

> My name is Jon Erickson, I am an associate professor in the English Department at Ohio State University. I've been meaning to write to you for a while, partially because I was asked by a publisher last year to review the proposal of your book [*Theory's Empire*]. I was very enthusiastic about your project, not least because I have been teaching critical theory in our department almost since the time I was hired, in 1990, both to grads and undergrads.
>
> I spent the 1980s in grad school at the University of Wisconsin-Milwaukee, getting one of the first degrees in "Modern Studies" there, out of the English Department, and connected with the functions of the Center for Twentieth Century Studies. My attitude toward Theory is a lot more sanguine than many of my colleagues', largely because I was so inundated with it in my time there, not simply in the forms of texts, but in encountering the famous theorists firsthand. Here are a few of those I encountered in lectures, classes, workshops, and even lunch: Lyotard, Jameson, Said,

Kristeva, de Man, Hartmann, Baudrillard, Stuart Hall, Dick Hebdige, Marjorie Garber, Mary Poovey, the list goes on.

What's more, there were the people who taught there: Andreas Huyssen, Teresa de Lauretis, Jane Gallop, Tania Modleski. There was only one professor, Ihab Hassan, who, while well respected for his work in postmodernism, was resistant to the over politicizing of every aspect of literary study. He was even called a fascist by a few radical Leftist students, which was upsetting to him. I have come to respect his principled stance, his willingness to stand by literature and the value of individual creativity in the face of ideological dogmatics.

In any case, I found your proposal exciting because after so many years of teaching the same material over and over, Barthes, Derrida, Foucault, Lacan, various Marxists, gender feminists, etc., etc., it was becoming clearer to me just how little sense much of it was making to me. This was abetted by the fact that I also read Anglo-American philosophy (in particular moral and political philosophy), stuff that is much clearer and more rigorous in its argumentation.

My interest in this philosophy was stimulated by my brother-in-law who teaches moral philosophy in a small college in Massachusetts, and who has been suggesting authors to me ever since I was in grad school. (I recall once giving him Baudrillard to read, and hearing peals of laughter coming from his office as he did so.)

What has happened in the last couple of years is that I started giving students in my "Foundations of Contemporary Critical Theory" graduate class critical essays and some bibliographies of works critical of the theory they were learning. When I looked over your proposal I discovered that several of the authors in your book were authors I recommended in my lists. …

We then wrote back to Erickson, and received some further comments:

> I was thinking about your question about why students are still so attracted to Theory. When I was in grad school, Theory was just coming in, so there were real fights with the old guard (who usually took the position of E. D. Hirsch), and so there seemed to be something real at stake. It was also the case that not everyone who was reading the new theory bought it all either; so, for instance, there were real arguments between Marxists and Foucauldians and Derrideans.
>
> Once all the new approaches became orthodoxy in the nineties, those tensions seemed to have disappeared, and people picked and chose their theories without worrying about contradictions, and one could be a Marxian Foucauldian without blinking. Now the attraction I think is this: on the one hand the rhetoric of Theory is still operating at that guerrilla warfare kind of pitch, which will always attract post-adolescents (up until their 30s these days) who want to appear anti-authoritarian and radical. At the same time it is completely safe, because it is, in fact, the orthodoxy of the academy that completely protects you from the nature of real life, and indeed, authorizes you. (I tell my students that my response to the bumper sticker "Question Authority" is: "who says I should question authority?") "Radical" ends up taking on the same kind of meaning that it does in style for skatepunks, for instance. I remarked in the seminar where I gave a paper [on this subject] that people wear the names of Foucault and Derrida and (above all) Deleuze & Guattari in their papers and conversation like they wear Tommy Hilfiger clothes. Theory has become "designer theory" in effect. (It actually seems all of a piece with how David Brooks describes bohemian capitalism in *Bobos in Paradise*.)
>
> I think the other thing is that there is some kind of mythic power attached to theory, as if it is some form of intellectual martial art: you learn the language like

> you would learn fighting moves. The only problem is that your opponents are all straw men, since it can't really be used in arguments with people who don't know what you're talking about. So it's basically a form of braggadocio among the cognoscenti. I think of the word "strategic" for instance, as in Gayatri Spivak's "strategic essentialism." Who among those not in the know, that one is presumably using "strategic essentialism" against, would have any idea, or care, what you are doing? (Outside of the fact that you're not being honest with them.) Replace the word "strategic" with the word "convenient" and it makes as much sense.

We have always known that some colleagues teach theory from a critical point of view, but more—whether those who came to maturity with Theory (and are now reaching retirement age) or others, perhaps newer to the profession and seeking to demonstrate their credentials—seem content to teach the "greatest theoretical hits" without inviting criticism, and often in fact discouraging or disallowing it. In recent years we've encountered few graduate students, and also few young colleagues, who are at all acquainted with earlier theorists, or with basic texts preceding the advent of Theory. No lessening of the expectation that new PhDs will always be able to "do Theory" is in the wind, and few are the departments that address this issue directly and ask whether indeed all their faculty need to have the same sort of orientation. We are thus pleased to see in John Holbo's collection that *Theory's Empire* is recognized by many contributors as addressing a need, whatever particular criticisms of the book one or another participant in the discussion may make.

Theory, with the capital T we specified in our introduction to *Theory's Empire*, it would appear, though still hanging on as a now-institutionalized, hardly transgressive presence in the academy, has come to a standstill. Nevertheless, Theory's hold over humanities departments, like its status as the preferred academic discourse today, does not seem to be waning—judging by the job ads, course descriptions, and dissertation topics we repeatedly encounter. Meanwhile, it is likely that serious challenges to received theorists' status will keep appearing—challenges such as Robert Irwin's recent re-reading of

Said's *Orientalism*, or the revised, enlarged and re-translated version of Foucault's *Madness and Civilization* that is raising questions about the French master's "isolation from the world of facts and scholarship," according to a recent review by Andrew Scull in the *TLS*. Whether or not these challenges will find their way into literature departments is a separate matter. So far, we see little sign of that at an institutional level. However, the kinds of comments we've quoted at length above suggest to us that some younger colleagues and soon-to-be-colleagues are indeed approaching the entire Theory scene from a fresh perspective, and that in a piecemeal way they are helping to restore some much-needed balance and rationality to the study of literature. To assist them in such an endeavor was a primary aim of our book.

April 2007

Appendix: Links, Comments, & Context

Most contributions to this volume started life as blog posts. Most posts had comment boxes; much of the life of the event lived therein. The comments are not included in this volume, but can be found, courtesy of the links below. Also, many posts have been edited; the originals may be of interest to a few academic archaeologists. For each title I have provided two links: the original, and a back-up which—in the event of breakage—should be good for the foreseeable future. Below that, I have also provided further links to Valve event archives and a few links to threads elsewhere that seem particularly (*le mot juste*?) … *emblematic* of the quality of discussion (for better and for worse).

1 Review of Theory's Empire
Mark Bauerlein

http://www.butterfliesandwheels.com/articleprint.php?num=134/
http://www.webcitation.org/5MVChNyvl

2 Theory of Everything
Michael Bérubé

http://www.michaelberube.com/index.php/weblog/theory_of_everything/
http://www.webcitation.org/5MRN5bTJv

3 Theory's Empire: Making Sense of the Theme
John Holbo

http://www.thevalve.org/go/valve/article/theorys_empire_does_the_books_theme_make_much_sense/
http://www.webcitation.org/5MVCrdpFh

4 Theory's Empire: Ersatz Theoretical Ecumenism
Scott Kaufman

http://www.thevalve.org/go/valve/article/theorys_empire_ersatz_theoretical_ecumenicalism_criticism_qua_criticism/
http://www.webcitation.org/5MVCxfY7T

5 Theory Tuesday
Michael Bérubé

http://www.michaelberube.com/index.php/weblog/comments/678/
http://www.webcitation.org/5MXek6n9V

6 Theory's Empire—Wrestling the Fogbank
Sean McCann

http://www.thevalve.org/go/valve/article/theorys_empire_wrestling_the_fog_bank/

http://www.webcitation.org/5MVDixy5T

7 Hostilities
Daniel Green

http://www.thevalve.org/go/valve/article/hostilities/
http://www.webcitation.org/5MVE4Gh0h

8 A Response to 'The Deconstructive Angel'
Adam Kotsko

http://www.thevalve.org/go/valve/article/a_respose_to_the_deconstructive_angel/
http://www.webcitation.org/5MVEAtKLx

9 Theory Thursday
John McGowan

http://www.michaelberube.com/index.php/weblog/comments/680/
http://www.webcitation.org/5MXpMjiWv

10 Book Notes: Theory's Empire
Tim Burke

http://weblogs.swarthmore.edu/burke/?p=60/
http://www.webcitation.org/5MVESvkux

11 Four Challenges to Postcolonial Theory
Amardeep Singh

http://www.thevalve.org/go/valve/article/four_challenges_to_postcolonial_theory/
http://www.webcitation.org/5MVEf9Jdo

12 Why I Love Theory/Why I Hate Theory
Jonathan Mayhew

http://www.thevalve.org/go/valve/article/why_i_love_theory_why_i_hate_theory/
http://www.webcitation.org/5MVEjlu8G

13 On Mark Bauerlein's 'Social Constructivism: Philosophy For the Aca-

demic Workplace'
Jonathan Goodwin

http://www.thevalve.org/go/valve/article/on_mark_bauerleins_social_constructionism_philosophy_for_the_academic_workp/
http://www.webcitation.org/5MVErKrN4

14 Post-Post-Theory
Chris Cagle

http://web.archive.org/web/20060114231328/http://leftcenterleft.typepad.com/blog/2005/07/postposttheory.html/
http://www.webcitation.org/5MVFUri4L

15 Essentializing Theory: a Testimonial
Christopher Conway

http://camicao.blogspot.com/2005/07/not-much-of-theory-head-but.html/
http://www.webcitation.org/5MVFan4Br

16 Anthropological Theory, Siglo XXI
Kathleen Lowrey

http://savageminds.org/2005/07/14/anthropological-theory-siglo-xxi/
http://www.webcitation.org/5MVFfOLkk

17 Two Months Before The Mast of Post-Modernism
Brad DeLong

http://www.j-bradford-delong.net/movable_type/2005-3_archives/001282.html
http://www.webcitation.org/5MVFmnFhn

18 Theory's Empire—It's the Institution, Stupid
Sean McCann

http://www.thevalve.org/go/valve/article/theorys_empire_its_the_institution_stupid/
http://www.webcitation.org/5MVGnDdxg

19 Theorizing Novels
Matthew Greenfield

http://www.thevalve.org/go/valve/article/theorizing_novels/
http://www.webcitation.org/5MVGqx5EQ

20 Thinking About Theory's Empire
Morris Dickstein

http://www.thevalve.org/go/valve/article/thinking_about_theorys_empire/
http://www.webcitation.org/5MVH2knTz

21 The Death and Discontents of Theory
Jeffrey Wallen

http://www.thevalve.org/go/valve/article/the_death_and_discontent_of_theory/
http://www.webcitation.org/5MVHAPI8v

22 Trilling's Taste, an Instance
Jonathan Goodwin

http://www.thevalve.org/go/valve/article/trillings_taste_an_instance/
http://www.webcitation.org/5MVHZ5imB

23 Teaching Theory's Empire
Jonathan Goodwin

http://www.thevalve.org/go/valve/article/teaching_theorys_empire/
http://www.webcitation.org/5MVHI1SB4

24 Morally Sound
Daniel Green

http://www.thevalve.org/go/valve/article/moral_content/
http://www.webcitation.org/5MVHoIECE

25 Literary Studies Without Literature
John Emerson

http://www.idiocentrism.com/theory.htm/
http://www.webcitation.org/5MVHsZvI1

26 Theory Tuesday III
Michael Bérubé

http://www.michaelberube.com/index.php/weblog/comments/689/
http://www.webcitation.org/5MVI37VRu

27 Bill the Butcher As Educator
John Holbo

http://www.thevalve.org/go/valve/article/is_there_a_fucking_knife_in_this_class/
http://www.webcitation.org/5MXuRvblK

28 T1 and T2
Mark Kaplan

http://charlotte-street.blogspot.com/2005/08/t1-and-t2.html/
http://www.webcitation.org/5MXuwiF7V

29 There Be Monsters—or, Rosa Parks: Not Psychotic

Sean McCann

http://www.thevalve.org/go/valve/article/there_be_monsters_or_rosa_parks_not_psychotic/
http://www.webcitation.org/5MXvCjQEo

30 What's So Scary About Theory?
Jodi Dean

http://jdeanicite.typepad.com/i_cite/2005/08/whats_so_scary_.html/
http://www.webcitation.org/5MXvUOf2V

31 Prosthetic Thoughts
Mark Kaplan

http://charlotte-street.blogspot.com/2005/08/prosthetic-thoughts.html
http://www.webcitation.org/5MXw7x6sc

32 Breaking News
Mark Kaplan

http://charlotte-street.blogspot.com/2005/08/breaking-news.html
http://www.webcitation.org/5MXwUzsvS

33 The Para-Costives
Mark Kaplan

http://charlotte-street.blogspot.com/2005/08/para-costives.html
http://www.webcitation.org/5MXwlFngD

34 Against My Better Judgment
Adam Kotsko

http://www.adamkotsko.com/weblog/2005/08/against-my-better-judgment.html/
http://www.webcitation.org/5MXwwwfrP

35 On Theory and its Empire, 2: the Politics of Capitalization
Kenneth Rufo

http://ghostinthewire.org/archives/2005/08/on_theory_and_i_1.php
http://www.webcitation.org/5MXxA3s2H

36 Conceptualization and its Vague Contents
John Holbo

http://www.thevalve.org/go/valve/article/conceptualization_and_its_vague_contents/
http://www.webcitation.org/5MXxnjCnR

37 Nussbaum v. Butler, Round 1

John McGowan

http://www.michaelberube.com/index.php/weblog/comments/701/
http://www.webcitation.org/5MXxV7w0T

38 Nussbaum v. Butler, Round 2
John McGowan

http://www.michaelberube.com/index.php/theory_tuesday_nussbaum_v_butler_round_two/
http://www.webcitation.org/5MXy9d4Yi

39 Nussbaum v. Butler, Round 3
John Holbo

http://www.thevalve.org/go/valve/article/precluding_untheoretic_prescripts_to_the_philosophic_figments/
http://www.webcitation.org/5MXyPE7Ae

The *Theory's Empire* Valve Event Archive Page (four pages worth). A number of posts did not make the cut for inclusion in the volume. Also, should the Valve pass away, the Web Citation links should still be good. (More clues for the curious.)

http://www.thevalve.org/go/valve/archive_asc/C41
http://www.webcitation.org/5PHwZUCWE

http://www.thevalve.org/go/valve/archive_asc/C41/P15/
http://www.webcitation.org/5PHwkMyJV

http://www.thevalve.org/go/valve/archive_asc/C41/P30/
http://www.webcitation.org/5PHwqAn1m

http://www.thevalve.org/go/valve/archive_asc/C41/P45/
http://www.webcitation.org/5PHx3G8pE

Some of the curiouser contributions our event encountered, on its way down the rabbithole, popped up in comments elsewhere. I cannot omit to memorialize two. The post associated with the first of these also contains numerous links to other posts, many not included in the volume. (More clues for the curious.)

Theory's Empire: Dissenting With "Dissent"
Matt Christie

http://pasaudela.blogspot.com/2005/08/theorys-empire-dissenting-with-dissent.html
http://www.webcitation.org/5PHxqg7NG

http://www.haloscan.com/comments/pasaudela2004/112327111926038007/
http://www.webcitation.org/5PHxuvaLB

Haloscan [Coda to the deleted "Coda"]
Mark Kaplan
http://charlotte-street.blogspot.com/2005/08/haloscan.html/
http://www.webcitation.org/5PHy5L0MK

Contributors

Mark Bauerlein is Professor of English at Emory University. He is author of *Literary Criticism: An Autopsy* (1997) and *Negrophobia: A Race Riot in Atlanta*, 1906 (2001). He blogs at Phi Beta Cons (phibeta-cons.nationalreview.com).

Michael Bérubé is the Paterno Family Professor in Literature at Penn State University and the author, most recently, of *What's Liberal About the Liberal Arts?* (Norton, 2006) and *Rhetorical Occasions* (U of North Carolina P, 2006). His well-known blog (www.michaelberube.com/blog) is in dignified retirement. He blogs at Crooked Timber (www.crookedtimber.org).

Timothy Burke is Associate Professor of History at Swarthmore College. He is the author of *Lifebuoy Men, Lux Women* (Duke Univ. Press, 1996) and *Saturday Morning Fever* (St. Martin's, 1999). He blogs at Easily Distracted (weblogs.swarthmore.edu/burke).

Chris Cagle is a Lecturer in Film and Media Arts at Temple University. His research examines the industrial and social history of postwar American cinema. He blogs at Category D (http://categoryd.blogspot.com).

Christopher Conway is Associate Professor of Modern Languages at the University of Texas Arlington.

Will H. Corral is Chair of Foreign Languages at Sacramento State University. In addition to editing *Theory's Empire*, he is the author of numerous books on Spanish American literature, and has been awarded two Fulbright research fellowships.

Jodi Dean teaches political theory at Hobart and William Smith Colleges. She has authored or edited eight books, the most recent of which is *Zizek's Politics* (Routledge 2006). She blogs at I cite (http://jdeanicite.typepad.com/) and Long Sunday (http://www.long-sunday.net/long_sunday/).

Brad DeLong decided to become an economist rather than a historian in 1981 when history graduate students took him aside to tell him the state of the history academic job market. He has been terrified ever since a Federal Reserve Bank Vice President introduced him not as the "economic historian" or "the macroeconomist" or "the Berkeley professor" or "the ex-Treasury staffer" but as the "weblogger" (http://www.j-bradford-delong.net/movable_type).

Morris Dickstein is Distinguished Professor of English at the CUNY Graduate Center. He is the author of numerous books and articles. His most recent book is *A Mirror in the Roadway: Literature and the Real World* (Princeton, 2005).

John Emerson is distinguished by an autodidactically exemplary degree of academic non-affiliation. He will soon self-publish a book, *Substantific Marrow* through Lulu.com. He blogs as Idiocentrism (www.idiocentrism.com).

Jonathan Goodwin is Visiting Assistant Professor at the University of Louisiana at Lafayette. He blogs at the Valve.

Daniel Green is an ex-academic. He blogs at The Reading Experience (http://noggs.typepad.com). And the Valve. His new book is *Tell A Story!*, available from Lulu.com.

Matt Greenfield is Associate Professor of English at the College of Staten Island, CUNY. He is co-editor of *Edmund Spenser: Essays on Culture and Allegory* and has numerous articles and poems. He blogs at the Valve.

John Holbo is Assistant Professor of Philosophy at the National University of Singapore, where he spends his days thinking about Nietzsche, Wittgenstein and literary theory. He is founder and 'editor' of the Valve. He also blogs at Crooked Timber (www.crookedtimber.org).

Mark Kaplan is a writer and lecturer living in London. He blogs at Charlotte Street (http://charlotte-street.blogspot.com).

Scott Eric Kaufman, a graduate student in the department of English at the University of California, Irvine, is currently working on a dissertation about the influence of evolutionary theory on early 20th Century American culture. He blogs at the Valve and Acephalous (acephalous.typepad.com).

Adam Kotsko is a doctoral student at the Chicago Theological Seminary. His current research interests include patristic and medieval theology and contemporary continental thought. He blogs at The Weblog (www.adamkotsko.com/weblog).

Kathleen Lowrey is Assistant Professor of Anthropology at the University of Alberta in Edmonton, Canada. She blogs at Savage Minds (www.savageminds.org).

Jonathan Mayhew is Associate Professor of Spanish at the University of Kansas. He is a specialist in Lorca and in contemporary Spanish poetry. He blogs at Bemsha Swing (http://jonathanmayhew.blogspot.com).

Sean McCann is Professor of English and American Studies at Wesleyan University. He blogs at the Valve.

Scott McLemee is essayist-at-large for *Inside Higher Ed* (http://insidehighered.com/views/intellectual_affairs). He also blogs at Crooked Timber (www.crookedtimber.org). In 2004, he received the National Book Critics award for excellence in reviewing.

John McGowan teaches at the University of North Carolina, is an editor of the *Norton Anthology of Theory and Criticism*, and the author of five books, including the forthcoming *American Liberalism: An Interpretation for Our Time* (North Carolina UP)

Daphne Patai teaches Brazilian literature and literary theory at U Mass, Amherst. She is the recipient of fellowships from the National Endowment for the Humanities, the Guggenheim Foundation, and the National Humanities Center. In addition to editing *Theory's Empire*, she has written and edited a dozen books, including *Professing Feminism: Education and Indoctrination in Women's Studies*, with Noretta Koertge(Lexington, 2nd ed., 2003).

Kenneth Rufo is an independent scholar who studies rhetoric and mediation. He lives in the Seattle, WA area, does media and advocacy consulting with Tea Leaf Media (tealeafmedia.com/), and blogs at Ghost in the Wire (ghostinthewire.org/).

Amardeep Singh is Assistant Professor of English at Lehigh University. He is the author of *Literary Secularism: Religion and Modernity in Twentieth-Century Fiction* (Cambridge Scholars Press: 2006). His eponymous personal blog is (www.lehigh.edu/~amsp/blog.html); he also blogs at the Valve and Sepia Mutiny (www.sepiamutiny.com/sepia).

Jeffrey Wallen is the author of *Closed Encounters: Literary Politics and Public Culture* (U of Minnesota P, 1998), and is professor of comparative literature at Hampshire College.

www.ingramcontent.com/pod-product-compliance
Lightning Source LLC
LaVergne TN
LVHW091041080826
845145LV00002B/584